The Romantic Life

The Romantic Life

Five Strategies to Re-Enchant the World

D. ANDREW YOST

Foreword by
Elijah Clayton Null

CASCADE *Books* · Eugene, Oregon

THE ROMANTIC LIFE
Five Strategies to Re-Enchant the World

Cascade Books
An Imprint of Wipf and Stock Publishers
199 W. 8th Ave., Suite 3
Eugene, OR 97401

www.wipfandstock.com

PAPERBACK ISBN: 978-1-6667-3013-5
HARDCOVER ISBN: 978-1-6667-2124-9
EBOOK ISBN: 978-1-6667-2125-6

Cataloguing-in-Publication data:

Names: Yost, D. Andrew [author]. | Null, Elijah Clayton [foreword writer].

Title: The Romantic life : five strategies to re-enchant the world / D. Andrew Yost, with a foreword by Elijah Clayton Null.

Description: Eugene, OR: Cascade Books, 2022 | Includes bibliographical references.

Identifiers: ISBN 978-1-6667-3013-5 (paperback) | ISBN 978-1-6667-2124-9 (hardcover) | ISBN 978-1-6667-2125-6 (ebook)

Subjects: LCSH: Romanticism | Romanticism in art | Romanticism in literature | Romanticism—Germany | Romanticism—Great Britain | Philosophy—German—18th century | Philosophy—German—19th century | Literature—Philosophy | Spirituality

Classification: PN603 Y67 2022 (paperback) | PN603 (ebook)

VERSION NUMBER 082222

To Tristan

A thing of beauty is a joy for ever:
Its loveliness increases; it will never
Pass into nothingness[.]

—John Keats, *Endymion*

Contents

Foreword

This is not a self-help book, at least as the genre is widely understood. In some ways, I think of it as an anti-self-help book, though this strange designation requires some explanation. Andrew Yost wants you to see that there is something beyond yourself and your well-laid plans, beyond what he calls (borrowing from David Foster Wallace) our "tiny skull-sized kingdoms," and beyond mere matter. In a word, this thing is *enchantment*. There is music all around us, which we can recognize if we can only loosen our iron-grip on control for a moment. It's not that our lives depend on it, if by life we mean bare, physical existence. But Yost, for the reader willing to enter into his thoughtful, loving exposition, shows that a truly meaningful life certainly depends on the recovery of enchantment.

This book, then, is not about "pulling yourself up by your bootstraps" or "nine steps to a better sex life." It's not self-help in that sense. Openness and surrender to reality, not grit or determination, is what this book recommends; connection rather than self-sufficiency; wonder instead of mastery. Those of us—and I suspect there are many—who feel that another social media post or another promotion won't satisfy the deeper stirrings of our hearts, stirrings that we manage to quell most of the time, will find nourishment in Yost's insights into what it looks like to live an enchanted life. Come, Yost beckons, all ye tired and burnt-out and jaded. In an age of pessimism, Yost unabashedly declares that there *is* more than what king-of-the-hill culture offers.

Drawing on deep learning and reflection, Yost is sincere without being sentimental and wise without being pretentious. He directs our gaze to his great teachers, the Romantics, whom he knows intimately. Using their poems, paintings, and philosophy, Yost reveals that the problems of our age are not completely unique to our age. The Romantics have already plumbed the depths of these dilemmas, and we would be prudent to attend to their investigations. The Romantics, Yost deftly shows, are not mere relics of intellectual or literary history. They are wise teachers.

This book provides concrete steps for readers to help them reimagine their habits, practices, and relationships so that they might step into enchantment. These small but actionable suggestions will result in something like "self-help," if by the term we mean surrendering to a richer, fuller way of living. It's the sort of self-help that comes from laying aside the incessant schemes for personal "improvement." Let me stress once again—this book is *not* about gaining more control. The pervasive illusion of control, rather, is a large part of the problem. If this sounds scary, it's because it is; but Yost, I assure you, is a trustworthy guide.

Yost begins with an acute examination of the stressors and distortions of the modern age. Many commentators make careers of endlessly decrying cultural decline without offering any solutions. Thankfully, Yost goes well beyond mere critique. His analysis of our cultural moment clears away the fog in order to remember (literally: re-member, *put back together again*) a way of being that finds the beauty, goodness, and truth in the little things of life—such as the beloved's smile—and in things as big as the night sky in all its brilliance. This book is an invitation and a challenge: choose what is meaningful, not what is expedient; invest in what is truly worthy, not in what is trendy; stop, listen, and enter in. Yost's work is sensitive, realistic, and in the best sense of the word, quixotic. He enjoins us to journey with him through a cynical world and find princesses to save, castles to storm, and dragons to slay. All of these things are lying hidden in plain sight, we just need to learn to see differently.

Through many conversations and through reading his work, Yost has taught me much about the contours and qualities of enchantment. I believe he will do the same for you. For some readers, he will convince you of the reality of enchantment for the first time. The great thing about this epiphany is that it is only the beginning of the adventure. The Romantic Life beckons. Will you take up the call?

Elijah Clayton Null
Denver
May 2022

Acknowledgments

The words of the Romantics have nourished my soul ever since I was a child. It is to them I owe the greatest debt, and to my grandmother, Ann, who gave me the gift of poetry when I was just a boy. I must also thank the members of The Wickers Club, Benjamin J. Peters and Elijah Null, who through their charity, wisdom, and insight shepherded me through the creation of this book, and the refinement of my thoughts on enchantment. The spark that inspired them came from a close study of the legend of King Arthur I endeavored upon with Ben, one bright and sunny spring, several years ago. After making our way through those wonderful tales, the writings of Chrétien de Troyes, Thomas Malory, Alfred Tennyson, and J. R. R. Tolkien, we were forced to ask the question, "Can such stories still enchant us?" I think the answer is yes, and I am grateful to Ben and Elijah for helping me explore why, and how. I am also thankful to my wife, Laura, for her patience and commitment as she listened to my meandering conversations while I worked out these ideas. I'd like to thank my dear friends Ty and Heather Keefe, who over the course of our friendship have always been gracious listeners and curious inquirers. It is hard to express my full appreciation to them, and others like them, who throughout my life have given me the gift of philosophical conversation. Finally, I'd like to thank Chloe for asking her father, Ramone, the profoundest question of all, the question that reminded me to explore just how enchanting life can be. Thank you, Chloe. I owe you one.

Introduction

Disenchantment and the Romantic Invitation

A Disenchanted World

Around 1802, in the days of the Industrial Revolution when business was beginning to boom and industry was on the rise, the Romantic poet William Wordsworth strolled about the English countryside and penned these lines:

> The world is too much with us; late and soon,
> Getting and spending, we lay waste our powers;
> Little we see in Nature that is ours;
> We have given our hearts away, a sordid boon![1]

Wow. That's heavy stuff. What does it even mean? We lay waste our powers? What powers? We've given our hearts away? To whom—or to what? And what's so bad about giving them away in the first place, as we sense in this sleazy word, "sordid"? It all seems a bit dramatic, doesn't it, William?

One hundred years later, in 1919, during a lecture to a large group of German students, the sociologist Max Weber declared that "the fate of our times is characterized by rationalization and intellectualization and, above all, by the disenchantment of the world." That sounds a bit like Wordsworth's point. They seem to be saying something similar; namely, that the world is awry, that something's out of joint. But what? Weber at least gives us a hint at the answer: the world is "disenchanted." But what does *that* mean? What are these two getting at?

Less than a century after Weber's declaration and about two hundred years after Wordsworth's, in 2007, the Oxford-trained philosopher Charles Taylor said that in the modern world we live according to an "immanent

---

1. Wordsworth, *The Major Works*, 270.

1

frame" which rests on "the presumption of unbelief."[2] Although a bit less dramatically, Taylor is echoing the concern of Wordsworth and Weber. Which is what? Well, there's a lot to be said about the immanent frame, but the upshot of Taylor's point is that somehow over the last five hundred years we've become disenchanted. Over that span of time we've gone from almost everyone believing in magic, spirits, demons, angels, folklore, witches, curses, blessings, etc., to basically no one believing in any of that stuff, or at least no one assuming that's the baseline structure of the world. Magic isn't the "default position" anymore. In fact, it's quite the opposite. According to Taylor, there is a baseline "presumption of *un*belief."[3] Whether we say it out loud or not, our modern world is marked by an implicit assumption that anything beyond what we can observe is made up. We just assume that what we experience is all there really is, that everything is "immanent," and that there is nothing "transcendent" or "beyond" our experience. Sure, you might still believe in ghosts or God, but according to Taylor that tends to be more of an add-on to a presumably secular and physical world, a world fundamentally made up of matter. Belief in God is one option among many, where five hundred years ago *un*belief in God was almost unimaginable. But now we all start with the unspoken assumption of unbelief.[4] For Taylor, the move from the presumption of belief to unbelief constitutes a seismic shift in the way we experience the world. It's another way of saying we've become disenchanted. So, what happened? How did non-belief become not only an option for us, but the default position? And what does this have to do with "laying waste our powers" and all that? As it turns out, a lot.

Wordsworth, Weber, and Taylor are all talking about the same thing: *disenchantment*. According to them, and thinkers like them (including yours truly), our modern experience of life—and by that, I mean our contemporary, "right now," everyday experience of life, yours and mine—is haunted by a deep and penetrating question: "Is this all there is?" Rarely do we ask the question out loud. Most of the time it remains hidden, lurking just beneath

2. Taylor, *A Secular Age*, 12–14.

3. Taylor, *A Secular Age*, 13 (emphasis added).

4. To be clear, Taylor is not denying that people believe in God. What he's saying is that our orientation toward the idea of belief in God has dramatically changed in the last five hundred years. Today, we see it something like this: belief in God is nice and if it helps, then go for it. But the underlying "sense" of our world is that God is not the basis of all reality. It's not about whether God exists but the intuitive way in which the world "feels" to most of us in the modern West. The world "feels" secular, right from the start. In fact, Taylor is very open to God. He thinks a lot of us are, and maybe even should be. But regardless of whether or not you're a Christian, we all feel "cross-pressured," to use Taylor's term, by the pull of secular immanence and the draw of something more, something transcendent.

the surface, a shadow in the background. It makes an odd house guest, like a cat you rarely see but whose presence you feel whenever you come home. The question is always there, prodding and poking. It leaves us feeling like something's just not right. Something's missing, something *more*. When the question does rise to the surface, it can be jarring. It rattles us because we know it's important, but we don't know how to answer it, or even how to begin to contemplate it, really.

Now, you might be tempted to say, "Not me. I've never asked that question," but what I'm trying to get at is that this question is not like other questions. It doesn't need to be asked to be posed. In other words, "Is this all there is?" occurs to us almost before thought, *pre*-thought, before we can even articulate it. It's a built-in condition of our modern experience, whether we admit it or not. Some of us answer the question with a resounding "no," and find satisfaction in religion. Others answer the question with a resounding "yes," and find satisfaction in science. But the point I'm getting at is that the question is always there, demanding to be asked. Our responses to it are myriad: depression, despair, frustration, anger, longing, love, desire, possession, anxiety, hope, etc. We don't really know what to do with the question. We've laid waste our powers.

One way to understand the experience of disenchantment is to take a look at what passes as assumed truth in the world, and to ask ourselves why we think that way, how we've come to settle into a certain view of things, almost without reflection. We need to look at the way people naturally talk about the world, and the way they see themselves in it. I'd wager that if we took a moment to consider that, what we'd discover is that the dominant, authoritative discourse of our modern day is *scientism*.

Scientism is not the same thing as science. Science is an empirical mode of inquiry that operates on the idea that we can acquire knowledge through structured observation of the natural world. Scientism is the idea that science is the best, most reliable, most objective form of knowing and that all other forms of knowing are secondary and subordinate to it. Science studies the material world. Scientism claims that because the material world is what science studies, that's really all that exists. Science uses a scientific method to examine the universe. Scientism argues that the scientific method is the only method that leads to real truth and should therefore be applied to all domains of human activity, whether it be the natural world, child development, happiness, ballet, poetry, or whatever. Science acknowledges its limits. Scientism privileges science above everything else and rejects claims that science has any limits at all. Scientism disenchants. Science does not.

If you're with me so far then you can see that there is a certain way of seeing the world, a certain orientation toward it, that reduces everything to matter, to stuff we can see, taste, touch, smell, and hear. It rejects appeals to more, to things hard to say, mysterious things we know in our souls but struggle to say with our mouths. This is the orientation of scientism. According to scientism, references to symbolic truth, intuitive knowledge, depth, poetic meaning, transcendent experiences, or imagination are references to essentially empty ideas unless they can be moored to perception. They must be observable to be real. Things like beauty, truth, and love only make sense when they are explained in terms of what we can empirically verify. Beauty? Yes, says scientism, that's the complex chemical reaction resulting from an influx of dopamine into your brain that occurs when you encounter a harmonious composition. Truth? Well, can you reproduce it in a laboratory? If so, then yes, it's truth. Love? Oh, you mean the right neurons firing and the right dose of norepinephrine that comes flooding in, which causes an increase in your heart rate otherwise known as "pitter-patter?" Yes, that exists. You see? All you need is science.

But then the question comes up: "Is this really all there is?" Is everything—all of it: fear, hope, nature, joy, war, sorrow, sadness, ecstasy, all of it—really just a matter of, well, *matter*? Is all that there is to life the complex machinery of physics unfolding into the cosmos, into the vast, nameless void of the ever-expanding universe? (Do you feel the force of the question now?) The trouble is that the claim of scientism seems to fly in the face of what we intuitively know to be true; that is, that my experience of the world, my family, the sun on my skin, my fear of death, my anxiety about losing my job, etc., certainly *include* the observable, but they are so much more. The fullness of the love you feel for your child is not reducible to a complex chemical reaction. We know this to be true, even if scientism tells us otherwise.

Disenchantment is marked by a disinterest in depth, subtlety, nuance, a surplus of meaning, the un-nameable, the ineffable, and the symbolic. Disenchanted discourses don't concern themselves too much with the truth of a myth or a fairy tale, unless to explain their meaning away through some pseudo-Freudian interpretation or in order to ridicule them for their failures to represent underrepresented identities, or to draw some other cynical conclusion. Subject to the gaze of scientism, disenchantment sees the world as fundamentally *reducible*. There is only one truth. Life is not full of abundance, an overflow of meanings, references, signs, and possibilities. Matter is all there is.

Let me give you a simple example to illustrate the way disenchanted, reductive thinking plays out in a normal conversation. Imagine you recently watched *Star Wars: Return of the Jedi* and were moved by the father-son conflict of Darth Vader and Luke Skywalker. Knowing that there are three more movies that explore Luke's development, you're excited to go and see them. Now imagine that after viewing all the *Star Wars* movies you meet up with a friend and explain your interest in Luke's character arc and your (disenchanted) friend says to you, "You know, I watched an interview with George Lucas once and he said that the story of *Star Wars* was really the story or Anakin's rise and fall. It's really about Darth Vader, not Luke Sky-walker." What your friend is suggesting here is that there is actually only one meaning to the story of *Star Wars*, and that is the meaning the director gave it in the interview. Whatever truth we glean from the films must be related to Anakin's rise and fall, or else it is misguided, wrong even. You see? Your friend is a reductionist: there's only one truth about the movie, and it's whatever the director intended.

But there's another way to look at things. You might respond to your friend that while it's all well and good that Lucas cared most about Vader, once he put the movie out into the world it is no longer up to him to decide what the movie is "really about." In other words, the movie has multiple meanings, a surplus of meanings even, and "what it's about" is an invitation offered up by the movie itself, as a work of art, not a single truth given to us by the director. In fact, that's precisely the point of movies in particular, and of art in general. Art "says" what cannot be "said," it provides us stories and images and songs and characters so that we can explore what it means to be human *without* feeling the need to come up with a single, clear, comprehensive answer. Why is an answer so hard to come by? Because being human is complicated. But disenchantment doesn't like that. It wants answers. It has an intolerance for layers. It seeks out complete explanations, reductions, and practical applications. It attempts to confine what's possible to the perceivable, and disavows references to the kinds of truths that can only be signaled toward through metaphor and simile. It tells us *Star Wars* means just what Lucas says it means, that science is the only truth, and that the best explanations are always the most practical. According to disenchantment, if you don't adopt a posture of reductionism then you risk looking like a backwater fool.

According to philosophers of disenchantment like Weber and Taylor, the way we got to this point is a complex story. It has a lot to do with narrative shifts in how we see ourselves in the world and the forces at play that are driving those shifts. One narrative that dominates our social imaginary today is that in the not-too-distant-past we were all a bunch of superstitious and ignorant peasants who more like children than adults believed in ghosts and spirits and God and magic. We believed in this stuff because we just didn't have the intellectual capacity or means to see the way things *really* are; that is, according to science. Whenever we encountered an experience we couldn't explain (e.g., a terrible drought, or a mysterious disease killing off our pigs) we had to fill in the gaps in knowledge with our own imaginations. We made up a bunch of stories, essentially, adding new creatures or beasties to the cosmos whenever we saw fit to do so in order to explain the unexplainable. But then science came along, giving us the light of reason vis-a-vis the scientific method, and forced us to look truth in the face, *and grow up*. But it's hard to grow up. It comes with a lot of pain and discomfort, and historically it has cost us the lives of many a scientific martyr. But after a while, we accepted the truth and matured into adulthood, putting away childish things and embracing the fact that all there is in the world is matter. Science is right, real, and the only objective way of knowing. Might as well admit it. That's the story most of us implicitly live by, or at least, were born into.

But that's just one narrative, and maybe not the right one. There are others. In *A Secular Age*, Taylor tells a different story, one that challenges the "scientific maturation" theory in favor of a more complex human history proceeding less as a growing-up narrative and more as a series of subtle shifts in the way we conceive and experience ourselves, God, knowledge, and reality. I won't go into Taylor's argument here. It's too rich and complicated for a cursory treatment, but I highly recommend the read. The point I'm trying to make is that part of the problem of explaining disenchantment is getting at the story of how we got here in the first place. What forces are at play that tell us existence is made up only of matter? What keeps us from seeing magic in the world? What are the dominant cultural discourses that trivialize, belittle, dismiss, or mock a view of life that yearns for something more, for enchantment? We'll explore these questions in depth in chapter 1, but suffice it to say for now, there are several major forces that hold a mighty sway over our current thinking.

Now is probably a good time to explain what I mean by "magic." It's a loaded term. Clarifying it will help sort out some things that will come up later in our conversation. Let's start with what we usually mean by "magic," which is something like a set of beliefs, rituals, and activities that operate on the presumption that there are unseen forces in the universe (some good, some evil, some both, some neither) that can be tapped into or manipulated to effect change. That's a very basic description of what we might call the medieval mindset (with no disrespect to medieval folks). Wordsworth and Weber and Taylor are right about the idea that the disenchantment of the world in some ways involved the dissolution of magic as a "real thing"; that is, that magic has largely been discredited as a legitimate part of a viable theory of reality. Nobody *really* believes in magic anymore, or so we say. If you do, you have a case to make about its reality and will almost certainly be met with intellectual resistance wherever you go. No, if we want to be enchanted we can't "go back" to a time when we presumed magic was woven into the fabric of the world. We can't go back to the medieval period. That sense of magic is lost to us. Our modern mode of existence, our way of experiencing the world has changed, dramatically, fundamentally, through-and-through, so much so that there is no way we can adopt a form of life from five hundred years ago. We need to resist the temptation of nostalgia as a means to re-enchantment.

So, what do I mean by "magic?" I want to argue that it's still possible to experience the world as magical without having to adopt the medieval mindset. By using the term "magic" I want to direct our attention to the "drive behind the drive" for magic proper; that is, magic as a supernatural power of manipulation. I want to consider what's *behind* the idea of magic, what draws us toward it as a concept, what makes it alluring in the first place. I think that part of the appeal of magic (and other, related ideas) is a deep-seated human attraction toward those elements of our experiences that are not fully articulable and therefore call for a creative-responsive engagement, an imaginative interaction with the world that draws upon the inventory of symbols, signs, stories, and significations that are culturally available to us in order to make associations that reveal the world from new angles, giving it new dimensions and textures that are otherwise unavailable to us from a strictly material perspective. In other words, magic is part of a broader human enterprise of imaginative engagement with the world around us. My use of the term "magic" is not about metaphysics. It's not a word that refers to a mystical force operating in the background or underneath what we experience in the everyday world. It refers to our desire to address the non-reducible aspects of our experiences. It's about using the imagination. And I don't think we have to conclude that goblins and ghosts exist if we want to take magic seriously. There's more to it than that, as we'll see throughout this book.

Now, let's turn to the idea of *enchantment*. That's what this book is about, after all. I want to make the argument that enchantment is not off the table, that we can and should imbue our lives with beauty, truth, and love, and other impractical—but invaluable—things. While going back in time and *adopting* the medieval mindset in order to experience magic is not the answer, there are answers expressed in other times, more recent times, that if *adapted* to our lives today might allow us to see the world with fresh eyes, with enchanted eyes. Of course, some modifications are needed to make these ideas relevant to our modern age. But they are not so foreign or remote as to be inaccessible. They are not as distant to us as, say, the medieval mindset. In fact, a lot of these ideas are still alive and well in our collective unconscious and we live them out today, or some thinner version of them, at least. To access them we need not to travel back in time, but to pay attention, to develop a sensitivity to the wisdom of the not-so-distant-past. Doing so offers a wealth of promise and opportunity. These ideas come to us from the eighteenth- and nineteenth-century Romantics, and they offer the possibility of re-enchanting the world. Which brings me to the central point of this book: *through the practical application of Romantic methods and insights we can once again experience the world as an enchanted place.*

Romance vs. Romanticism

The word "romance" is a tricky one. What does it really mean? For most of us, it points toward that vague, warm-and-fuzzy feeling you get when your lover whispers sweet nothings into your ear, or when you're sharing an intimate meal and everything seems just right: the candles, the wine, even the waiter's outfit exude an amorous air. "Romance" makes us think of two people's tantalizing chemistry, surprise vacations to the south of France, or starry-eyed gazes. It's exciting, mysterious, and, well, a bit cheesy. Maybe even *very* cheesy.

But the thing is, we want it. We like it. We desire it. Despite our cynicism toward the magic of romance, most of us secretly hope we find it. We dream that one day we too will feel its fluttery touch. That, in a nutshell, is the modern notion of romance. But the word hasn't always meant that. It has interesting origins. By most etymological accounts, the word "romance" comes to us from Old French, meaning, "in the vernacular." It used to refer to a kind of story known as a verse narrative, a long tale written in the common language using a certain poetic structure and style. "Romantic" works were entertaining tales of knights-in-shining-armor doing chivalric deeds like slaying dragons and rescuing maidens. But modern romance means something else, something a little bit different, although our usage is not totally unrelated. When we use the word "romance," we mean the loving behavior between two people who are "made for each other," two people who when together form a harmonic whole. "Two become one," we say, or "they were destined to be together." Sure, there is some residue of chivalry and fairy tales clinging to our sense of the term, but the core of the word's meaning has something to do with how two people lovingly interact with one another.

Where did we get this idea? Where did we get the notion that romance has something to do with lovers merging with each other? Not from medieval romances, that's for sure. In medieval romances there was a lot of swashbuckling and adventure and sex, but not a lot of metaphysical union. The idea that romance is about joining of souls and harmony between lovers has different roots, roots that lie not in the medieval period, but in the eighteenth and nineteenth centuries, a period that historians now call the Romantic period. During the Romantic period, the idea of "romance" came to mean something much more than Old French stories of knights and castles. Thanks to poets like William Wordsworth, Percy Bysshe Shelley, and John Keats, "Romanticism" came to mean something deep and transformative, something quite shocking, in fact. And *that* is where our story truly begins.

Romanticism as a Historical Movement

Romanticism with a capital "R" and romanticism with a small "r" are two different ideas. Capital "R" Romanticism refers to a historical movement that took place during the so-called "long eighteenth century," from about 1750–1850. It was a counter-cultural movement. The Romantics were a group of poets, thinkers, and writers who had had enough of Enlightenment rationalism. They pushed back against the values and ideas of the preceding era, arguing that hyper-intellectualization and the myth of progress had gone too far. But more about that in a moment. Small "r" romanticism refers to the idea we just described, the modern idea that love is often accompanied by a set of amorous behaviors serving to enhance, energize, or charge a relationship with moments of relational intensity. It's important not to confuse the two. This book is about Romanticism, not romanticism. While we'll certainly discuss romantic ideas along the way, this book is about the lessons of the Romantic period, lessons we can apply to our modern lives in order to imbue them with meaning and beauty, in order to make them more enchanting.

This book is about Romantic paths to living an enchanted life. An enchanted life is more than the amorous life, a life spent in love with someone else. The enchanted life includes love, of course, but it goes beyond love too. The enchanted life encompasses a broad swath of experiences, including our relationship to nature, the way time "feels" to us, how we think about beauty and truth, how we encounter each other, our personal feelings, our self-expression, and so on. Romanticism has a lot to say about these things. We might even go so far as to say that the time is ripe for a Romantic revival. There are uncanny parallels between the way people experienced their lives just before the Romantic period erupted (and erupt it did) and the way modern people experience their lives today, people like you and me.

Prior to the Romantic period, reason ruled the day. Reason, most people thought, was the key to human progress. We call this era the "age of Enlightenment" (roughly 1715–89) because of its focus on rationality, logic, and intellect, rather than tradition, revelation, and belief. For Enlightenment thinkers, dogmatic religion, folktales, magic, superstition, and subjective feelings had led people to a sort of mental and cultural enslavement; that is, they were enslaved by their own ignorance. "Enlightenment," the philosopher Immanuel Kant once said, "is man's freedom from his own self-incurred immaturity." Enlightenment thinkers argued that humanity could only progress through rational change. Enlightenment was liberation. Indeed, the American War for Independence and the French Revolution were both directly inspired by Enlightenment ideas of liberty, equality, and fraternity.

A lot of this might sound familiar. After all, just like in the Enlightenment, most of us today see reason as the best way to acquire truth, and very few of us still believe in magic. But belief or disbelief in magic only scratches the surface of what the Enlightenment was really about. At its core, the Enlightenment rested on the idea that the only true form of knowledge was rational knowledge, which itself was acquired through a combination of empirical observation, mathematics, and formal logic. Science, especially Newton's newly discovered laws of physics, were understood to govern *all* of existence and purported to render the *entire* universe knowable, all the way down to the behavior of specific atoms. As the famous epigram by the Enlightenment-era poet Alexander Pope goes, "Nature and nature's laws lay hid in night, / God said 'Let Newton be!' and all was light."

The reach of "Enlightened Reason" knew almost no bounds. Like a sheet of cellophane, Enlightenment thinkers stretched it across just about every domain of human activity. Art, commerce, politics, and ethics were all subjected to the principles of rationality. As the twentieth-century historian Isaiah Berlin tells us, for a person living during the Enlightenment, the general view was that "life, or nature, [was] a jigsaw puzzle" in which all the pieces fitted together into "one coherent pattern."[5] We just needed the key of reason to unlock the picture and see the whole. Although Enlightenment thinkers were not uniform in their specific ideas—there were among them a variety of different opinions and perspectives—there was also a common, underlying view that "virtue consists ultimately in knowledge"; that is, rational knowledge, and the secret to living a happy life lay in the ability of a person to deduce through reason who she is, what she needs, and how best

---

5. Berlin, *The Roots of Romanticism*, 23.

to obtain it for herself.[6] In other words, Enlightenment thinkers lived the rational life, not the Romantic life.

It's interesting to examine the ways in which this assumption about knowledge plays out in activities that many of us today now think of as essentially "non-rational" activities. Take art, for example. According to Enlightenment principles, the task of art was to perfect nature. Nature, they argued, seeks perfection, as all things do; that is, perfection according to the order of reason. Art's aim was therefore to convey to us the rational perfection that was imperfectly expressed in nature. "Just as mathematics deals in perfect circles," Berlin tells us, "so the [Enlightenment] sculptor and the painter must deal in ideal forms."[7]

In ethics, Kant argued that the right moral action is the one that is most rational. Consider lying. Lying is always immoral, Kant said, because if you lie it leads to a logical contradiction, which would lead to an ethics of absurdity, and that cannot stand. Think about it. In order for you to lie, the person you're lying to must assume you're telling the truth. The assumption of truth-telling is a condition for the possibility of lying. But in lying, you are saying that everyone should lie, because your actions are a prescription for what you think is right conduct. But if everyone followed your lead and lied, then no one would assume anyone was ever telling the truth. And if no one assumed anyone was ever telling the truth, well, no one could ever lie, because lying requires the assumption of truth telling. So, lying leads to the inability to lie: a logical contradiction. Therefore, according to Kant, lying is immoral. Always. Every time. Even if you have Anne Frank in the attic and a Nazi at the door. That's the degree to which reason ruled the day in the Enlightenment.

You can imagine how stifling this line of thinking can become. It leaves out something very important about what it means to be human. It bottles up or suppresses the more spontaneous, chaotic, or non-rational aspects of our human natures, aspects that are not always "bad" but can be great sources of creativity and truth. The Enlightenment mode of thought did not take seriously enough that side of human being. Still, we shouldn't paint with too broad a brush stroke here. Enlightenment reason produced powerful results. Enlightenment thinkers made enormous contributions to Western civilization. Out of the Enlightenment came the natural sciences, modern physics, calculus, medicine, and chemistry. Empiricism, reason, and science brought us cures for diseases and buildings less likely to collapse. They also brought a new sense of rigor to our concept of knowledge. By insisting that every

6. Berlin, *The Roots of Romanticism*, 25.
7. Berlin, *The Roots of Romanticism*, 28.

person has within them the ability to reason for themselves, Enlightenment thinkers empowered everyone, from the highborn to the low, to govern and choose their own way of life (so long as it was rationally grounded).

The idea that we all have the ability to reason strikes a heavy blow against the oppressive powers of dogma, establishment, and divine right. Reason has its place, its purpose. But reason has its limits, too. Science is not the only way to truth. As the Romantics were keen to point out, there are truths outside the purview of science, truths essential to human being but not reducible to material things or knowable through empirical observation. The first wave of Romantics attacked Enlightenment rationality on precisely these grounds. Isaiah Berlin recounts how one of the earliest Romantics, Johann Wolfgang von Goethe, claimed that Enlightenment scientists would treat beauty like a butterfly, if they could: they'd catch it, pin it down, scrutinize it, and then let its brilliant colors fade as they search for its "ideal form" in its lifeless little body.[8] The Romantics found this approach wholly unacceptable. It suppressed the deep truths of human being, truths as wild and unrestrained as nature, as sincere and genuine as our subjective feelings, and as penetrating as an ineffable secret passed on through poetry. There is according to the Romantics an unbridled vitality to life, a vitality that flows, desires, creates, and struggles. It resists the scientist's pin. Ironically, the Enlightenment's attempt to liberate through reason had instead led to a stifling feeling of bondage and oppression.

So, Romanticism came crashing in. The age of reason had run its course. It was time for something new. It was time for the human soul to once again emerge, to express itself not according to the daylight of rationality, but according to the night of mystery. What, then, was (or *is*) Romanticism? What did it have to say? What were its tenets? And how is it relevant today? Let's take a look.

Romanticism: A Cluster of Compelling Ideas

Romanticism is notoriously hard to define. For everything you say about it is, there is a counter example showing how that's not quite right. Rather than chasing down a definition destined to fail, let's consider Romanticism as a cluster of ideas. That way, we can discuss themes in the movement without feeling the need to overstate what Romantics shared in common or to confine Romanticism to artificial boundaries. Romantics weren't into boundaries anyway. They were rule breakers, not followers. If there was a boundary to transgress, they'd transgress it. Nevertheless, there are some

---

8. Berlin, *The Roots of Romanticism*, 43.

shared ideas among Romantic thinkers, giving them a similar enough shape that we can point to a "Romantic revolution" and speak of it as a serious form of life. So what are these ideas?

Sincere Self-Expression

Romantics took their feelings seriously. They did not adhere to a hard line between reason and emotion. The idea that such a line even exists comes to us from Plato and has been passed down through the Enlightenment. The Romantics rejected it. Instead, they saw the human person as a swirling confluence of thoughts, feelings, imaginings, judgements, passions, sensations, desires, reasons, and contradictions. As the Romantic philosopher Friedrich Schiller put it in 1793, the "beautiful soul" was one in which "sensuousness and reason, duty and inclination harmonize, and grace is its epiphany."[9] To eschew one set of human capacities and revere another does an injustice to the sweeping wholeness of being human. Feelings, the Romantics argued, reveal important insights about what it means to be alive in the world and should not be pent up in a rationalist cage or suppressed as baser, more animalistic instincts. Sincere feeling warrants self-expression. But feelings can be dangerous, of course, and the Romantics knew that too. We are an impulsive lot. We are prone to "acting out," as they say, and can do ourselves great harm when unbridled passion erupts within us. But even in its most dramatic and self-destructive forms, the Romantics believed that human passions disclose an important truth; namely, that to be human is to be *expressive*.

We can see the implications of this so-called "expressivist turn" by comparing Enlightenment and Romantic theories of art. Where, as we have seen, Enlightenment philosophers viewed the aim of art as the perfection of nature depicted in ideal forms, Romantic thinkers saw its goal as aesthetic expression. Enlightenment art was a complex form of copying, or what we might call *mimesis*. In it we see balance, precision, order, and geometry. Buildings stand erect under straight and narrow columns. Portraits depict regal men and women, full of self-restraint and self-control. Music was mathematical. The best art followed rules. The particular foibles or idiosyncrasies of the artist were no matter. But for the Romantics this view of art was too confining, too abstract, too oppressive. Art, they argued, was its own end, its own goal. Art was sacred. Why? Because art is always someone speaking. It is someone expressing themselves. And self-expression is at the heart of what it means to be human. The sincere expression of one's self

9. Schiller, "On Grace and Dignity," 368.

through art is the revelation of truth. As Rousseau writes, "it is the history of my soul that I have promised to recount, and to write it faithfully I have need of no other memories; it is enough if I enter again into my inner self, as I have done till now."[10] The artist no longer carried his canvas around like a mirror, ready to copy what nature reflected. Instead, the artist's canvas was a flowering meadow, an open space for sincere expression to blossom and come forth.

The Power of the Imagination

When we think of the imagination we tend to think of make believe. "It's just my imagination, running away with me," the old song goes, suggesting that what one imagines is somehow less real than what one perceives. The imagination is interesting, to be sure, but it's not giving us anything real. It *reproduces* reality in the form of mental images. It recalls past events or conjures fantasies. At its worst, imagining deludes. Its images and affect can create something nefarious, threatening, or scary even, something that "isn't really there" but that still has an impact on you. "Oh," we say, "you're imaging things again." But this sense of the imagination as a source of fiction or just vague impressions, as a somewhat trivial mental faculty that simply reflects back to the mind things it once perceived or combining ideas into fantastic creations (horse + narwhal = unicorn) is a very modern conception of imagination. It's an old one too, interestingly. In between this ancient and modern idea of the imagination lies the Romantic one. The Romantics thought the imagination was a powerful creative faculty. Imagining, they claimed, was one of the key ways of imbuing the world with meaning, of experiencing it as an enchanting place.

In his wonderful little book, *The Romantic Legacy* (1996), philosopher Charles Larmore explains just how important the imagination was to the Romantics, and just how relevant it is to us today. The Romantic imagination, he argues, is fundamentally a "creative-responsive" faculty.[11] Unlike our modern view of the imagination, which sees it primarily as a source of fancy, the Romantics saw the imagination as the key to experiencing beauty, truth, and love in a world grown cold. The imagination creates by transforming experience, by poeticizing life through meaning-making, reference, symbolism, and signification. It gives life a "charge." It "amplifies" it. In fact, the Romantics argued that we don't really have a choice in the matter. We can't help *but* imagine. It's always operating in the background,

10. Rousseau, *The Confessions*, 262.

11. Larmore, *The Romantic Legacy*, 7–16.

pulling together our sensations, experiences, language, and interactions into a cohesive whole and making meaning out of them. Even the rigid Enlightenment philosopher Immanuel Kant acknowledged the imagination's productive capacity, calling it "that mysterious power hidden in the depths of the soul." How's that for stuffy Enlightenment thinking?

But the imagination doesn't just create, it also responds to what is given in experience. Imagining is not just freewheeling make-believe. Imagining is grounded in what really does appear to us, what we experience; that is, the world that rises up and meets us at every moment of every day. The world is the source of our imagination's content. The imagination interacts with our experiences, combining them into a unity and allowing us to generate a sense of magic in our lives. It reveals to us a world full of symbols, metaphors, and meanings. It beautifies what we see and hear, taste and smell, think and consider. As Wordsworth wrote, the imagination allows us "to see into the life of things."

Nature's Revelation

Perhaps the most common association we make with the Romantics is an abiding concern with nature. Unsympathetic critics of the Romantic period often scoff at the Romantic obsession with landscapes, forests, and streams, seeing it as mere pastoral nostalgia or a predictable reaction to the Industrial Revolution. Sadly, "love of nature" is now a Romantic trope. It's certainly true that the Romantics loved nature; or really, "Nature," but not in a cheesy or cliché sense. Like "Romanticism" with a capital "R," "Nature" with a capital "N" means something different for the Romantics than "small-n" nature, means to us.

When we think of "nature," we think of the environment. We think of outside: birds, trees, flowers, mountains, clouds, and so on. To us, nature is a living ecosystem, and we mean that in the scientific sense. The basic idea is that nature is all the stuff "out there," beyond the city limits or nestled within a city park, operating according to the rules of science. But Nature, for the Romantics signaled toward a deeper concept of what's going on "outside." It's an aesthetic word, not a scientific one. Or more precisely, it's a word that refers to a peculiar way truth reveals itself, rather than a word that refers to an ecosystem or a backyard. That takes some explaining. Nature, for the Romantics, is *the very fact of becoming*. It is the vitality of existence opening itself up before us. Nature is inexhaustible, not in the sense that its "natural resources" (oil, minerals, lumber, etc.) will go on forever, of course they can be used-up, but in the sense of its inexplicability; that is, its *meanings*. No matter what you say about it you can never say enough. And it continues to say more than we can ever express. Nature is the power of life itself, an ever-unfolding excess. It evades or eludes or overflows any concept that might contain it. Much to the dismay of Enlightenment rationalism, Nature according to the Romantics could never be reduced to "a thing." As the English poet Samuel Taylor Coleridge put it, scientific accounts of Nature try to carve it up into knowable pieces, they "contemplate nothing but *parts* and all *parts* are necessarily little—and the Universe to them is but a mass of little things."[12] But Nature always resists such divisions, such attempts at control. Nature is, as Berlin writes, "unembraceable."[13]

The idea that Nature is an ineffable force, a power both subtle and profound, one that can never be explained, controlled, or reduced to an object is at the heart of the enchanted life. Some moderns may not feel any real connection with Nature, and that is understandable. Going outside is not for everyone. For some, the Nature aspect of Romantic thought is less appealing than the ideas of imagination or sincerity. "Nature is full of bugs," someone might say, or "It's dirty and uncomfortable out there." These sorts of feeling are legitimate, of course, but the Romantic view is not quite about camping and hiking. It's not just for hippies or homesteaders. Quite the opposite, in fact. Romantic Nature has less to do with *where* one is and more to do with *how one sees and feels one's surroundings*. For the Romantics, the term "Nature" included grand mountain vistas and vast ocean horizons, but also pedestrian garden pansies and evening twilight in a city suburb. Nature is not always "out there," a place you visit every couple of years during family vacation. It is a pervasive force. It reveals its truth all around us, all of the time. It's something you can experience through the comfort of a living-room window. What is key for the Romantic view of Nature is that Nature is *truth unfolding*. It is not a thing. It is an unyielding act of love. And by paying attention to it, by "tuning-in to it" we can transform our encounter with the world, and enchant our lives. The Romantic obsession with Nature (and it *was* obsessive, though in a good way!) was something quite personal. It was about learning to see the ever-flowing truth of creation, which is active in all things. Love of Nature is about attunement with the truth of one's self as an expressive and vital life. Viewed this way, Nature is the doorway to symbolism, beauty, and sublimity, all of which are right there, right outside your window, and within you, too.

12. Coleridge, *Collected Letters of Samuel Taylor Coleridge*, 387.
13. Berlin, *The Roots of Romanticism*, 103.

Poetry and Poetic Contemplation

Poetry is a tough sell these days. To many, it seems confusing, obscure, and inaccessible. You're told from a young age that poetry is important, but just about every time you try and read it, it seems impossible to understand. It's like you know that something profound is being said but you can't figure out *what*, exactly. Poetry can feel a little elitist too. Some of these biases toward poetry and poetic contemplation are justified, but some are based more on stereotypes than actual experiences. They arise from caricatures of what we think poetry is, or from *bad* experiences with it. Remember when Mrs. So-and-so made you read Shakespeare before you were ready? It came off as incomprehensible gibberish, not art, and you haven't given it a second look since.

But if you can muster the courage to engage poetry again, claim the Romantics, you might discover something new. There is more to it than flowery language and sing-song rhymes. For the Romantics, language in general and poetry in particular constituted a universe by themselves.[14] The word "poetry" referred not only to what we traditionally think about when we think about poetry (verses composed in a stylistic manner with lots of metaphors and similes), but also an act of aesthetic creation that participates in or expresses the power of life itself. The English Romantic poet William Wordsworth defined poetry as "the spontaneous overflow of powerful feelings," which "takes its origin from emotion recollected in tranquility." The German Romantic Friedrich Schlegel thought of poetry as "an overall symbolic vision of the world in which all things point at the absolute."[15] For the Romantic philosopher Friedrich Schelling, poetry was tied up in symbolizing. It was the act of "raising finite representations to an infinite meaning."[16] Importantly, none of these definitions describe poetry as an intellectual act. Creating poetry is exactly that: an act of *creation*, not an act of rationalization. And we have already seen how important creation was to the Romantics: Nature is the great creative force. The imagination participates in Nature through its creative-responsive activity. The expression of sincere feeling is the creative act of human being *par excellence*. Poetry, therefore, is the supreme aesthetic act of creation. Art is the ultimate way to participate in the Great Unfolding that is existence itself. It puts one in tune with the entire cosmos. The world sings in and through the poet, or so the Romantics thought.

14. Dupré, *Quest of the Absolute*, 5.
15. Dupré, *Quest of the Absolute*, 11.
16. Dupré, *Quest of the Absolute*, 10.

Romantics used to draw a metaphor between the poet and this weird instrument called an aeolian harp. To "play" an aeolian harp you set it on a windowsill and let the wind blow through it. When it does, the harp sings the natural tune of the air. Nature alone plucks its strings. To the Romantics the image of the aeolian harp was the image of the poet. Through her Nature would sing. Beauty expresses itself in and through the poet's soul, going in as inspiration and coming out as poetic creation. Remember that according to the Romantics *we all have imaginations*. We all have the poetic capacity. Each of us can express ourselves creatively and pay attention to Nature's expression around us. Each of us can imbue life with meaning and symbolism and receive the meaning and symbolism Nature has to offer. We are *all* aeolian harps.

Our task is to poeticize the world, to enchant it. And we don't need to be a tortured soul or lyrical master to do it. We only need to engage in poetic contemplation. By that, the Romantics meant that the enchanted life is a thoughtful life, a reflective life, a life that pays attention. In thinking "poetically" we see the magic and charm of being. We make insightful connections between our past, our present, and our future by drawing upon the inventory of symbols, ideas, images, words, paintings, music, folktales, etc., that have formed us from childhood. Poetic contemplation looks for beauty in the world. It seeks it out and imaginatively engages in what gives itself to us in experience. A flower is never *just* a flower because a flower is *not* just a flower! But seeing the world through poetic eyes takes practice. We must develop a sensitivity to our surroundings. While the poet may have a knack for it, the rest of us need to hone our poetic attention and learn to see as much with our souls as with our eyes.

Transcendence, the Absolute, and the Sublime

As we've seen, the Romantics found the Enlightenment account of the cosmos unsatisfying because it eschews powerful human experiences that cannot be reduced to a concept. The Romantics took the Enlightenment to task on this point from another angle, arguing that in addition to aesthetic ineffability there are other experiences that push us *beyond* rational thinking, experiences that overwhelm our entire consciousness and saturate us with a sense of awe and terror, but also, peculiarly, delight. These experiences are what the Romantics called *sublime* experiences. We encounter something breathtaking, like a domineering mountain vale in the midst of a winter storm, a soft moon twilight descending on an open field of springtime flowers, or the overpowering push-and-pull of ocean waves tugging at the shoreline. We are struck by the vastness of the scene and our own smallness in the face of its incomprehensible grandeur. We are forced to recognize the finitude of our existence and the trivialities of our mundane life.

These experiences, say the Romantics, are an experience both of awe *and* of pleasure. On the one hand, when we encounter the sublime we encounter the truth of our own impotence in the face of the raw power of existence. We are human, all too human. *Merely* human. Existence can crush us at any moment. The great American Romantic Herman Melville described in *Moby-Dick* this power as expressed in the ocean, "panting and snorting like a mad battle steed that's lost its rider," one that "dashes even the mightiest whales against the rocks, and leaves them there side-by-side with the split wrecks of ships." (Lord, that's good stuff.) On the other hand, when we encounter this awe-inspiring force, we also feel a peculiar affinity with the scene. We're drawn to it. It gives us perspective about our own troubles and helps us see their big-picture insignificance. The whole scene moves us.

But there's more. The sublime encounter often places us on a terrifying and tantalizing ledge in which our rational faculties are overrun by what appears before us. It is as if we are compelled into a non-rational, imaginative mode of consciousness, just by the sheer grandeur of the landscape or seascape. Melville says that you can go to any coastline in the world—any lake, stream, or oceanside—and there you'll see people "[p]osted like silent sentinels . . . fixed in ocean reveries." "There is magic in it," he says. For many Romantics, the feeling goes even further: they describe the sublime as a sort of dissolution. In the sublime, we dissolve into Nature itself, losing our own sense of individuality, particularity, or identity. We sense that we too are *part* of the mountain, the valley, and the ocean. We merge with it and experience ourselves at one with the Absolute, even if only for a brief moment, just for an instant.

The sublime reveals a wealth of wisdom. First, it shows us that there are truths beyond rational cognition. The emotional upheaval that we experience at the base of a roaring waterfall is not reducible to a mere psychological state. It does something "philosophical" to us. It lures, challenges, moves, and terrifies us. Second, it puts us into a space of what the Romantic poet John Keats called "negative capability," a space where we are able to stand in the face of uncertainty, mystery, doubt, and contradiction without trying to explain it away or rationalize it. A sublime experience is a mixed experience. It brings together things within us that don't always find a happy co-existence, like simultaneous feelings of pleasure and fear. Unlike watching a horror movie, in which we intentionally suspend our disbelief in order to experience "fun fear," the sublime induces in us the very justified feelings of awe and terror because it is in fact true that the tumultuous ocean waves could take us over if we were exposed to them. But that truth delivers a deeper insight about life than a horror movie can. It is more immediate and visceral. It encompasses our bodies. We are literally surrounded by it, not at home on a couch with popcorn and a guard dog. So a Romantic would never say of the sublime, "it's all in my head." They wouldn't try and psychologize it. The sublime is not a mental state. It is a rapture of your whole being. And finally, experiences like the sublime (and for some Romantics, the beautiful too) open us up to something more than matter, something more than the immanent frame in which we live. The sublime can impel us toward transcendence, which is a fancy way of saying that the truth we encounter in a brooding summer storm reveals to us that there is indeed a vast and infinite existence beyond our own, immediate life, or our entire lifetime, or history, or time itself, even. It's the Great Mystery of Becoming that calls us forth from our location *in* time and space, but that goes beyond it. It is the call of the Absolute.

The Romantic Invitation

Now we can begin to see why the time is right for a Romantic resurgence. There are important commonalities between the Enlightenment experience of the world and our modern condition. But our modern form of life goes even further than that of our Enlightenment counterparts in its distaste for all things enchanted. As we will see in chapter 1, in part thanks to the rise of capitalism, we have a cultural aversion toward "slow thinking," reflective contemplation, careful aesthetic observation, and sincere expression. We tend toward five-minute TedTalks rather than the day-to-day rumination required for the truth of a poem to do its work on us. We want the answer *now*, not subtly revealed over the course of a lifetime. The speed of modern life conceals from us the layered truths of our own experiences, rich truths that call for reflection and attention, not immediate consumption. The pace of Romantic life opens a space for those truths to reveal themselves, and the time is right to allow them the chance to resurface.

We could also use a break from materiality. I don't mean materiality in the sense of owning too much stuff (although that could be reined in too). What I mean is that we could benefit from a discourse that isn't rooted in the "Yeah, but can you prove it scientifically?" kind of mindset. As I've already said, there's nothing wrong with science. It's a marvel, truly. But it isn't the *whole* story. There are "immaterial" experiences that warrant consideration, that we should take seriously, like the profundity of the sublime or the way sincere expression can touch our souls to the core and

activate our sympathies. These immaterial experiences are legitimate sub-
jects of conversation, contemplation, and consideration and although they
do not come to us through scientific inquiry they nevertheless add a great
deal of depth and meaning to our lives. The Romantics bravely suggested
that we embrace and explore "useless" things like beauty, truth, and love. We
should be thinking about them, a lot. As the philosopher David Foster Wallace said, critical thinking doesn't just mean using critical thinking skills,
it means being critical about what you *choose* to think about.[17] You have to
be picky about where you direct your mental energies. The time is right for
us to direct them toward ideas that imbue our lives with meaning, toward
ideas that recognize the sacredness of the question, "Is this all there is?" and
respond to it.

But perhaps the biggest reason that the time is right for a Romantic
resurgence is that we are disenchanted, and because life is richer when it
is enchanted. Romanticism offers us a way to experience an enchanted
world. As we will see in the next chapter, our disenchantment runs deep.
Our lives are inundated with messages and images and headlines and apps
that distract us from seeing the magic of existence, that suggest we scroll
on—just keep scrolling—rather than pause, and look around; rather than
stop, and consider. The frantic pace of modern life makes us anxious, and
anxiety makes us tense, and tension causes us to snap, and snapping releases
rage, and rage makes us afraid, and fear makes us anxious. And on it goes.
We're all outraged, but about what? Racism. Oppression. Bigotry. Greed.
Consumption. Hatred. Ignorance. All of it. None of it. It's hard to even say
anymore. We simply carry around a baseline, undirected anger waiting to
spring forth at someone or something that rubs us the wrong way. Even
if *you* don't feel that way, you know someone who does. You sense their
anxiety and cross-pressures. But what if there is another way? What if there
were a set of practices, a form of life, a way of encountering things that high-
lighted and revealed their depth? What if there was an approach to life that
looked for and invited experiences of beauty, truth, and love, on a regular,
day-to-day basis? Wouldn't that life be enchanting? If the answer is yes, then
you've picked up the right book because that is precisely what this book is
about. *That* is the Romantic invitation.

How This Book Can Change Your Life

To the modern ear this may all sound nice, but also a bit idealistic. These are
interesting ideas, someone might say, but what would the Romantics have

17. Wallace, *This is Water*, 14.

us *do*? What does the Romantic life actually look like, practically speaking? Those are good questions. As we'll see, the answers are complex but they all fundamentally rely on one maxim: *embrace your humanness*. The Romantics believed that it is our humanness—our capacity to have rich and symbolic experiences, to engage fully in the act of living, to seek truth, to take joy in beauty, and to love one another—that provides the conditions for the possibility of an enchanted life. This is not just some pie-in-the-sky ideal. For the Romantics, enchantment is something you *do*. It is a form of life. And throughout their works the Romantics provide practical strategies, methods, approaches, and ways-of-being to help us experience the world as an enchanted place.

To that end, this book provides step-by-step instructions on how to use Romantic methods in order to experience enchantment. Chapter 1 focuses on the problem of disenchantment and explores in detail the Romantic invitation. It looks at the forces at play in a disenchanted world, forces like scientism and capitalism, which have their own way of "enchanting" us but not in the positive sense in which we've been using the term. It then takes a detailed look at Romantic ideas and provides case studies and examples from the Romantics themselves, so you can get a sense of their own language, lives, and lessons, right from the source. After that, each chapter becomes a practical field guide for enchanted living, focusing on one Romantic strategy you can use to experience the world in an enchanted way. Chapters 2 through 6 follow a common structure. First, they'll look closely as a specific modern problem. Second, they'll discuss the Romantic response to that problem. Third, they'll distill from that response a practical strategy the Romantics came up with to address it. And fourth, they'll offer you a chance to apply the strategy in a practical exercise. Each chapter is designed to move you from your modern experience, to the Romantic reply, to the practical application of the idea, so that you end each chapter with a clear sense of how to actually live the Romantic life.

Here's a quick summary of the strategies we'll cover. Chapter 2 explores the power of the imagination and how to use it to see things with fresh eyes. Chapter 3 explores our relationship with Nature and how to tap into its special sort of truth. Chapter 4 looks at language and the role of sincerity in an age of snark. Chapter 5 teaches the art of poetic contemplation, of slowing down and adding texture to your everyday experiences. Chapter 6 teaches the importance of transcendence, taking seriously the sublime and providing strategies for recognizing and reflecting on it. Chapter 7 rounds out the discussion and shows how even in modern life there are seeds of enchantment planted all around us, seeds we can cultivate and grow and share with others. Fairy tales, holidays, seasons, meals, etc., all provide fertile ground for re-enchantment. The last chapter ends with a send-off, so to speak, a nod to the trajectory of the Romantic life that, if carried forward and applied, makes for good living.

Maybe Wordsworth wasn't being too dramatic after all. Maybe it's time to lessen our obsession with "getting and spending." Maybe it's time to stop "lay[ing] waste our powers" and to once again imagine, dream, contemplate, express, transcend, and reclaim our hearts, and our humanness. What do you say we give it a try? The Romantic life awaits.

1

How Not to Become a Star

Chloe's Question

I'd like to begin with a story. It's not a particularly unique story, which is why it's so relevant. It's the kind of story that many of us could tell. It's a true story, but the important truth it delivers has less to do with its facts and more to do with the underlying feelings it communicates. Here's how it goes.

Once there was a little girl named Chloe. Chloe was born to nice parents in a small suburb just outside of Cincinnati, Ohio. Chloe's father was a lawyer at a midsize firm and her mother was a management consultant for a large, international company. Both were doing well in their careers, thanks to their reputable college degrees, hard work, and a little luck. Chloe grew up in a comfortable house, but it wasn't opulent. She had plenty of friends and plenty to eat. Her parents drove Toyotas and shopped at Target, just like the rest of us. She took ballet classes, played soccer, and decorated her room with Disney dolls and Lego constructions. By all accounts, she lived a completely normal life. Chloe's parents didn't go to church because they didn't like organized religion, and besides, they never went to church when they were kids so they really didn't see the point in it. They celebrated holidays, of course, but Santa Claus and the Easter Bunny took center stage over Jesus of Nazareth or the Prophet Muhammad. Chloe's parents had a standard view on things: they assumed the world was made up of atoms, science told them the truth, the goal of life was to be happy, and it was important to be your authentic self. That was their basic view. It's not a bad view, after all. Most of us hold it.

One day, when Chloe was about six years old, she began to wonder about death. Her friend at school told her that her grandmother had died over the weekend. Chloe felt sad for her friend but wasn't sure what to make of her grandmother's death. Until then, death seemed like a pretend thing, something that might happen to one of her toy figurines when they were on an adventure, but they could always come back to life. This seemed different, and it troubled her. *What if it happens to my grandma?* she thought. *Or my mom? Or me?*

That evening, Chloe asked her father about death. They had just finished reading *Cinderella* and were sitting on the edge of her bed.

Chloe just blurted out: "What happens when you die?"

Her father was caught off guard. He paused.

"Well, what do you mean?" he stammered, "Where did you come up with that?"

"Sara. Her grandma died this weekend. She's sad about it, and so am I. Where did her grandma go? What happened to her? What happens when you die, dad?"

Chloe's father wasn't sure what to say. He had always known the question would come, and he'd given it some thought, but never the kind necessary to articulate a good response. He knew the truth, of course: that when you die your heart stops beating and your brain stops working and your body becomes a lifeless mass of matter and you grow cold and stiff with rigor mortis and they bury you in the ground. People gather around you and lament your passing but they also accept the fact that you're dead and that all creatures die, lions and worms and birds and everything else. There is no exception. One day we all close our eyes and slip into oblivion. That's all there is to it. The end.

But he couldn't just say that to Chloe, of course. She was six for goodness sake. That would have been too much. She wasn't ready for the truth. But what *could* he say? He wasn't about to tell her some made-up story about how when you die you don't really die but instead go to heaven and live with your grandma and grandpa and Jesus. That's not true, he knew that, and he owed it to her not to deceive her, especially given how young and impressionable she was. He didn't want to lie. What could he say? He was stuck. He had to think fast.

"You become a star," he said.

"A star?" asked Chloe, the upward intonation of her voice suggesting curiosity, and relief.

"Yes, a star," he repeated, committed now. "When someone dies, they become a star. Their soul goes up into the sky and stays there, shining down on us. It's sad when someone dies, but it's not the end. You can see their love burning bright in the sky. It's true you can't just go to their house or hug them anymore, but when you become a star, it's kind of beautiful too. Their love keeps on going, shining on in the sky."

Hey, he thought, *that was pretty good.* He even felt a little proud of himself.

Chloe was starting to come around, but she still seemed worried.

"Will *you* become a star one day daddy?" she asked.

"Yes, I will. One day, honey. But not for a while."

"And mommy too?"

"Yes, mommy too."

Chloe paused. Maybe she wasn't coming around after all.

"And me? Will I become a star?"

"Yes, Chloe, one day we all become stars. But it's a long way off for you, and me, and mommy."

Chloe's eyes began to well-up with tears. She sniffed and hung her head low. She began to cry.

"But what if I don't *want* to become a star?"

What Disenchantment Feels Like

It's tough to be a child. It's tough to be an adult, too. Sometimes it feels like there are no good answers. Maybe there aren't. One thing I find truly remarkable about Chloe's story is the way in which her father tries to deal with this feeling. He senses that there are no good answers to the question of death but he still tries to provide one. He feels like he owes it to Chloe to "tell her the truth" about existence—that we live and die adrift in an inherently meaningless, cosmic void—but he knows that, as meaning-making human beings, we need more than that to be able to get up in the morning. Whether it's ignorance, or God, or a story about a star, he knows that we need *something* to carry us through our material existence. Now, he has his own biases against which stories he's willing to tell (e.g., he has a vague distaste for Christian mythology based on his own experiences with Christians growing up), but he still feels the need for a story. He's "cross-pressured," as Charles Taylor puts it. He's tugged in two directions: toward the truth of scientific materialism on the one hand (death is a biological fact) and toward a desire for eternal, immutable truths on the other (love lasts forever). So he adopts a middle ground. He assumes a position in which he implicitly holds that existence is reducible to matter, that there is nothing else "out there," but he allows himself recourse to symbolism as a means to convey a story about being human that preserves in some sense the possibility of inherent meaning.

But these two approaches are at odds. After all, if only matter exists, then love is just an overly valorized, complex chemical reaction going on in our bodies. We can dress it up all we want, write poetry about it, and call it a star, but it's really just biology. At the end of the day, like Sara's grandma or stars themselves, love burns out. Lovers die. People forget. We all end up food for worms. You see? There are no good answers. Trading Jesus for a star doesn't solve the problem because the problem isn't about religion. It's about disenchantment.

There's another story to tell here. A less dramatic story, perhaps, but one as relevant to our understanding of disenchantment as Chloe's. There once was a time when people didn't think the way Chloe and her dad think, the way most of us think today (even if only implicitly). About five hundred years ago almost everyone presumed belief in something "out there," a transcendent order that was outside of our control, that moved unseen throughout existence and could impact our daily lives. Magic, God, angels, spirits, demons, goblins, and ghosts of all kinds existed in a world of their own, a world that overlapped with ours but was not reducible to it. To folks five hundred years ago, existence was made up of much more than matter.

Back then, when a child asked, "What happens when you die?" there were a number of "good answers," and by good I don't mean satisfactory to us, in the modern period, but satisfactory to them, in their own time and place. You go to heaven. Your spirit lives on. You can communicate with your loved ones even after death. You can pray for them and affect their location in the afterlife. They can pray for you, and affect yours, and so on. The point I'm trying to make here is not that they were right and we are wrong, or that we should "go back" to the way medieval people thought about the world five hundred years ago. We can't and we shouldn't. What I'm trying to get at is a point similar to the one Charles Taylor makes in *A Secular Age*: there was a time in the not-too-distant past when *un*belief in a world "out there" was almost unimaginable, and now there is a *presumption* of *un*belief about anything being "out there." In other words, we presume a deep, existential and metaphysical immanence. We all have this unspoken idea that what we can experience with our senses is all that there really is, and that anything else is an add-on, an option, maybe even just a feel-good story to make life more bearable. A star story, so to speak. Unbelief is the baseline, everything else is up to you. God, angels, divine energy, or whatever you want to call them are star stories, myths we tell ourselves. You can choose which, if any, you want to adopt. Or, you can "grow up" and face the facts of a material existence. But we sense that doing so is difficult. The truth is hard to swallow. We know that without some kind of star story we'd all be Chloe, grasping at straws for an explanation about what makes life worth living, while at the same time struggling with what we know to be true: that life is nothing but matter and there is no inherent meaning in our lives. It's a tough spot to be in, and we all feel the cross-pressure of it, even if we don't recognize it.

Now, this is where the story starts to split. It gets complicated, and layered. When we ask ourselves how it is that we went from a presumption of belief to a presumption of unbelief, we find ourselves in a bit of a quagmire. The reason for the quagmire is that there are competing narratives as to how we ended up this way, and depending on which way you "lean" you're more or less likely to adopt one narrative over another. For example, the basic secular story as to how we ended up with unbelief as the baseline and God as one option among many goes something like this: five hundred years ago, we were mostly uneducated, illiterate, ignorant peasants who didn't understand the world because we didn't have access to scientific achievements. So when things went wrong or events happened that we couldn't explain we made up stories to explain them, conjuring all sorts of creatures and magical forces and witches and curses to make sense of whatever the world threw our way. It was a patchwork effort, but eventually the various explanations came together and formed a comprehensive whole, and part of the whole involved an entire universe of unseen forces, including God, the great Unseen Force of Good who was "out there" orchestrating things but could also come "in here" and work his own sort of divine magic. All of this made a great deal of sense five hundred years ago. Unfortunately, it's all false. The world isn't *really* like that. We know this to be true. And how do we know? Because we have science. Thanks to the curiosity, genius, and stubbornness of a few generations of scientifically minded heroes like Galileo and Newton, we were able to overcome the dogma of superstition and shine the light of scientific reason on the world. And when we shined it, it was miraculous what we *didn't* see. There were no ghosts, no goblins, no witches, and no God. We could all grow up now and stop believing in fairy tales. Science ushered in a new age of maturity, of knowledge, and of truth. Now, to believe in anything other than what science can prove is childish. Non-scientific beliefs betray a kind of childishness in the person who believes them because they suggest the person can't accept the facts, things as they really (scientifically) are. Belief is an inability to face up: existence is composed of matter and that there is nothing "out there" except more matter, spinning and swirling around in the ever-expanding void of the cosmos.

That's the story of secular materialism. Some philosophers call it *scientism*: the idea that science is the best form of knowing and that we should privilege it over all other forms of knowing. If something can't be scientifically proven, it's second rate. This should all sound familiar. It's what most of us think, and it is what Chloe's dad thinks because he's a secular materialist too, even though he would probably never use those words to describe himself. *He* actually doesn't think he's *anything*. He thinks he's just accepting the facts, and that's what he's training Chloe to do too.

It's funny though. There's a lot going on in that little story. For one thing, Chloe's dad thinks he's only telling one story, the star story, to Chloe. But he's actually telling *two* stories. He's telling the star story, sure, but he's also telling *himself* a story about the way the world is, a secular story. Without even knowing it he is reifying his own unbelief by framing all of his experiences according to what Taylor calls "the immanent frame." The immanent frame is a certain orientation we moderns take toward the world, basically by default. The immanent frame is the implicit way in which we view the world and explain it. Immanence means "right here," what's before us, what appears right in front of our eyes. Contrast that idea with transcendence, which means something "out there," something beyond or immaterial, something we can't necessarily see, taste, or touch. According to our secular orientation, everything is immanent. We frame our existence with a disposition toward immanence. There is nothing transcendent. At least, that's one way to spin it, and it's a common way. It's Chloe's dad's way, and it will be Chloe's way too, eventually, because that's the story she'll grow up hearing. He's catechizing her a secularist. The star story is a band aide. One day she'll learn the truth: stars are luminous spheroids of plasma held together by their own gravity. They're not souls, and they're not love. Chloe is destined to be disenchanted.

Disenchantment is part of our modern, secular condition. It's the sense that comes along with living within an immanent frame. It's a way of implicitly perceiving the world. What's important for our purposes is not only what disenchantment is, intellectually, but how it "feels," how we kind of carry it around in the background of our lives, all of the time. Disenchantment often goes unnoticed because it's so embedded in the way we move about the world that we hardly know it's there. It's "thick," so to speak. It's part of the very make-up of the modern experience, it's in its very structure. It informs our reactions, thoughts, and impressions without us recognizing it. Our relationship to disenchantment is like a fish in water. There's the fish, just swimming about and minding his own business, when another fish swims up and says, "How's the water today?" The fish replies, "What water?" That's what disenchantment is like for us. It's the water. But we can learn to see the water. We can recognize that we're swimming in it, and unlike the fish, we can do something about the way we experience it. I think we can even change the water. But before we get into that, let's plunge a little deeper and take a look at how the water we're currently swimming in feels.

Everything's an Object

The secular, material world is full of objects. It's full of things. When we look around we see a bunch of stuff: a coffee cup, a Subaru Outback, a tree, a bird, another person. Everything is composed of matter, has its own independent existence, and is not dependent upon us in any way in order for it to *be*. But we *can* control the objects. We can master the world by knowing it. Any object can be dissected. We can strip it down to its constituent parts. A car is just an assemblage of different mechanical pieces. A person is just a complex composition of blood and guts and bones. Happiness is a brain state, an influx of serotonin, dopamine, endorphins, and oxytocin.

There's another thing about viewing the world as full of objects: whenever we do strip something down to its constituent parts—to its *real* parts— all we find is more manipulable matter. The exercise of dissection confirms our orientation toward immanence. That coffee cup is made up of clay, which is made up of mud and water, which are made of molecules, which are made of atoms, and so on. We can make a million mugs. The Subaru is a bunch of mechanical parts ready for mass production. The bird is feathers and flesh and the tree is twigs and bark and cells. We can grow both. Even the other person is essentially a material object, albeit a complicated one. Whatever "it" is, it's *really* just an object made of matter. And if it can be taken apart, it can be controlled, and it can be reconstituted or created *by us*. Making something an object makes us masters over it.

This is an interesting perspective when you think about it. On the one hand, it feels obvious, like it's the logical implication of science: the only things that exists are things we can observe. But most reputable scientists wouldn't go that far. They'd say that science studies the observable universe, but not that science is the only form of knowing, or that the only thing that exists is the observable world. We'll discuss that idea later, but for now let's stay focused on how disenchantment feels. It feels like a world made up of objects. But on the other hand, because of our lived experience and the complexity of our own inner lives, we feel like *not everything* is reducible to being an object. Some things resist objectification. We have deep emotions, things move us, we have a vision for our lives, a love for our families, and hopes and fears that we carry with us. We "sense" things as much as we "observe" them, maybe even more so.

My point is that when we "look outward" all we see are objects because we have internalized a certain scientific view of knowing the world; but when we "look inward" we see a vast confluence of experiences, feelings, senses, sensations, projections, imaginings, memories, and so on. These "things" don't feel like things at all, they feel like states of being, or modes of experience, or a non-objective flow. Sometimes, despite our intuition that our lived experience is not reducible to materiality, we try and explain it in those terms anyway. That's a disenchanting move. For example, we might say that the sense of awe we feel standing in front of a mountain landscape is really explained as a brain state. Or we might say that the grief a child feels over the loss of a loved stuffed animal is essentially a psychological expression of familial attachment. In either case, what we're doing is subjecting *ourselves* to the scientific gaze, rending *ourselves* an object. And in doing so, we are trying to master ourselves (and others too). We can rationalize all of existence. But when we do that we run the risk of concealing parts of ourselves that deeply matter, that aren't simply matter; that is, the experiential parts that we know but cannot quantify, like our experience of the eternal, the moral, or the true.

A Sense of Urgency

Another way we "feel" disenchantment in our lives is in its pace, in our sense of time. Modern life is frantic. I once heard it said that "structure drives behavior." There's a lot of truth to that. The idea is that people will behave in a way that comports or conforms to the structures in which they find themselves. And what's more, they will begin to internalize the structure so that the shape of their thought takes on the "structure of the structure," so to speak.

Let me give you an example. Consider a high school classroom. The room has one entrance and four walls. The white board and teacher's desk (which is bigger than all the other desks) are at the front of the room. The students' desks are all in a row, running from the front of the room to the back of the room. Students enter. How do they behave? Like subservient workers, that's how. They file in, take a seat, turn to the front of the room, and submit to the teacher's authority. The structure steers them. They must walk in a certain direction (single file lines toward the back), lower their bodies before an authority (sit down), and acknowledge that authority as it imparts knowledge (face forward). What's more, the structure seeps into the psychology of the students. They internalize it, adopting an acquiescent disposition toward the room's power-broker. At least, that's the idea. The student's behavior conforms to the structure of the room. I know a lot of modern classrooms don't look like that anymore but that only strengthens my point: teachers (rightly) decided to change the thinking of our students in order to make them more open, innovative, and creative, and so they changed the structure of their rooms to facilitate that sort of behavior, and to *internalize that way of thinking*. Structure drives behavior and it forms thought. That's a big deal in terms of how disenchantment feels.

There are innumerable structures around us that drive our frantic, disenchanted behavior. These structures create in us a sense of urgency with no clear purpose, no clear goals. We're in a hurry, but we don't know why, or where we're trying to go. Think about how you use your cell phone, for example. Almost every social media site, app, or webpage is designed to make you flick your finger, just one more time. *Just one more flick.* Keep the page scrolling. Don't slow down. It's okay to "go down the rabbit hole" and chase link after link. What do we discover there, buried in each hole? More flicks, more scrolls. The literal structure of the device itself—the phone—a three-by-six-inch piece of metal and plastic, compels you to keep scrolling, to always wonder what else is there, just below the bottom border of the screen. Go on, slide your thumb from the bottom to the top. *Flick.*

The entire structure of things like social media drive our frantic behavior, so much so that we internalize the structure into our own thought patterns. Our minds flick through things without ever stopping, without slowing down to contemplate or even consider something in detail. When we're at a party talking with friends we're anxious for them to be quiet so we can tell *our* story. Our minds flicking through stories-like-this-one that we might share. When we're alone with ourselves we're thinking about the next thing we have to do, the next flick of action, the next item on the list. When we sit down to watch a movie we flick through Netflix (ironic name, no?), impatiently screening the catalogue until we find a show that might settle our minds, even if only for a short sixty minutes.

The pace of disenchanted life is the pace of the never-ending scroll, the constant flick, the anxiety that comes with always needing to know what's on the next page, what's beyond the bottom of the screen. As we'll see later in this book, enchantment calls for poetic contemplation, a kind of "magical focus" on what lies before us, versus disenchantment, which is marked by a vague demand, a sense of urgency that presses us onward with no clear destination. We have to keep going, just keep going. But do we? Enchantment says, "no": there's more than enough time for a pause. In fact, everything depends upon taking one.

Then there's "confetti time." Have you ever had an hour of your day look like this? You've just put the kids to bed or finished that last work email. You're finally done. It's time to relax. You've been looking forward to a glass of wine and a new book, or taking a bath, or taking a walk, or trying something new. It's time for leisure, and you're ready to go. Your phone pings. You get an email, then another. Something's up at work. You check your phone and respond to one of the emails, then turn back to the book (or hobby).

You read a few sentences. The dog barks. You get up and let him out. In five minutes, he'll want back in. You read a few more sentences. He barks. You let him in. While you're up, you get a text. It's from your mother. She has a leaky faucet. You tell her to call a plumber. Back to the book. A few more sentences. Instagram dings: new comments coming in. You flick for five minutes, skimming pointless banter. Back to the book. Out of nowhere, you remember you wanted to check Etsy for a cheap end table. You grab your computer. You look at furniture. You end up disappointed. None of it's right. Back to the book. Slack pings. Your works friends want a happy hour. You reply. Back to the book. A few paragraphs in you wonder whether the kid's sleeping. You check the monitor. He's fine. You're relieved, but still a little worried. You're always a little worried. You need a break. Back to the book. Another text. This goes on for the remainder of the hour. Time's up. Leisure's over. Better get ready for bed.

What the hell just happened? You lost your chance at pleasure to what Harvard professor Ashley Whillans calls "confetti time," ripping up your moments of leisure into little fragmented bits of unenjoyable moments that deny you the pleasure you sought in the time set aside. Confetti time leaves you unfulfilled and stressed out. But it also disenchants. You never experience the magic of a moment spent doing something you love. You forget that life can be deeply enjoyable, that slow, focused concentration or getting lost in a task is incredibly rewarding. Instead, your leisure time is spent worrying about what's going on "out there," out in the world of social media, or mainstream media, or work, or whatever. Confetti time cuts twice. It makes you feel an unsettled sense of urgency, and it denies you the time it takes to stop and realize *that you feel a sense of urgency in the first place*. Confetti time conceals the very fact of confetti time. It's insidious in that way. It takes a great deal of effort to not only *see* confetti time for what it is: the shredding up of joyful possibility, but to *do* something about it. It's funny (and maybe even a bit embarrassing) that it takes a Herculean act of will to put down your cell phone for an hour. But it does. It's tremendously difficult. That's how deep disenchantment runs. It's seeped into our minds, so much so that we are unable to allow ourselves the leisure we so desperately desire, even when we know what's denying it to us. We clutch to the chains that bind us. We desire what shackles us. That's what disenchantment *feels* like.

Foundationlessness

Another hallmark of disenchantment is the feeling of foundationlessness. Like the other "feelings" of disenchantment we've discussed, the feeling of foundationlessness is less an emotional state and more an embedded "sense," something we experience *before* we think about it. It's not like normal feelings, like pain or happiness or sadness. It's a "background" feeling. It's always there, even when we don't recognize it. It's the water we swim in.

Foundationlessness is the sense that there is no stable ground to our existence, no inherent meaning or general principle of reality. It's the impression we get of the world when we adopt what secularism claims is "the standard view of things." Let me give you an example. Back in the medieval period, people experienced the world as a *place*. There was an order to things. In fact, most cultures at one time or another had a place-model of the universe, but we'll focus our attention on Western cultures because that's our starting point. During the medieval period most people assumed the world was ordered according to The great chain of being. God was the source of everything, and to varying degrees the rest of creation flowed from God. A hierarchy of being emerged. Angels were at the top, because like God they were immutable spirit. Humans followed, a mix of spirit and matter. Then came the animals, then plants, and finally, lowly minerals. You don't have to be a medieval Christian to see the importance of this model of the universe (in fact, it probably originated with the Greek philosopher Aristotle). The point is that for the medieval person existence had a foundation: God. And the cosmos had an order, a hierarchy of being that located humanity within it. God was the ground and we had a place in the grand scheme of things.

But now, we don't. The bottom's fallen out. As the German philosopher Nietzsche declared, "God is dead." Where once we saw God and the great chain of being as a viable explanation for existence, we no longer assume that there is any explanation at all. We simply *are*. We just exist. We are floating in space, not rooted to a place. Secularism tells us that we are infinitesimal and insignificant biological creatures crawling around on a planet adrift in an ever-expanding universe. Do you sense the difference there? Can you imagine how existence must have "felt" for a medieval person versus how it "feels" for us? I'm not suggesting one is better than the other (not yet, anyway), I'm just pointing out that there is a way to experience the world as having a foundation, and a way to experience it as foundationless, and that our current existence is marked by the latter.

This "space" versus "place" distinction is important. Unlike a place, where something fits or belongs, a space is a void into which anything may be put. Existence is a space. We are here, but there's no sense of belonging. Our "being here" feels like a crap shoot, a fluke, a lucky (or unlucky) turn of the cards. We're here because of an accident of nature and we'll be gone soon, and nothing will really have changed. Our family and friends may be sad but they too shall pass. We are foundationless.

And like the structure of a cell phone or a work day, we internalize the experience of foundationlessness. It plays out in everything. Beauty is subjective (there's no objective grounds for calling something pretty). Wisdom is a cultural construct (there's no outside way to evaluate a life insight). Truth is relative (unless it is empirically verifiable, but then we're back to spaces and voids). We *want* a foundation, but *we don't want* one too. We want to be able to point to a truth, but we are afraid that claiming there is one will in some way be oppressive to others and to ourselves. And we think we've learned from our past, historical mistakes about claims to grounded truths—they've led to a lot of heartache, war, genocide, and bigotry—and so we eschew them in favor of the vague purgatory of secular humanism that says we can never settle, we can never have a foundation. The trouble is, as the philosopher Emmanuel Levinas pointed out in his brilliant essay "Reflections on the Philosophy of Hitlerism," people *yearn* for a foundation, for a lived sense of belonging. Denying that yearning opens the door for radicalism and horror. It may go some way in explaining the current rise in nationalist populism today. But that's another book.

So we sense the world lacks a foundation. There is no truth, no God, no (objective) beauty. We do not belong, we simply are. It is up to us to make something out of the void of existence. The French philosopher Albert Camus likened our modern condition to the Greek hero Sisyphus, who after having offended the gods was condemned for eternity to push a giant boulder up to the top of a mountain only to have it roll back down the other side. Sisyphus's existence was absurd. It made no sense. It had no inherent meaning. Sisyphus had no place in the world. He simply occupied a space. Now, according to Camus, if we can imagine Sisyphus happy, if we can imagine him taking joy in rolling the boulder up the hill then we can imagine for ourselves a meaningful life. But this is a different sort of meaning than the meaning delivered by the great chain of being. Models of existence like the great chain of being deliver meaning from "outside" of us. We always already find ourselves in a place. But Camus's existentialist sense of meaning is a human creation. We are all Sisyphus and our task is to find joy in the absurdity of rolling the boulder up the hill, in the inherently meaningless—that is, foundationless—nature of our existence. We must find a hero from "within" because there is nothing to imbue life with meaning from "without." The plight of Sisyphus resonates with most of us because we are born into a secular humanist worldview that decides for us before we even show up that the world into which we're thrown lacks any and all foundation. And that's how it "feels" to be modern, to be disenchanted.

Outrage and Suppression

At this point you may be thinking to yourself, "Gee, modern existence is pretty awful. It feels more like a disease than living." That may in fact be true, but there are bright sides to being modern. It's not all bad. For example, we have a thirst for justice that drives a lot of our political discourse, even though it often comes off as angry and divisive. There is a common, underlying conviction that we should treat people fairly, that we should do right by others. The disagreement is in what that means, but the thirst for justice is a modern conviction. And we are more connected with each other than we've ever been. That's a good thing too, generally. It allows us to have a heightened sense of awareness of our "footprint" in the world. It makes us more sensitive to others and calls us into responsibility toward them.

But often times these convictions become muddled and confused because they trade on a discourse of undirected outrage and suppression. What I mean by that is that disenchantment as an experience of urgency, objectification, and foundationlessness coupled with a deep drive for a better world creates in us a tension, and that tension needs a release. We feel a sense of tension because we *want* there to be more to life, we *want* there to be a grounding truth (call it God, Justice, Equity, Freedom, whatever), we *want* to slow down and savor things, but all around us are structures that drive our behavior to the contrary. We're swimming upstream, so to speak. That can be maddening. It makes us feel an undirected outrage at the fact that we experience the world as unsatisfying but want satisfaction. So we pop off at strangers and Facebook "friends." We tweet our shock to the world when some political blowhard blurts out bigotry. Or we string a series of Instagram hashtags together in order to snarkily express our disgust at a frenetic president. But all this to no avail. Nothing works. We're on to the next outrage, the next outburst, and our discontent comes with us. Disenchantment denies us the possibility of something more, but we still want it, badly. Instead, we're left with a nagging anger and feeling like we're never actually heard. It's ironic: we live in a time where there are more outlets for self-expression than ever before (Facebook, Snapchat, TikTok, Onlyfans, Twitter, YouTube, Whatsapp, the list goes on) but no one actually feels heard. We're angry and we have a thousand ways to express it, but they all seem more like a muzzle than a mouthpiece. We're outraged, and we're suppressed.

The World Is Flat

Another hallmark of disenchantment is the sense that the world is "flat." What I mean by this is that disenchanted thinking eschews symbolic thinking. It doesn't have an interest or the tools it takes to look for depth, for *layers of meaning.* Disenchanted thinking doesn't take seriously, or at least relegates to a subordinate status, appeals to the symbolic, appeals to what the poet Robert Bly calls the "more than true." Symbols point to things beyond themselves. They are coded with lots of meanings. The American flag, for example, refers beyond itself through its images and colors: the red stripes symbolize hardiness, valor, and spilled blood. The white represents purity and vision. The blue is justice and perseverance. And of course, when combined in a flag those symbols are at play with each other, constituting a whole host of possible meanings: rebellion, pride, freedom, failure, hope, disappointment, oppression, liberation, conflict, colonialism, unity. The meanings don't have to be consistent on an enchanted read. Enchanted thinking acknowledges that symbols are not discursive messages. They speak with many voices. When you look at the American flag you can see a colorful piece of cloth and maybe even feel nationalist sentimentality, but when you look at it symbolically you see a variety of possible references, all swirling about in a milieu of meanings. Enchanted thinking says things like, "What might this remind me of?" or "What might this stand for?" or "What *else* could this mean to me?"

Disenchanted thinking privileges a single explanation, reduction, and literalism. In this way it is "flat" thinking. It wants to provide a complete account of something and then make use of it, to convert it into some practical value. In philosophy we call this "instrumental reason." It says things like, "What does this *really* mean?" or "Did it *really* happen?" or "What can I *do* with this?" Enchantment sees depth and multiple meanings as a good thing, something to be celebrated, an invitation to explore the various possibilities of a thing's meaning. Disenchantment sees multiplicity as confusing and unnecessarily messy. It's inefficient. Disenchantment looks at things through a single, usually literalist, lens. The American flag doesn't mean both freedom and oppression. It can't, those are contradictions. It can mean only one thing (and the result is to either put your hand over your heart or take a knee). Disenchantment lacks the tools to see depth, multiplicity, and even simultaneous contradictions. All the disenchanted thinker has is a hammer, and everything looks like a nail.

Let me give you a more complicated example, one more directly related to the Romantic strategies we'll discuss later. Consider fairy tales. Some people read the old Grimm version of fairy tales but most of us get

the Grimms' stories retold by Disney. We don't really explore the meaning of
a fairy tale. Our fairy tale conversations (if we even have them) are usually
about how violent they were originally, how Disney has made them more
palatable for our delicate children, etc. Sometimes we critique the Disney
versions for re-enforcing gender norms we now find oppressive, or to the
contrary we might celebrate how valiant Disney's efforts are to use the fairy
tale medium to overturn those same oppressive gender norms. The point
is that, for us, fairy tales are a thing to be analyzed, critiqued, or explained.
They do not speak for themselves. We speak over them, or about them. But
if you read a fairy tale you see that they are full of mystery, symbolic references, and nuance. There is innuendo in a bower-enclosed princess. There
is an invitation in the woodcutter's hut. Fairy tales speak with many voices.
But on our modern, disenchanted account we try to explain them away or
critique them rather than revel in the multiplicity of meanings they offer
up. This has less to do with fairy tales themselves, of course, and more to
do with the disenchanted way we talk about them. And that's exactly what
I'm getting at: the discourse around symbolic thinking is disenchanted and
disenchanting.

Something similar happens with Santa Claus or Jesus of Nazareth.
"They're not real," we say, or "He wasn't who others say he was," and so
we don't use them to teach our children the deeper truths of life (I'm not
suggesting Jesus wasn't a historical person, I'm suggesting we reduce his
importance to his historicity). We fail to see them as symbols, in addition to
whatever else they are. Santa is a myth and Jesus was just a teacher, so there's
no use going on about it. That's what disenchantment says. But what we miss
when we say these things is that Santa Claus is more real than reality. He is
(at the very least) the spirit of human generosity, gift-giving, and surprise.
He is a watchful father and a playful friend. He is mirth and hearth and
wonder. His truth is more true than the truth (or falsity) of whether there
is *in fact* an old man who lives in the North Pole and delivers presents on
Christmas Eve. The same is true of Jesus. You don't have to be a church-
going Christian to appreciate and ponder the depth of love symbolized by
Jesus healing sick children, praying with poor people, and making his death
into a sacrifice. At the very least, Jesus demonstrates for us the capacity of a
person to be kind, loving, and sacrificial. That is a truth of Jesus that is truer
than his status as a historical figure, a wise Jewish teacher who antagonized
the authorities. He may or may not be that too, but there is no need to reduce and then dismiss the plurality of truths given over by the symbol of
Jesus's life. To do so is to disenchant.

But that is precisely what we moderns tend to do. The world is flat. It
has one meaning (if any). Symbolic thinking isn't worth the time it takes

to engage in because it's based on a literal falsehood. The underlying event (Santa's location, Jesus's divinity, a fairy tale's plot) isn't real, and so we need not spend time considering it. That's disenchantment.

Skull-Sized Kingdoms

The philosopher David Foster Wallace, whom I referenced earlier, once described the modern experience of alienation as the experience of always living inside your own head, rarely (if ever) breaking out of your "own, tiny, skull-sized kingdom." We're alienated from each other because we struggle to get outside of ourselves and so we feel a deep sense of loneliness at the center of our existence. There's a lot of truth in that. The "problem of other minds" is a perennial problem in philosophy. *How can I get outside of myself? How can I really know what's going on out there, in other people's heads? How do I know I'm not really alone?*

This "problem" is a big one, and disenchanted thinking only hardens it, offering no good solutions. According to "the problem of other minds," we struggle to overcome our own existential alienation because we cannot transcend our personal subjectivity. We can't break out of the Matrix. We experience existence first and foremost from "within" ourselves. I am my body. I am my mind. I am my own experiences. Day in, and day out we live as though we are indeed at the center of the universe. It's as though the world *actually does* revolve around you. We struggle to get outside of ourselves, and maybe we never can. Even the most empathetic or compassionate person among us experiences the world from within her own mind. A great chasm seems to separate "me" from "you." And so, according to Wallace, we lord over our own tiny, skull-sized kingdoms and carry with us an innate sense of alienation. Even in our most intimate activities, like making love or laughing together, we sense this distance that separates us. As the Irish poet W. B. Yeats said, "the tragedy of sexual intercourse is the perpetual virginity of the soul." That seems to hold true not only for sex, but for all human interaction.

The distance we feel between ourselves and others tends to disenchant, or to be magnified by disenchantment. But it doesn't *have* to. One way the distance of the other plays out as a disenchanting force in a modern, secular context is in our inability to ask questions, to have true conversations with each other. Question asking is an art. Done right, it reflects a desire for something other than one's self, a desire to explore the wilds outside your own kingdom. But most of the time when we are in a conversation with another person, say, at a house party or a barbecue, we're listening not with the intent to "get outside" our kingdoms but with the intent to express what's "within" them. We're waiting for the other person to stop talking so we can speak. You see what's going on there? The insulated, modern mind alienates itself and in so doing denies itself access to others.

But others can be a great source of enchantment. When you stop trying to find a story from your own experience that connects to what the person at the barbecue is saying and instead become curious about the other person in and of herself what you may discover is a wealth of interesting things, insights, fears, tensions, desires, and hopes. You may even find joy in the presence of the other person. That's what Aristotle thought true friendship was: taking joy in the virtue of the other person. Asking questions invites new experiences, invites the other to reveal herself, to try and bridge the chasm that separates us. It's one small way to get outside yourself. Now, some people may not interest you, and that's ok. Not everyone is full of fascinating mystery (actually, they are, but we'll get to that later). My point here is that it is our tendency to live within our own heads that denies us the possibility of the "more" that is the inner life of the other, and that forecloses possibilities of encountering joy and beauty. It forecloses enchantment. Curiosity, question asking, and putting one's ego aside may not always enchant, but it makes enchantment possible.

Disenchanting Forces: Three Examples

Now that you have a sense of how of disenchantment feels, the next, natural question is something like, "Well, how did we end up this way?" There are lots of reasons. What I'd like to do here is look at three disenchanting forces at play in the world we live in today, rather than give a historical account of the rise of disenchantment. The story of disenchantment is contested. Not all scholars agree on how we got here. But I'm convinced that describing modern life as disenchanted is illuminating, and so rather than rehash the philosophical and historical stories in the previous chapter about "how we go here," in this chapter I'm going to provide a brief explanation of "what's keeping us here." I'm going to explore three forces in modern life that I think disenchant, and perpetuate disenchantment. These forces turn us away from depth and profundity and try to keep us in the shallow end. They make us feel all the things we've just discussed.

One last note: I'm not a conspiracy theorist. I'm not arguing that there is a secret cabal somewhere in the Swiss Alps orchestrating an international disenchantment propaganda campaign, and they're hypnotizing all of us into an existential stupor. Disenchantment is subtler than that, it's more complex and insidious. I'm suggesting that there are economic, social, and philosophical structures underlying our modern way of being that form a confluence, one that both promotes a disenchanted worldview and obfuscates our ability to see it. I don't think there is a master puppeteer, or if there is, it's all of us, by virtue of the fact that *we* create and perpetuate these structures. So what are those forces? Let's take a look at what I think are The Big Three.

Suffocating Scientism

Recall that *scientism* (not science) is a view *about* science, not the view *of* science. Scientism is a popular position: a lot of people hold it today. It says that science is the only objective—and therefore best—way of knowing, and all domains of human activity and experience should be subjected to the scientific method because, well, it's "right." And by "right," scientism means that science accurately describes the way things are in the world, and does so completely. We don't need to resort to any other way of knowing to get to the Truth, with a capital "T." Everything, according to scientism, is scientific. Everything that can be known can only be known through the scientific method. Scientism claims that because science studies the observable world, the observable world is the only thing that exists. But as we will see, there are a whole host of other ways of knowing, other modes of consciousness, other dispositions and attitudes that we can adopt that reveal truths not reducible to empirical explanation, modes like imagining and poetic contemplation.

There's one key point to make about scientism before moving on to explain how it disenchants: *most scientists are not proponents of scientism.* Scientism is a cultural assumption about knowledge that's been absorbed into the mainstream, popular, secular worldview. But most scientists don't see science as the only source of knowledge. Scientists readily admit the limits of science and scientific inquiry but are intrigued by what there is to know within those limits. They would not make the "strong" claim that scientism makes; namely, that empiricism is the only way of knowing. That's important to remember. Enchantment is not antithetical to science, but it is antithetical to scientism. Enchantment and science are not mutually exclusive, but enchantment and scientism are.

A major way that scientism suffocates us and leaves us disenchanted is by forcing a scientific explanation on everything we experience, everything about the world that we find magical. Another way of describing how scientism disenchants is to by saying that scientism cannot rest in "negative capability," as the Romantic poet John Keats called it. Scientism wants to *explain*, and it must do so according to an empirical framework.

Take love, for example. Google "the science of love" and see what comes up. There are a whole host of university-funded studies, articles, research projects, and peer-reviewed publications that attempt to explain love as *essentially* a complex chemical reaction. They usually get a lot of press around Valentine's Day, and they go something like this: You want to know what love really is, right? Let's look at the science. According to science, love occurs when a certain kind of object appears before the human subject (one that arouses sexual attraction and induces our desire to procreate; in other words: a pretty person) at just the right moment, triggering a series of hormone infusions into our bodies.

First, there is lust: the hypothalamus stimulates doses of testosterone and estrogen from the testes and ovaries. You experience the physical sensation of sexual arousal and a desire for sexual gratification thanks to this immediate burst of chemicals. Next comes attraction. Brain pathways open up, and for a few weeks after your first dose of lust hormones you start to have this feeling of being "overwhelmed" or "taken" because you've "met someone." You're "lovestruck." But what's really going on here is your brain's hypothalamus gave you a jolt of dopamine and norepinephrine. Of course, you might get a reduction in serotonin, which leads to a decreased appetite during the attraction phase. But that's temporary. The need for fuel will kick back in. Finally, there's attachment, which arrives in the form of oxytocin (the "cuddle hormone") and vasopressin. These two hormones promote long-term bonding, which leads to procreation and the ability to pass your genes on to the next generation. You see? It's simple. The reason you think "love" is something magical is because you just don't understand the science. It's a matter of human chemistry, biology, and evolution. That's the answer to the question, "what is love?"

Is it, though? Does this account really capture what we *experience* when we experience love? It does explain the science, that's for sure. But is that enough? Does the scientific account say anything meaningful about the existential longing you feel in the depth of your soul for companionship? Does it speak to the truth of spending a lifetime together with another person, and then holding their hand as they take their last breath? Does it illuminate in any real way the moment of eternity you experience when your lover smiles at you and offers you a bite of his ice cream? I don't think so. I'd wager you don't either. Chemistry helps us see some things, but not enough. You'd never know that from scientism's perspective though. That's the arrogance of scientism: it claims that all you can know, you know through science. There is nothing else. That is disenchanting.

There are lots of examples like this one. Scientistic reductionism takes on basically the same structure when it gives an account of something. Religion is a combination of an innate, human need to create meaning (anthropology), the pursuit of social cohesion as a survival mechanism (sociology), and a desire to belong to a group (psychology). It's a human enterprise explainable by (social) science. Beauty, like love, is a chemical cocktail induced by the appearance of the form of some object. You're not really "moved" by a painting, it's a dopamine trigger. Even your griefs, fears, and anxieties amount to empirical phenomena. The lived reality of all of these things is reducible to biology, chemistry, matter, etc. You get the idea, and like many other people, you sense that there's more to things than that. Well, there is. But the discourse of scientism can suffocate with its relentless reductions. As we'll see, to experience the world as an enchanted place you have to be on guard against scientism, *but that doesn't mean you reject science.*

Capitalist Confusion

Scientism is not the only disenchanting force in our modern world. Capitalism plays an important role too. I want to be clear at the start that what I'm *not* saying is that capitalism is "all bad." It's not. In explaining disenchantment, I'm not actually advancing a covert Marxist critique. But I am trying to point out the way capitalism and its ideologies seep into our discourses and set our values. We "think capitalistically," whether we like it or not. It's no coincidence that we value hard work, productivity, ingenuity, practical application, money, and material stuff: these are the things capitalism needs us to value in order to keep the economic engine of capitalism running. We valorize risk-taking and energetic entrepreneurs, and we loath indolent, ivory-tower academics. The former contribute to the economy, the latter contribute only ideas, which are basically useless, unless they can be monetized. Economic idleness is the worst sort of vice. It's those kinds of assumptions embedded in a world structured by capitalism that I want to point out, particularly as it relates to disenchantment.

But capitalism is paradoxical: it *both* enchants *and* disenchants. It disenchants by rendering the world a smorgasbord of resources, products, and items for us accumulate and consume. We see the world as full of commodities, and we—the consumers—are called upon to gobble them up. Something is valuable if we can *use* it. We can hear capitalism speak through us when we say things like, "Yes, but how can we *apply* that in real life?" or "That's good in theory, but what about in *practice*?" or "Yeah, but is it *worth* anything?" The implication of these questions is that something is valuable if its convertible; that is, if it has an exchange-value and can be transformed into something useful, the most useful transformation being, or course, transformation into money.

Capitalist-style disenchantment happens when we see the world like this, when the supreme values are exchange and practical application. Privileging practicality and transactional worth above all other values has the effect of devaluing things that have historically enchanted, things like art, beauty, poetry, and moments of quiet contemplation. None of these things exist to make money. None of them find their value in conversion or usefulness. Capitalism disenchants by telling us that enchanting things are not valuable, so pursuing the beautiful or the true is a waste of time, or worse, an exercise in idleness. In order for the pursuit of beauty and truth to be a legitimate enterprise you must find a way to package and sell it. Write a book. Get it published. Make some money. Beauty and truth are not ends-in-themselves. But there's something important about the relationship between an "end-in-itself" and enchantment. We sense that when our motivations are merely monetary, when they do not emerge out of a genuine concern for something, we lose out. The thing is cheapened in some way. Capitalism disenchants by always prodding us with the question, "Can you make some money on it?" That's what I mean when I say that capitalism commodifies everything: it keeps whispering to us that the things we do and love must be *economically* valuable to be *truly* valuable.

Of course, valuing practical application is not bad. This book is about the practical application of Romantic ideas, after all. But *privileging practical application and economic value over all other values is where things start to go awry*. It's not much different than science vs. scientism. One offers a certain way of seeing and knowing and is satisfied to operate within its limits (i.e., science), the other makes the more audacious claim that the best and truest way to see and know is just one way, and we should apply that way to everything we see (i.e., scientism). Likewise, most of us do value practical application, usefulness, and exchange-value *among other values*, but capitalism presses us to value them the most, above all other values, and to evaluate the ultimate worth of things according to their standard. Capitalism disenchants because it reduces all things to their transactional value. It does this not only to everyday things like cars and trucks, but to all things, like animals, art, and even each other.

Capitalism is tricky though. There's a paradox here. On the one hand, capitalism disenchants through the reduction of all things to their transactional value, but on the other hand, capitalism enchants; or better, *re-enchants* (in its own, insidious way, or course). It says, "Yes, all things find their ultimate value in use and exchange, but look at the marvels we've created by seeing it that way! Look how amazing the world is when we're all motivated by money!" To a certain point, that's true. Capitalism has indeed created marvels, and is a marvel itself. There can be no doubt that because of capitalism we have thrilling and intoxicating things right in front of us: a weekend trip to the Caribbean, FaceTime with friends halfway across the world, a thousand and one kinds of cereal from which to choose. That's not sarcasm you're hearing. I mean it: capitalism has for many delivered on the promise of a more comfortable, easier, and materially satisfying life. It's also driven invention and innovation in a way unprecedented before the Industrial Revolution. The form of life capitalism offers is very, very seductive. Capitalism re-enchants by suggesting to us that what we've lost in its use-value reductionism, we've made up for in pleasure, comfort, joy, and fun.

Capitalism also re-enchants by *dazzling* us. It's shiny, and it likes shiny things. It's always offering us something new. It promises us that our perpetual consumption and desire yields technological progress, which in the end is better for humanity. We do our *duty* by consuming. But don't think about that for too long. The flashiness of capitalism insists that everything be fast and novel. There's always another experience coming down the pike. We just have to try it. There's always another version of the iPhone. We just have to have it. The time it takes to reflect on whether all this so-called "progress" is, in fact, actually better for humanity is not afforded to us. Before we have a chance to ponder it, the next shiny thing is shoved in front of our faces. Isn't this fundamentally what marketing is about? Marx was wrong. Religion isn't the opiate of the people. Advertising is.

"But!" you might say, "We're solving problems left and right thanks to free-market competition. It spurs innovation. Isn't that a good thing?" It can be. But it comes with a cost, a big one. It seems there's no problem too big for capitalism. We always assume "someone is working on it," someone out there is burning the midnight oil trying to solve or resolve our issue. Your dog's unsafe in the car? Someone's inventing a doggy seatbelt. You're tired of dropping off the laundry? We're working on an app for that. If you have a problem, rest easy knowing that someone, somewhere, is trying to fix it. Capitalism re-enchants by telling us capitalism can solve all our problems, that it's the best economic system we can come up with. Sure, it makes everything a commodity, but that incentivizes problem-solving through profit, and *that's actually a good thing because, well, look around at how amazing everything is!*

A lot of people find this logic convincing. I can see why, honestly. Sometimes I do too. But take a second look. Are we actually solving problems? In a way, yes, but in another way, no. It's true we cranked out a COVID vaccine in a year, but we also created a media apparatus that made us all want to kill each other because of it. Both are products of capitalism. Are we replacing one set of problems with another? Are the new problems "better" than the old ones? Some yes, some no. The answer isn't so simple. It's worth problematizing the narrative that says capitalism fuels human desire and that improves everyone's lot. For example, how long can the world hold on environmentally while we extract its resources in order to get rid of all our discomforts? How much is enough? At what point do we say that to be human is to experience some discomfort, and that's ok. We don't need to solve every problem.

There's one more thing worth problematizing about capitalism before me move on. Capitalism re-enchants via the promise of innovation. But does capitalism actually produce innovation? Or does it produce *iteration*? Does it give us something new, or does it give us new ways to do the same thing? How many times can we see the same superhero movie? How many ways can you make a car? How many different kinds of ketchup do you need to taste before you make the right choice? Is a new iPhone really progress? *Progress toward what?* Faster flicks? Higher-def forms of narcissism (portrait mode selfies!)? On second look, capitalism looks more like endless repetition than innovation. Capitalism dizzies and distracts us by giving us more of the same, which in turn perpetuates an unrestrained desire to consume it all. "New" turns out to be another version of "old." And this bedazzlement and "problem solving" conceals from us the deeper moments of truth and beauty that we might otherwise experience. In this way, capitalism both dis-enchants and re-enchants.

Deteriorating Deconstruction

This last force of disenchantment I'd like to discuss is a tough one. It's quite subtle and hasn't fully worked itself out yet in the popular discourse, but it's there. And like capitalism, it disenchants but then (tries to) re-enchant. It's a bit heady as an idea, but stick with me and I'll bring it around.

In the 1960s and 1970s a new way of doing philosophy started to pop up, first in France then later in America and across the European continent. This way of thinking is called "deconstruction" and has evolved into a broader, more general view of the world today that we call "postmodernism." The French philosopher Jacques Derrida was the first to articulate a full deconstructive program. He argued that most of Western thought since Plato had been obsessed with what he called "logos," the stable, unchanging ground of all of existence, the thing that is "really real" and is always there, the center of things. We've been looking for the logos for eons, it seems, but the good news is we believe that we've been progressing toward its eventual discovery (if we haven't already discovered it, that is). But what Derrida argues is that there is no logos, there is no ground, or if there is, it's not the stable thing we think it is. According to Derrida, language always plays a constitutive role in what makes up the "real," and linguistic meaning is inherently unstable. Words make sense by referring to other words. Language is an endless play of *différance*, an endless referral to something else. Because the "thing" we're looking for is constituted by language, and language is always deconstructing itself, the "thing" is never fully here, it never fully arrives, and we can never cling on to it with the philosophical certainty we desire.

These ideas—that there is no stable meaning to language and no underlying structure to reality—are deeply insightful, and in many ways true. But the story of deconstruction takes a disenchanting turn. Soon after Derrida's articulation, deconstruction spread like wildfire. In fact, it's still spreading today, but often in a watered down, less reflective form. It shows up in our everyday thinking. For example, we have this general assumption that "everything is relative." What's right and wrong? Most people would say it's "just up to the individual" or "the culture" in which they live (whatever "culture" means). There is no "real" right or wrong. Morality is inherently unstable. How about the meaning of a book, or a movie? Relative. There is no meaning buried in the book. Meaning is not like a gold nugget, "in there" somewhere, just waiting to be mined. No, it's up to the reader to imagine for herself what the book is about. It's a matter of how it speaks to her, personally. A text's meaning is never settled. Personal identity is very similar. There is no fixed "essence" to who you are. You can be whoever you want to be, whatever you want to be. Identity is socially constructed, and so it can be deconstructed and reconstructed in any way you want. Identity is always in flux.

Insightful as it may be, this postmodern way of thinking can play out in paradoxical ways. Let's stay on the topic of identity for a moment. It illustrates these paradoxes well. The question of identity is a hot-button issue in America. Everyone is calling into question the (oppressive) forces at play that define gender and sex roles for our culture. New genders are popping up all over the place. At the time of writing this book, Facebook has at least fifty-eight identity options users can select, including androgyne, bigender, cis, intersex, non-binary, pangender, trans____, and so on. A lot of people list their preferred pronouns in their email signatures, signaling to others how they'd like to be identified. The plethora of gender options and pronoun notices point to an underlying postmodern view of things; namely, that identity is always deconstructing itself. It's fraying at the seams.

But here's where things get weird. According to Derrida and other deconstructionists, any time you use language to constitute reality, you end up making a double move: you both affirm and negate the thing you're constituting. Whenever you claim to be X, you're also implicitly claiming *not* to be Y, or Z. As soon as you say you're one thing, you're also saying you're not something else. "I'm a man" also means "I'm not a woman," and so on. But when you look at those things, you wonder whether in claiming to be X, you really meant not-Y and not-Z, too. Did you? Maybe so, but maybe not. So you end up in this perpetual attempt to capture all the affirmations and negations that you "really" meant. You come up with fifty-eight different ways to categorize yourself and others. But according to Derrida, there's no end to this activity of categorizing and recategorizing, of chasing the ghost of identity, because the categories themselves are always deferring to another category to generate their meaning. They're inherently unstable. They're fraying at the seams. Each new identity category reveals the instability of the others. The point I'm trying to make is not that we should or shouldn't differentiate genders *ad infinitum*. That's not for me to decide. The point I'm making is that the proliferation of genders and identities testifies to the postmodern assumption that, as the poet Gertrude Stein once said, "there is no there, there." There is nothing underpinning identity. There is no ground. And that has had the effect of leaving us disenchanted.

We have a similar problem with truth. What is truth? Up until recently, the popular, secular position was that, like meaning and morals, truth was relative. True for you might not be true for me. The way I perceive things and the way you perceive things are different. Who's to say which perception is *really* true? No one can see the whole picture. We're trumpeting the German philosopher Friedrich Nietzsche's proclamation from a hundred years ago: "there are no facts, only interpretations." But then a funny thing happened. The very people who generally pushed back against the postmodern view of things—most conservative folks—began to adopt it. There was a time in the not-too-distant-past when political liberals saw themselves as the great emancipators, wielding the sword of deconstruction to destroy oppressive power structures by revealing their socially constructed and inherently unstable "foundations." But now political conservatives are making the postmodern move and claiming "alternative facts" and bias, bias, everywhere. The irony is that the most postmodern thing that could happen is that the anti-postmodernists adopt deconstruction as a tactic. And that's exactly what *did* happen. In a sense, we've become a victim of our own deconstructive enterprise. No one has a leg to stand on. In the great post-truth era of fraying identities, relative ethics, and ungrounded truth, we cannot appeal to any stable source to make a claim about the world. So what do we do? We join a tribe, and we shout at the other tribes. Everything is in a perpetual state of un-doing. Some might even say deterioration. At least, that's what it *feels* like, doesn't it?

Postmodernism and deconstruction disenchant by un-doing everything, by denying grounds and stability and by living in the free space of play. While this sounds nice, it also comes with a cost, as we can see. We feel disenchanted within postmodernity because we cannot look around and see beauty, truth, or love anywhere. Every time we claim we see something beautiful there is a deconstructing voice that says it's not *really* beautiful because beauty is relative, it's a biased perspective, maybe even an oppressive, patriarchal construct. We're afraid to say something is beautiful for fear we might offend someone, or that in doing so we're endorsing some idea that has an insidious underside, that it's oppressive to someone because it originates from some patriarchal, colonial, or you-name-it motivation. What's worse, we run the risk of looking like a fool for even thinking in the first place that there is such a thing as beauty. Beauty's not real, says the deconstructionist. It's just a construct. Only an ignoramus would say something is beautiful. Awe is replaced with cynicism. Like capitalism, we might say that postmodernism in some ways actually re-enchants, too. Deconstruction does a good job of freeing us up from historically oppressive constructs, and opening a space of possibility, of a future. But when the instability revealed by deconstruction becomes the obsession, and when we wield only one weapon for social critique, we end up with a lot of smashed bits and nowhere to stand. In that sense, postmodernism feels more like a disenchanting force than a re-enchanting one.

Answering Chloe's Question

Let's return now to Chloe's question. Given what we've just discussed, I hope it's clear that hers is a deep one. In fact, it's The Question, as far as this book is concerned. Her version of The Question was "How do I *not* become a star?" There are lots of other ways to ask it too. Here's a few more: Is this really all there is? How can I escape all this madness? What should I do about the fact that one day I'll die and become food for worms? Is my life meaningless? If so, so what? Is there anywhere that I belong? Will I ever figure out what I really want out of life? How should I live? What is "The Good Life," anyway? How can I get the most out of life? Are there any other options aside from all this materialism? Is there any other way to *be*?

Despite their differences, these questions all emerge from a common experience of the world, an experience of disenchantment. They articulate a deep set of concerns about what it's like to live in space rather than a place, how it feels to *always feel* the perpetual press of consumption, and what follows from the fact that everything is fraying at the seams and it seems like there is no center. These questions give voice to a fundamental tension that characterizes our modern, secular, materialist worldview. They give voice to disenchantment.

That last version of The Question is an especially insightful one. Is there any other way to *be*? It represents an opening, an inquiry into possibility, a reach for a future ripe with meaning. We hope the answer is yes, but we don't know how to find out how else we can live, how we can discover different "forms of life," as the Danish philosopher Søren Kierkegaard put it. We look to popular culture, movies, music, politics, etc., but because all of these are products of the underlying, disenchanting forces of scientism, capitalism, and postmodernism they simply reaffirm our anxieties rather than address them. Even worse, they often perpetuate them. We don't know where to look for answers, and so we make them up. We come up with star stories and hope they do the trick. But they don't, at least not for long.

Like Chloe and her father, we are stuck. We sense there are no good answers within the immanent frame, or from within a disenchanted mode of existence because the forces of disenchantment deny us the tools necessary to adequately address the types of questions we're asking: existential questions. We have to break out. We have to look elsewhere. We need to revive and re-engage ideas that have always been sources of enchantment but that have been papered over by modern consumer culture and materialist-style secularity. Romanticism is one such option. There are others, of course. But the strength of Romanticism is its abiding concern with beauty, truth, love, mythology, symbolism, the imagination, values, contemplation, poetry, narrative, and a whole host of other "useless" things that we have always found enchanting, that historically we have used to experience the world as an enchanted place. Without something more, the forces of disenchantment leave us unmoored, adrift in a flat world, silently outraged, alone and alienated. It doesn't have to be this way. Romanticism offers a way out of disenchantment, or better, a way *beyond* it. The Romantic Life can lead toward a life of enchantment.

The remainder of this book will focus on that: it will teach you how to go beyond disenchantment by looking closely at five strategies the Romantics used to enchant the world and how to apply them in your own life, how to *be* Romantic. This is a book about hope, not cynical resignation. We will look to eighteenth- and nineteenth-century Romantic philosophers, poets, and writers to see how despite our "age of outrage," frantic pace, and almost religious deference to science we can still address our desire for meaningful experiences that imbue life with beauty, truth, and love. Romantic thinkers were keen to this impulse and developed a rich philosophy that cultivated and responded to it. According to them, the ineffable truth of a poem or the sublime awe of a mountain landscape gives depth and texture to life in a way that scientific and economic materialism cannot. Let's see how they do it.

2

The Imagination's Power

Conjuring Beauty in a Cold World

Imagination, Make Believe, and Delusion

"You're imagining things," you say to your friend as you walk past a graveyard, though he swears he sees something in the dark. A mother says to her toddler, "Tell your imaginary friend so-and-so to come and sit down. It's time to eat." The word "imagination" is often preceded by another, smaller word: "just." "It's *just* your imagination." What do we mean by this? What do we think we're doing when we imagine? Are we doing anything important? Generally, the answer is no. What we mean—whether implicitly or explicitly—is that we're making stuff up. Imagining is make-believe. It may be fun to do it, but the thing you're thinking about—the thing you're imagining—is not really real. It's a figment, a fancy, a fiction.

That doesn't make imagining bad, of course. Nobody thinks we *shouldn't* imagine simply because it's make-believe. Imagining can be fun. We might even encourage it, especially in our children. "Let's imagine you're a super hero!" or "Imagine if you could play the piano like that!" we might say. But we also recognize the hazards that come with imagining. Our imaginings can blind us to the facts. "You imagine you'll be fine, but if you don't save enough money, you'll end up in trouble," you tell a teenager; or, "you're letting your imagination run away with you," you say to a jealous lover. Some imagining can be even worse, slipping into delusion. The person who fails to distinguish between her imaginings and reality can lose touch with the world around her. And sometimes, imaginings become hallucinations, dangerous symptoms of an underlying pathology.

We can see from these examples that there are a number of ways to think about the imagination. It is quite powerful. "Power" might seem like a strange word here but given its ability to influence our perceptions of reality, it's hardly an overstatement. The imagination *does* have a power. In fact, it *is* a power. It is the power to reconstitute the way we experience the world. Perhaps there's more to the imagination than meets the (mind's) eye.

Let's start with what seems obvious. The imagination is a mental faculty. It's a faculty in the sense that it's a capacity our minds have, it's one of our mind's abilities, along with the ability to reason, to perceive, or to form judgments. But imagining is also an activity. It's something that we *do* with our minds. In other words, when you imagine something, you sense that there is something "going on up there," in your head. But what *is* going on up there?

Try it out, imagine something. Imagine a yellow canary. Now, make it sit on the branch of a tree. Now, have it ruffle its feathers and tweet out a short song. What, exactly, is going on there? In imagining, you're initiating and controlling some kind of action, some agency, some creative power. Through the act of imagining you're able to draw from a store of previously perceived experiences and call up images of them, assemble them in new ways, move them about, change them, etc. You can make things. You can move them around in a future not-yet-defined. The imagination goes beyond memory in the sense that memory is tied to some event that (ostensibly) happened in the past, some actual set of facts that once occurred. But in imagining, we sense that we can free ourselves from what has actually happened or what we've actually perceived and are able to create *new* things, unmoored from direct perception. What we create takes its reference from perception, but isn't limited to it. This creative aspect of the imagination was key to the Romantics, as we'll see, and they challenged the notion that imagination happens "just in your head" or, even more radically, that there is a bright line between what we imagine and what is real.

One last thing to note about the imagination: pay attention to how when you imagine something, it appears somewhere, but "where," exactly, is hard to put your finger on. It's like the imagination conjures things in some quasi-real mental "space"; that is, somewhere in your consciousness. But where *is* this space? That's a really tough question. We've been stewing on it for ages. What's important for our purposes is to notice that the imagination is its own mode of consciousness, and that it has its own mental "real estate." To imagine is to orient yourself to a certain way of experiencing the world. The yellow canary you just called up definitely exists, and it exists "there," in that nebulous mental space of the human mind. You can "see" the canary, but it's in an in-between state. We know it's not real in the same way a canary outside your head is real, but we know it's not "unreal," either. It's not like it doesn't exist *at all*. The canary has what philosophers call a *metaphysical status*: its own nature of reality, its own kind of being. As we look closer, we see that imaginings blur the line between what is real and what is unreal, or at least call it into question. Maybe imagining isn't such a childish activity after all. Philosophers don't think so. There's a long history of people trying to figure out what is actually going on when we imagine. A basic understanding of their views will help us appreciate—and then apply—the Romantic way of imagining, which is a way that brings about enchantment.

Mirrors and Lamps

Prior to the Romantic period, the dominant theory of the imagination was that it operates much like a mirror, reflecting images of reality back to the mind. When we imagine something, so this theory says, we are calling forth a faded impression of something we once perceived. Imaginings are copies of reality; paler, inferior copies. This mirroring or *mimetic* theory of imagining has its roots in Plato (424–328 B.C.), who thought imaginings were "the poor children of poor parents," reflections of the material world, which according to Plato reflects the eternal, immaterial world of Ideal Forms. To him, imaginings were of even less importance than the normal, everyday world, which was itself less important than the abstract world of ideas. That's all you need to know about Plato to see that for him (and generations of philosophers to follow) the imagination was relegated to an inferior status among the mind's various faculties. Imagining was viewed as a shabby mental act, one prone to mistakes and fancies and at worst, deceptions. It does not lead us to truth. Quite the opposite. It leads us astray because the reflections it produces are incomplete, they are several steps removed from the thing that caused them, and *that* is the thing we want to know about.

Despite two thousand years of separation, the philosopher David Hume (1711–76) agreed with Plato that the imagination operates like a mirror, reflecting back to the mind less intense copies of sensations. But unlike Plato, Hume argued that the ideas we have in our heads are *all* images generated from sense impressions. All of them. The imagination to Hume is a sort of image-making factory that produces images from sensations and associates those images in our minds. The implication of this idea is that since all ideas are images, and reason's ideas differ only by degree of vivacity from other sensations, reason itself is subject to sense impressions and can make no reference to an "outside world."[1] All we have are sensations given to us as images. The result? Radical skepticism. To Hume, the imagination is the "undercurrent of the mind" that provides the illusion of cause and effect, identity, and being-over-time by relating images one to another. It tells us nothing about external objects, things "outside" of our minds.[2] So much for objective truth. That's heady stuff, I know. But you don't have to be a scholar of eighteenth-century philosophy to appreciate the fact that, for major thinkers in the Western tradition like Hume and Plato, the imagination is no trivial matter. Big things are going on "up there."

Then along came Immanuel Kant (1724–1804). Kant's *Critique of Pure Reason* is one of the most important texts in the history of philosophy. Awoken from his dogmatic slumber by the force of Hume's skepticism, Kant set out to examine the very structures of consciousness; that is, the conditions that allow for the possibility of experience to happen in the first place. If that feels a bit esoteric, hang on. I'll bring it around.

Kant wanted to know what had to be in place for all of this stuff, all these sensations that you experience every day, things like smells and colors and objects, etc., to come into your mind and actually make sense to you, to appear as a coherent world. Think about it for a minute. If the world is always throwing at us reams of sense data: a tree there, a person here, the sound of a dog bark, the color orange, cold, dark, warm, pleasure, etc., there must be something in the mind that binds it all together, something that unites all the information we take in into a single whole, a world that makes sense to us. Otherwise, we would just be inundated with a barrage of incoherent sensations. It would be chaos. Stuff would just be coming in to our minds with no order or structure: brown furry thing, bark, ouch, warm, glow, bright, sour, wet, etc. It would be a hot mess. Nothing would make sense.

But that's not how we experience it. We actually experience the world as a relatively structured place. I'm able to distinguish between objects and people and moments in time pretty easily. What is the thing that does the ordering? What brings it all together? *That* was Kant's question. You see? And what Kant discovered lurking behind all of it was one, mysterious force: *the imagination*. The imagination, according to Kant, was both a "mirror" and a "lamp." As a mirror, it reproduces images of things you perceive—like dogs and cats and the smell of bunt cake—but it also "shines" onto existence, illuminating your experience like a desk light sitting behind you. It pulls all your sensations together into one synthetic whole, into a

1. Kearney, *The Wake of Imagination*, 165.
2. Engell, *The Creative Imagination*, 53.

unity of perceptions, which makes up your "world." Now we can begin to understand why the word "power" is appropriate to describe the imagination. It is more than just a mental faculty that creates unicorns. It's not just reflecting things back to your mind that you've see with your eyes. It is an "art hidden in the depths of nature," as Kant put it, a mysterious, creative force that brings together an entire world for us, *the* world. Taken to its logical conclusion, Kant's insight shows that there is no meaningful distinction between what we imagine and what is real.

The Romantic Imagination

The Romantics took Kant's discovery quite seriously. Over the course of the next century, they built upon it, expanded it, and reveled in it. To them, the idea that through the imagination we create the world translated into an aesthetic injunction to give all of existence a poetic charge, *to make the deliberate decision to experience the world as a place rich with meaning, truth, and beauty.* The Romantics saw the human capacity to imagine as our greatest source of power. It was for them *the key* to living a truly enchanted life.

On the Romantic path, the creative power of the imagination was like a waterfall's rush, pouring over into the world, flooding it with unfathomable depths of meaning. But it wasn't all rush and force and power to them. The Romantics were sensitive, or more precisely, they developed a sophisticated sensitivity to the subtle play of the imagination and its ability to poeticize everyday life. The imagination is in many ways a "quiet power." With only a light touch, the imagination can turn mundane moments like a rainy spring day or a slowly budding seed into the whisper of an eternal truth.

The Romantics were nothing if not bold. They wanted to see what it really meant for us to have a constitutive role in the way the world appears to us. If Kant was right, then we have almost as much of an influence on what we experience as the "outside world" has on us. When stuff comes into our minds it is compiled together by the imagination to form a comprehensible whole. The imagination acts on our sensations as soon as they arrive. So if you think about it, the imagination plays a vital role in *the formation of the world*, in the way we experience anything, everything. The mind is an active force, gathering together experiences and making a world out of them. And we do this without thinking about it, without even trying. It just happens. We don't notice that it's happening because it's built into the very structure of our minds, but all the time the imagination is creating a world for us, responding to and constituting what we experience as "the world." That's an exciting proposition if you're an artist or a poet. But remember that for the

Romantics *we all imagine, all the time.* Imagining isn't reserved for Greenwich Village painters sipping lattes in their studio apartments. We all have the power to imagine. Each of us has the power to poeticize the world, to enchant it.

Let's look at some examples of how the Romantics used the imagination to enchant the world. From them we can glean several techniques that we can then use in our own practice as modern-day enchanters.

Novalis and the Art of Romanticizing

Novalis, a youthful Romantic known for his piercing gaze, put it this way:

> The world must be romanticized. . . . Insofar as I give the commonplace a higher meaning, the ordinary a mysterious appearance, the familiar the dignity of the unfamiliar, and the finite the air of the infinite, I romanticize it.[3]

Here we can see exactly what the Romantics thought we should be doing with our imaginations. If we toss out the idea that the imagination is just a mirror, and embrace the idea that the imagination is an active force that creates a world, then we can see that imagining becomes an activity of imbuing experience with *meaning*. We have a certain amount of control over how we experience the world. We can choose to experience it as full of depth and beauty. To use Novalis's word, we can "Romanticize" it. Notice what he says here: to Romanticize (or to use my word, "poeticize") the world is to give things we normally experience a "higher meaning," to make the ordinary mysterious, or to give the familiar the "dignity" of the unfamiliar (dignity is a great word here because it reminds us of the magic of being alive, of the sheer beauty of existence). We can do all this with our imaginations by making conscious associations between what we are experiencing and other things we have experienced, things we've found moving throughout our lives, and by using those associations to layer meaning upon meaning onto our experiences.

3. Novalis, *Werke*, 2:334.

Portrait of Novalis in 1799.

Let's say for example you're walking the dog during twilight. It's spring-time, the air is warm, and little crocuses are poking their purple flowers out of the ground. You look up and see in the sky a pale, ethereal moon shining down at you. Now, you could "see" all of this with a materialist eye: twilight is the time of day when the earth's rotation in relation to the sun blocks some of the light making its way through the atmosphere; a crocus, or *crocus vernus*, to be exact, is a resilient plant capable of blooming in cold conditions; and the moon is an astronomical body orbiting the earth as its only natural satellite. All true, and a bit dull. Or you could "see" it as a poetic moment: twilight is the time of in-between, where the discerning light of day gives way to the blurred merging of night; the purple crocuses echo the colors of evening, suggesting a harmony and potential oneness of all things; and the moon's pale glow lays over the world like a soft blanket of . . . of what? Not quite light, but not quite darkness either. The moon's pale glow is a translucent blanket, softly descending upon a world that has found a subtle unity. You see? That's the imagination at play. That's choosing to "see" the depth of the world around you without reducing it to matter. It's not make-believe. *It really is twilight.* The crocuses and the moon *really are* there. But through the imagination you can creatively respond to the world in such a way that it *appears* with meanings, depth, and symbolism. And *you really do experience it that way.* That's what it means to Romanticize the world.

Novalis isn't the only Romantic to see the imagination's poetical power working this way. His remark gives us the Romantic idea in a general sense, but other Romantics demonstrated the enchanting power of the imagination by focusing on their encounters with specific objects and items, things they ran into in their everyday lives. For example, Percy Bysshe Shelley, the erstwhile husband of the famous Mary Shelley, author of *Frankenstein*, wrote some enchanting lines about a quite unassuming songbird. By observing and imaginatively interacting with it he ends up poeticizing it, inscribing the otherwise forgettable creature with a depth of meaning, significance, and beauty that is not apparent on the surface of things. The visions of beauty that Shelley experiences emerge from his creative interplay with the world around him, and his imagination. Let's take a look at how he achieves this, and then we'll extract from his examples practical tools for achieving it ourselves.

Percy Bysshe Shelley and Imaginative Associations

In "To a Skylark," Shelley describes his encounter with a little brown bird. Have you ever seen a skylark? Google it, and prepare to be wholly unamazed. They are the most normal looking bird you've ever seen. They're completely common. Save for a little triangular tuft of feathers on the top of their heads, they are indistinguishable from just about every other backyard warbler. Sparrow, skylark, nightingale: they all look the same. At least, that's one way to see it. Another way is to, well, *listen* rather than see. The skylark's song is stunning for its complexity, duration, and variation. The skylark is an early riser, singing all day long and throughout the year songs that on average last two minutes. The skylark does not tweet. It doesn't chirp. It proclaims. It welcomes, and at a startlingly fast pace. The skylark's song can include up to five hundred syllables in a single serenade. That's *a lot* of syllables.

Joseph Severn, *Posthumous Portrait of Shelley Writing Prometheus Unbound*,
1845, oil on canvas.

As the story goes, Percy and Mary were walking one summer evening
along a country road in Livorno, Italy. They heard a skylark singing from
somewhere in the hedges. They never saw the little creature but its jubila-
tions were enough to set young Percy's heart aflutter. When he returned
home from the jaunt, he set to work on a poem about the skylark, so struck
was his imagination by the "blithe spirit's" song, as he would later describe
it. In the poem, he provides a series of similes that compare the skylark
to different images and experiences, trying to "get at the thing" that is so
marvelous about the birdsong. Here's one of them:

> Like a glow-worm golden
>> In a dell of dew,
>> Scattering unbeholden
>> Its aërial hue
> Among the flowers and grass which screen it from view[4]

Just think about that image for a minute. It's beautiful. Picture it in your
mind (imagine it!). Shelley is comparing the skylark to a firefly, or as we call
them where I'm from in southern Ohio, lightning bugs. His description of
the glow-worm is just about as beautiful as the skylark's song itself, the thing
he's actually writing about. Shelley paints an imaginary picture of a firefly

4. Shelley, "To a Skylark," 1216.

hidden among the flowers and grass that "screen it from view" so that all we can see is its "aerial hue"; that is, the soft golden light it emits from its body. Shelley implies that the hue, like any light, sparkles a bit when it bounces off the dew in the meadow, refracting its glow in a warm bath of color. To Shelley, the skylark's song is not just a backyard bird's random tweet. Mixed within his creative-responsive imagination, it becomes a glow-worm's soft flash, a pulsating expression of its inner nature, a flicker of Being itself expressed through the briefest blink of light. This simple comparison between the glow-worm's light and the skylark's song opens up to a new insight about the world, a new way of hearing the skylark's song. Because Shelley *made* the comparison, we hear the song differently, from a different angle, so to speak. It gives the bird's song another layer of meaning, a deeper intonation. We are able to appreciate the way both creatures spread out across the earth a song or light that seems to flow from them, naturally and without thought, something like the experience of inspiration. It's not a scientific comparison of their biology, but *a metaphorical comparison* between their ways-of-being. The comparison is meant to enrich, not inform. In fact, imagining is a lot like the glow-worm's glow or the skylark's song: it is our human ability to transform our surroundings by imaginatively spreading out across our experiences layers of meaning and beauty. Our imagination is just like the firefly's "aerial hue" or the skylarks "profuse strains." We have our own glow, our own song. We have the imagination. And the neat thing is that Shelley shows us this by using *his own* imagination. So there is a triple effect at play in just these few brief lines. And you thought poetry was boring.

Shelley's imaging doesn't stop there. If glow-worms don't do it for you, he tries another comparison:

> Like a rose embowered
> In its own green leaves,
> By warm winds deflowered
> Till the scent it gives
> Makes faint with too much sweet these heavy-winged thieves.[5]

Here, Shelley draws a more organic, more botanical comparison between the skylark and an "embowered" rose. "Embowered" means the rose is hidden, that it's tucked away or enclosed. Enclosed in what? In its "own green leaves." So the flower has bloomed but is nestled within its own foliage, cradled and hidden from sight. But then come along some "warm winds" that pick up its scent, carrying the rose's other beauties out into the

5. Shelley, "To a Skylark," 1216.

world. We can enjoy the rose with our different senses. Its beauty cannot be subdued.

And what happens to the rose scent once it takes flight on the wind? Well, it "makes faint with too much sweet these heavy-winged thieves." This line is intentionally ambiguous, which is nice because it resists our temptation to reduce the poem to one meaning, to "figure it out," to disenchant it. There's no clear "it" there to figure out. It could be that the "heavy-winged thieves" are the warm winds themselves, which steal the rose's perfume and carry it away to a lucky passerby who gets a faint, joyful whiff of its marvelous aroma. Or, it could be that the "heavy-winged thieves" are bumble bees that pick up the rose's scent on their wings and steal it away to other locations. Or they could be something else. But remember: this is a poem about *a skylark!*

Shelley is telling us that the skylark is like this embowered rose, a rose that is both caressed by and caresses the wind (or bees, or something else) with its sweet bouquet. The work Shelley is doing here is *imaginative* work. He's creatively responding to the world around him *by making new comparisons between ordinary things* and then looking at the insights they reveal. What does he discover? Beauty. Truth. Magic. It's everywhere: in the skylark's song, the glow-worm's glow, the rose's scent. Because Shelley is openly engaging the world with his imagination he is able to see meaning, truth, and beauty all around him. He hears one thing, the skylark, and then makes associations between that and other things around him. "Oh, it's like this!" he says, then "No, it's like that!" each time adding a new layer, a new insight into "what it's like" to simply be alive, to be attentive to this world, to walk with your lover on a warm spring day, and to hear a sweet birdsong from the undergrowth. It's so simple, and yet, it is at the same time the fullness of life itself. He could probably go on forever, but we don't need him to. Even in these brief passages we see that he's teaching us to appreciate the power of the imagination and the joy—the enchantment—it can bring to everyday experiences.

Shelley ends his series of similes with a bang. He writes,

> Sound of vernal showers
>   On the twinkling grass,
> Rain-awakened flowers,
>   All that ever was
> Joyous and clear and fresh, thy music doth surpass.[6]

6. Shelley, "To a Skylark," 1216.

By now you're really seeing what he's up to, what he's saying about the imagination's creative-responsive capacity. I won't belabor the point. But I do want to make a couple of observations about *how* the imagination operates in its Romantic form so that in the enchantment strategy section we can come back to those observations and put them to use.

In this stanza, Shelley gives us another delightful image to compare with the skylark. He says that the skylark's music "surpasses" the sound of a spring rain ("vernal" means spring, "showers" means rain) falling on "the twinkling grass." If you've ever sat on your porch and listened to the sound of a spring rain fall onto the newly greened grass then you know exactly what he's talking about. It's a marvelous thing to behold. When the next spring rain comes your way, give it a try. But Shelley says the skylark's song is *even better* than that. He says the skylark's song exceeds the beauty of "rain-awakened flowers" too. Imagine: flowers softly slumbering until the spring rain lightly lands on them, giving them a subtle shake. *Wake up*, it whispers. And they do, petals open up, and like sleepy-eyed children, they take in the mothering rain that nurtures and falls on them. It's such a lovely image.

But the skylark's song is even better than that! says Shelley. (This must be one hell of a birdsong.) In fact, the skylark's song surpasses all that "ever was joyous and clear and fresh." Now, that might seem a bit extreme, even for the most poetic ornithologists among us. But the point here is that there is a sense of rapture that accompanies Shelley's experiences, not only of the bird's song, but also of the imaginative interplay of images, metaphors, and sounds he conjures in relation to it. The beauty of the skylark's song can never be fully said. It offers too much experience. It saturates our senses. Shelley can only make comparisons, "It's like that . . . ," and then try again. It is as though the poem itself *is* the skylark's song. Through it, Shelley is showing us how to use the imagination to enchant the world.

Shelley ends "To a Skylark" with a powerful promise, a nod to the imagination's incredible potential. He writes:

> Teach me half the gladness
> That they brain must know,
> Such harmonious madness
> From my lips would flow
> The world should listen then, as I am listening now.[7]

That's just so good, isn't it? Shelley is saying that if the skylark could teach us the source of its inspiration we would be able to let flow the same kind of beauty that flows from it. The world would pay attention to that

7. Shelley, "To a Skylark," 1217.

beauty, as he is paying attention to the skylark's beautiful song now. That's a really nice way to end the poem. It gets at the heart of the matter; namely, that we actually have within us our own "skylark's song"; that is, the imagination. By imagining, by making connections, drawing metaphors, and letting loose our creative-responsive powers we can see into the depth of things. And what we discover in those depths is a *surplus*, an excess of meanings and insights, a bounty of beauty, and an inexhaustible wellspring of inspiration. The world gives us too much to take in, there's always more "out there" than we can ever conceptualize. We need other ways to engage the world, ways rooted in art and sentiment, not just science. While conceptualization has its place, the world always seems to exceed any nice little intellectual package we try to put it in. It resists reduction, as scientism would have it. The fullness of life dizzies, but unlike capitalism it does not do so with the intent to distract us from what appears before us, but with the invitation to explore it. And when we accept the invitation we are welcomed into an enchanted life, one dripping with layers of truth and beauty, like tree limbs after a spring storm. We find ourselves at home, in a place; not adrift in space.

Stendhal and the Unsubstitutable Other

The enchanting power of the imagination is not just limited to birds and bees. It can transform the way we experience other people, too. That's pretty radical stuff, but it's true, at least according to the Romantics. For Stendhal, a nineteenth-century Romantic novelist, the imagination allows for the possibility of falling in love. Through it, we are able to experience another person as "the beloved": radically unsubstitutable, one-of-a-kind, unique among all other people. In his 1822 work *Love*, Stendhal describes what he calls the process of "crystallization," in which through the imagination the lover imbues the beloved with a special significance. He comes to experience her as radically particular, as *this* Other, rather than an other. She becomes for him the unspoken ground of his existence, a generative source of meaning in his life. Stendhal writes,

> Leave a lover alone with his thoughts for twenty-four hours, and this is what will happen:
>   At the salt mines of Salzburg, they throw a leafless wintry bough into one of the abandoned workings. Two or three months later they haul it out covered with a shining deposit of crystals. The smallest twig, no bigger than a tom-tit's claw, is

studded with a galaxy of scintillating diamonds. The original branch is no longer recognizable.

What I call crystallization is a mental process which draws from everything new proofs of the perfection of the loved one.[8]

At first glance, this might sound like good old-fashioned amorous delusion. We call it being "lovestruck." You know the story. Your friend "meets someone." She is infatuated. She can't stop thinking about him (or her). Like the "leafless wintry bough," her beloved—that is, the otherwise completely normal person—is taken up by the lover's imagination and becomes "covered with shining deposits of crystals" (in other words, she's sees him for more than he really is). She tells you there's no one else like him. She's "blinded" by love, and starts to obsess. When she describes him, it's as if there's no way he's actually like that. He sounds too good to be true. You know in your heart she's seeing things that aren't really there. We even have a word for this: she's "romanticizing" him—which is a *bad* thing—or at least, a naïve one. But keep in mind that this is "small-r" romanticizing, not the "capital-R" Romanticizing we've been discussing in this chapter. (That distinction is key to this entire book.) Reducing the lover's imaginative envisioning of the beloved to "mere infatuation" is exactly the kind of disenchanting over-simplification the Romantics are warning us to avoid. So, what's going on then? What's all this stuff about a "wintry bough" and salt mines? What's that got to do with love, the imagination, and enchantment?

There's another way to look at this process of crystallization, of course. I think Stendhal's point is a bit subtler than the simple "it's just amorous delusion" account of things. Stendhal's view of the imagination is more in line with Novalis's and Shelley's views, and equally as sophisticated. He's trying to explain how *through the imagination* the lover creatively responds to the beloved's appearance, from within the lover's world. On this read, Stendhal is not saying that the crystals are a delusion, but that *for the lover* the beloved *actually appears as the crystallized branch does: studded with beauty, with proofs of the beloved's perfections.*

The distinction between "reality" and "the imagination" dissolves here because, as we have seen, according to the Romantics, the imagination plays a creative and constitutive role in what makes up reality in the first place. This is a hard point to wrap your head around. What Stendhal and the other Romantics are saying is that through the imagination's aesthetic interplay with the world around us *we forge it into being;* that is, whatever we see, taste, touch, smell, and hear is always in some way already influenced by the imagination. The imagination is like a "nest" of meanings into which our

8. Stendhal, *Love*, 45.

experiences "land." The imagination "is there first," so to speak, and shapes the very way we experience the world.

So in the case of the beloved, it's not as though the lover first experiences him as a "normal" person and then she consciously decides to ignore his human imperfections and makes stuff up in her mind about him, conjuring a beautiful image of his visage that isn't really there, one she then chooses to be attracted to it. (That'd be idolatry, not love.) No, to her, he *actually appears* like that. His "normalness" appears as "unnormal." Like the skylark's song or the spring rain, the presence of the beloved in the lifeworld of the lover is an interruption that captures the lover's imagination without her even knowing it. She is enamored by him, yes, but precisely because of the way he appears to her within the confluence of his being and her imagination. That's pretty cool, isn't it?

It's a complex point, but an important one. Here's the upshot: love is not a delusion. The lover's amorous imaginings are not make-believe. They are not lies a lover tells himself in the throes of passion. They are part and parcel of his actual experience. They are inseparable from who the beloved is to him. That's deep, and it testifies to the power of the imagination as the capacity to open us onto beauty and enchantment. For the Romantics, birds, skies, glow-worms, houses, friends, lovers, etc., are all in some important way constituted by the creative-responsive activity of the imagination.

Let me say one last thing about the imagination's relationship to the world before moving on to the next section about its practical application. Remember: according to the Romantics, the imagination is *both* creative *and* responsive. It allows us to "give the finite the air of the infinite," as Novalis said. It can do this because the infinite really does appear within the finite, the imagination is responding to that fact. As "Romantic" as this sounds, it really is true that the great mystery of being is present in a simple flower. And the Romantics aren't the only ones to pick up on this. The Buddha once gave a famous "lecture" to his students: he silently held up a single, white flower. He didn't say a word. There is a perennial truth at play in the Romantic impulse to imagine. The point I'm trying to make is that the imagination is not happening all in your head. It's not just make-believe, fancy, or delusion. By now, you get that. Your imagination is *responding* to stuff that really is "out there," that is actually appearing to you in your everyday life. But it can respond *creatively* to it by making associations and connections with other moving experiences, digging deeper and asking questions of meaning, highlighting and imbuing your life with beauty, and rendering the world an enchanted place. It is the skylark's song that comes to Shelley from somewhere in the grass, somewhere "out there." He didn't just make it up. It is the beloved's appearance in your life that happens *to you*. You don't just conjure him out of thin air. The Romantic imagination is always in some way tied to perception, to what appears to us, but it is not moored to perception. Its creative aspect is free to draw from the rich inventory of symbols, meanings, images, and truths we've experienced in our lives, and it can forge new meanings and insights out of those experiences. *That* is how the imagination enchants the world.

Enchantment Strategy #1: Using Your Imagination

Now let's talk about how to put all of this into practice, how to experience the world as an enchanted place. What I'm going to offer is a set of practical ways to kickstart and use your imagination. Of course, it's always been there, running in the background, but I want you to bring it to center stage. The good news is that once you learn how to consciously invoke the imagination in your daily life, you'll be able to do it naturally, almost without thinking. And it's fun. It's exciting to see the world with fresh eyes. At first, you'll need to engage in some deliberate imagining, which isn't difficult but it does require intention. Then, however, you'll begin to see that connections come easily to you, that it's actually pretty easy to think of the skylark's song as like a glow-worm's glow. Then you're off and running. The world will be full of opportunities to generate beauty and depth. You'll find that imagining comes naturally because, well, if Kant is right, it is the most natural thing we do. It's as natural as breathing, in fact.

Learning to use your imagination will happen in stages. First, you'll need to give it a jolt. Then you'll start to get your legs underneath you and routinely make illuminating connections and associations between things in the world. Eventually, you'll internalize imagining so much so that it will become a natural impulse. Almost without effort, you'll find yourself thinking things like, "Ah, that moon tonight is like a ghost's eye gazing down at me. It's like that time when I was a child and felt alone but also brilliant, in my own way," and so on. These sorts of thoughts will be a joy to you. In fact, at this stage in using your imagination you may not have any lucid thoughts about the connections you're making at all. You may just experience a deep intensity within you, something ineffable and profound that moves through you, along with images and sensations and a kind of satisfied knowing that cannot be put into words. There may come a point where you carry beauty with you always, thanks to the work the imagination has done *on you*. As the poet John Keats put it,

> A thing of beauty is a joy for ever:
> Its loveliness increases; it will never

Pass into nothingness; but still will keep
A bower quiet for us, and a sleep
Full of sweet dreams, and health, and quiet breathing.[9]

Let's take a closer look at each of those stages.

Step 1: Kickstart your Imagination

Recall what Novalis said about "Romanticizing" the world. To do so, he said, we should give the commonplace a higher meaning, give the ordinary a mysterious appearance, and the familiar the dignity of the unfamiliar. We've seen two examples of how that's done in Shelley's similes and Stendhal's crystallization. But what's the technical thing they're doing? How do they develop the capacity for enchantment? The first thing they're doing is *looking*. This may come as a surprise because we tend to think of imagining as all in our mind, not something coming from outside of us. But both Shelley and Stendhal, and Novalis too for that matter, point us outward, to the world around us, as the source of inspiration. To kickstart your imagination the first thing you need to do is *look around you*. Look closely. Notice things you may have never noticed before or that have become so mundane and commonplace that they evade detection: the sound of a creak in your floor, the space between the branches of a tree, the soothing sensation of a memory of your mother.

Now, pay attention to all the associations that those mundane experiences conjure up for you. Perhaps the creak in your kitchen floor reminds you of a time when you were a child in your room, afraid of the dark. There you were, just hoping someone would check in on you. Then you heard a creak outside the door (just like the one in your kitchen floor). In a flash of double intensity, you were shot through with the fear that someone was there as well as the relief that it was your father looking after you. Someone had come to check to make sure that you were okay.

Think of all the meaning packed into that little creak. There's so much more there than a childhood memory. It says to you: youth, darkness, fear, wood, loneliness, threat, blanket, father, protection, relief, security. It says all of that, and more. Thought imaginatively, that little creak takes on a life of its own. Kickstarting your imagination means learning to pay attention to the associations that emerge from the interplay of the world and your symbolic experiences. It's giving yourself a jolt, a push to think one layer deeper about what something means to you beyond the brute fact of its

9. Keats, "Endymion," 1398.

occurrence. Perhaps you notice in the space between the tree branches the way the sun shines through, and it dawns on you that the light and the tree branches intertwine so as to form a natural frame, encasing a raven that's sitting in the tree, just beyond them. You notice this serendipitous play of Nature in harmony and think about how your life is framed by things too: work, family, aspirations, desires, projects. And of course, ravens have their own set of significations: omens, promises, cleverness, warnings, diligence, etc. Who knows what the raven might say to you?

The point is that you can kickstart your imagination by first looking closely at the world as it appears and paying attention not only to the world itself but also *how it triggers a flow of images, symbols, associations, connections, and references* that are just underneath the surface of observation itself, floating just one layer below, in the realm of interpretation. These associations are a rich source of enchantment. They add a great deal to the way we experience life when they rise to the surface. And you're not limited to looking, of course. The other senses are just as potent. What we smell, taste, touch, and hear (recall the skylark, which was never actually *seen* by Shelley) all conjure associations for us. But imagining is a two-way street. It's creative *and* responsive, so the world stimulates your creative energies by instigating the imagination's response, and then you respond creatively by adding to the mix of meanings that arrive for you. You become conscious that the world is inviting your participation in it and active engagement in constituting it. Soon, the world becomes a deep and vast ocean of poetic opportunities. Beauty peeks out everywhere. Go ahead, take a stroll outside, sip some wine, read a short poem, listen to a birdsong, gaze at your lover, think of a warm memory, and *pay attention*. Invite your imagination to play, and pay attention to the things it wants to show you. You're on your way to an enchanted world.

Step 2: Practice Making Connections

Now that you've kickstarted your imagination and you're keen to its back-and-forth flow, you're ready to ramp up your creative side and practice actively making connections. In the first step we focused on noticing the way the imagination almost intuitively makes associations. In the second stage, your task is to play a more active role in generating novel associations.

Pick something that moves you. It can be anything, but just choose one thing. You don't have to know why it moves you, exactly, but it should be something you're drawn to for some ineffable reason. For me, it's the morning. (More on that in a bit.) This "thing" could be as simple as a star or a house plant or as complex as a friend or a father (I'd stay away from lyrical music for this exercise though, it's a bit too complex for what we're trying to do here.) Now, focus on that thing and develop a sensitivity to its poetic meaning to you, notice how its symbolic layers unfold, and pay attention to how you imaginatively generate other, deepening associations to it.

I'm a morning person. I've spent a lifetime wondering to myself what it is about the morning that I find so alluring. I know the beauty of that question is that there will never be a sufficient answer. For me, the morning exceeds any single explanation. But the question yields enchanting fruit each time I ask it, so I keep asking it. Like Shelley and his skylark, I take joy in thinking about the morning, in imagining what "it's like" in order to enrich my relationship to it; that is, to enchant it. I might wake up one summer morning, grab a cup of coffee, stand on the front porch, and *consciously* think something like this: "The morning air is crisp. I feel it on my skin. It's cold but promising, like a stone tomb left open, its chilled fingers pushing me outward. 'There is more to do,' the stony air says. The world is alive, but still." Then I draw from the inventory of images and associations I've gathered throughout my life, and continue to think, "Sleep is like death. I was just asleep, but now I am awake, alive. The morning calls me to rise from my tomb. The morning is the call of life." That idea, "the call of life," conjures for me an image of a newly planted vegetable garden. (Funny, I know. But I like vegetable gardens. Who knows why?) Now a vegetable garden brings to mind the ideas of nourishment and of Eden, and I think of Adam and Eve leaving the garden to go out into the world. And then the lines from John Milton's *Paradise Lost* come up: "the world was all before them[.]" I breathe deeply and I think, "Yeah, it's like that." It's very satisfying, and the morning remains to me a close friend.

Now, you might be thinking, "I was with you until Milton. I don't know anything about Milton, and I don't have any lines of poetry memorized. I can't do that." But don't be put off by my particular string of associations. Not everyone needs to memorize Milton to experience the enchantment of the morning. That's not what I'm suggesting. Milton is no different than the vegetable garden: they're both deepening associations that open onto new meanings in my experience. You must find your own. Trust your instincts. Make connections between things that please you. It doesn't matter what other people imagine.

Still, it's an interesting question: Why is one person drawn to Milton and another to mayflowers? Why does anyone like Milton at all? Or poetry, even? It's hard to say exactly why Milton's poetry speaks to me, but it does, and I'm aware of that, so over my lifetime I've cobbled together little bits and pieces of his poetry that mean something to me and I call them to mind when I'm actively engaging my imagination. They add another layer of depth to the experience. My advice to you is to "find your Milton," whatever it is: songs you enjoy, the "feel" of colors, encounters with nature, paintings that strike you, or even warm memories, like the time when your father expressed his love to you or the pleasure you felt watching your friendˢ say "I do" at their wedding. "Finding your Milton" means stockpiling cultural, aesthetic, and experiential reference points that touch you so you can draw upon them when you're actively engaging the world with your imagination. They are your inventory of enchantment. Your "Miltons" are like a spring in the wilderness that releases a subtle stream of insights, some of which can never be said out loud, only sensed, in your body and in your soul.

Stage 2 of using your imagination is about finding your Milton and channeling your Shelley, intentionally making connections that deepen your engagement with the world. It's about deliberate "Romanticization"—in the way Novalis uses the term—that is, to give the familiar the dignity of the unfamiliar. Doing so allows you to experience the joy of a beautiful thing. If you find yourself thinking phrases like, "It's like that time when . . . ," or "That makes me think of . . . ," then you're probably on the right track. In fact, four of Shelley's stanzas in "To a Skylark" begin with "Like a . . . ," so if it's good enough for Shelley, it's good enough for us. The key in Stage 2 is to consciously make imaginative connections. Here, we're emphasizing the creative side of the imagination. But don't take on too much. This exercise is about quality, not quantity. It has a more meditative pace to it. You're trying to squeeze out all the symbolic juices you can during your encounter with the object. Try doing it once a day, for a week. It may take you only three or four minutes to Romanticize something. Maybe less. Take your time and don't feel pressure to do anything special besides actively engage your imagination and make connections. Try and make connections that please you. Draw on associations that you like to think about. For me, it's poetry, and Gothic literature, and memories of my father, or the feel of the seasons around me. For you it may be something different. That's just fine. Don't feel a need to draw from any highfalutin references like Homer's *Odyssey* or Milton's *Paradise Lost*, or whatever. Just find your *own* Milton, and enjoy the enchantment of something beautiful.

Step 3: Embrace the Flow

The word "metaphor" means "to carry across." We use metaphors to make connections between two things in order to draw out their differences and similarities, and in doing so, learn something true about them, something difficult to say with straightforward language. A "simile" does the same thing but uses "like" or "as" to make the comparison. Both similes and metaphors enrich, rather than inform. They point us toward an insight you cannot say directly. For example, it's one thing to say, "Boy, I am really in love with you," and quite another to say, "O, my luve's like a red, red rose, / That's newly sprung in June: / O, my luve's like the melodie / That's sweetly play'd in tune."[10]

The second "saying" gets at the part of the experience of love that we all know but struggle to put into words—love's freshness and excitement, the sense of liveliness it brings to us, and the feeling that you're open to a new set of possibilities—but that isn't captured by the simple phrase, "Boy, I am really in love with you." In fact, it's precisely *because* we can't say directly what love is like that we speak of it in metaphor and simile. Hindus have this great phrase, "neti, neti." It means, "not so, not so." You usually hear it after someone says something about the Ultimate. A Western version of it might go something like, "God loves like a father, but not quite, not exactly." The phrase implies that no matter what someone says about the Divine, it's never enough; it's always insufficient. It's a partial truth, but there's always more to say because the Absolute exceeds any sole description. Love is like that too: it's always an excess, a surplus. We draw connections to roses and melodies and the month of June to try and get a sense of what love is about. But we know that love can never be fully said, and so we go on with more love songs, more love poetry. Love is . . . , neti, neti.

There is an interesting connection between what a metaphor or simile do, the insights they invite, and the feeling they give when you read them. They produce an almost intuitive sense of meaning as they carry us across the comparison. It's as if this sense lies "beyond" or "below" the words. In Stage 3 of using your imagination you'll start to notice that your creative-responsive engagement of the world takes on its own flow, its own stream of imaginings, associations, and connections. You'll sense that paying attention, making metaphors, drawing similes, and conjuring images comes more naturally to you now and that you have a heightened awareness of your imagination at play. Now you can revel a bit. You can really enjoy it. Embrace that. Embrace the "net, neti" nature of beauty and imagining, the part where you make a connection, relish it for a moment, then let it pass.

This stage is important because it's the moment where your attunement to the unspoken part of imagining, the truth of the metaphor that can only be expressed through signaling, through "pointing toward," comes to the forefront of your experience. You're no longer setting aside chunks

10. Burns, "A Red, Red Rose," 264.

of time to focus on one experience in order to consciously Romanticize it. Instead, you see beauty everywhere, and your imagination is always working, at play with what appears before you. You learn to enjoy each imagining as it comes, if only for a bit. You glean some insight from it and then let it go, leaving behind little deposits of truth along the way. At this point the world appears enchanted because everywhere you look you see (or maybe just sense) a world rich with meaning. Your life takes on a new depth and texture. The robin is never *just* a robin. Water is never *just* water. Sunshine is never *just* sunshine. Although in Stage 3 you may not consciously say to yourself, "The sunshine is like . . ." (although you might), you will know in your soul that sunshine is more than electromagnetic radiation given off by a ball of glowing gas somewhere in the void of space. You will experience sunshine as an ineffable truth, a friend that walks near you, comforting you and nudging you on. The sunshine will land on you and say a thousand things all at once: life, pleasure, fruit, birth, growth, glow, eternity. It will stir your imagination until you know what you've always known but only now remember: sunshine is indeed a thing of beauty, a joy forever.

Love presents an interesting case study on the influence of the imagination and how we experience our lives. The imagination's relationship to love is a subtle thing. Like all imagining, the imagination operates in the background of love, synthesizing our experiences with reference to the beloved, even if only implicitly. Think about it. Think of someone you love. Think of an erotic love, not your child or a sibling or God or your parents. Notice how the horizon of your life seems to unfold according to that person? It's as if the imagination shapes a world for you-as-lover that is grounded in, or takes its orientation from, the presence of the beloved. It's like you experience your life as though there was the "time before," the "time of," and the "time after" the beloved (which takes the form of your death or hers). That last part is tragic, I know, but it proves the point that with love, the imagination projects a horizon of existence centered around the life of the beloved, the *fact* of his or her presence in your life. And if you're not in love or never have been, the absence of love itself becomes a kind of presence in your life as well. *When might it come?* you ask.

Stendhal playfully describes the amorous imagination at work in *Love.* He notes that for a person in love the beloved is often imagined as someone who if she were present would add a sweetness to an experience. When she is not physically present, she is imaginatively present. She is present in her absence, so to speak. Stendhal imagines being on vacation without her and thinking, *"Would that the beloved be here beside me in the cool orange groves beside the sea at Genoa!*"[11] His words might sound a little anachronistic to us but the idea is that you imagine the beloved when she is absent and "can't imagine" your life without her in it. And of course, the lover "crystallizes" the beloved as she appears to him, beautiful, unique, and without substitute. All of that happens almost unconsciously, thanks to the flow of the creative-responsive imagination.

Step 4: Reflect & Bless

One of my favorite Romantic poets, Samuel Taylor Coleridge, had this interesting habit of ending poems by "blessing" things, things that provoked his imagination and inspired him to recognize beauty. It's a funny idea, to bless something. Unless you're a priest, or someone sneezes, you usually don' bless something. It seems a little silly, like there's no real power in it. But it's not, and there is. For Coleridge, blessing was not about granting a special gift or passing on a good vibe. It was *a way to note the sacred*, to acknowledge the presence of a thing as a giver of life, and to thank it for revealing its beauty to you, for enchanting you. At the end of "This Lime-Tree Bower My Prison," Coleridge finds himself admiring the soft arrival of twilight in a shady garden grove. He's just missed out on a hike with his friends. He's brooding a bit, and thinking of the striking landscapes his friends must have seen without him. A raven flies over. He writes,

> [W]hen the last rook
> Beat its straight path along the dusky air
> Homewards, I blessed it, deeming its black wing
> Crossed, like a speck, the blaze of setting day,
> While ye stood gazing; or when all was still,
> Flew creaking o'er your heads[.][12]

The "ye" in the second-to-last line is Coleridge's friend Charles, who had gone on the hike without him. The "your" refers to his other companions traveling with Charles. Coleridge is moved by the twilight scene and the silent flap of the raven's wings. He imagines his friends noticing the rook too, as it flies by him, wherever he is, and it unites Coleridge and friends in a moment of mutual perception, connecting them together like an imagined bridge. The raven *is* metaphor: it imaginatively carries them across the landscape and joins them together, despite their distance, despite their dissimilarity. Coleridge blesses the raven for this insight. He reflects for a

11. Stendhal, *Love*, 46.
12. Coleridge, "This Lime-Tree Bower My Prison," 633.

brief moment, and then offers up an act of gratitude, acknowledgement, and recognition. To bless something is to say, "Yes, there you are, and I am richer for it. Thank you." You might consider adding a little blessing into your life. You might consider acknowledging the beauty of life when it strikes you. Consider a small gesture, a word, or a phrase that is meaningful to you. You can keep it private. It doesn't have to be anything dramatic. A simple nod might do, or a word that resonates with you. Maybe just touching a finger to your heart. The point is that you take a moment to acknowledge the Great Mystery before you, which is given over by something as small as a skylark's song, a raven's wing, or the morning air.

One last note here. It may seem easy to skip this reflection piece, to just "think" the blessing for a second, and then move on. But reflection helps you internalize what you've learned, clarify your insights, and fold the activity of imagining into your sense of self. It increases the odds that what you discover will stick with you. There are a number of ways to reflect on your Romantic experiences. One way is to talk to others about them. You may have a friend who like you is curious or who feels the weight of disenchantment but doesn't know what to do about it. Many of the Romantics were close friends with each other: Wordsworth and Coleridge were known for their tight nit companionship and Percy Bysshe Shelley married Mary Wollstonecraft Godwin, so fond were they of each other. The point is to be on the lookout for a kindred spirit with whom you can connect. By reflecting on your imaginative experiences with others you not only reinforce your own insights, but also nudge others into a richer experience of life, giving *them* the tools to open themselves to enchantment. Friendship itself can in fact be a source of enchantment. Reflection is almost always rewarding so even if you don't have a friend to discuss your experiences, consider other means of communication, like a journal, leaving yourself voice memos, quiet contemplation, or simply taking the time to ask yourself, "What just happened?" "What was that like?" and "What does it mean for me?" Those sorts of questions cement the insights you've discovered into your mind and embed them in your heart.

Concluding Thoughts

Perhaps the most important thing to understand about the Romantic imagination is that it is not the source of delusion, make believe, or fantasy but *a creative-responsive faculty ripe with possibility*. Some philosophers and historians criticize the Romantics for having an inflated view of the imagination, for over-stating its creative potential and falling into a kind of narcissistic or dream-like revelry. But I think that's unfair, and I think it's inaccurate. Sure, some Romantics overstated the imagination's power, but at the core of their belief was the idea that as human beings we have the capacity to enchant the world, and we should, because experiencing the world through enchanted eyes gives us access to the Mystery of Being. The Romantics understood that the world is much more compelling than secular materialism would have us think, and that life's beauty and abundance is worth paying attention to, worth celebrating. If they're right about the productive aspect of the imagination and its pivotal role in constituting the world we inhabit then we miss the point entirely when we claim imaginings are delusions, and that all there is, is matter. Quite the opposite: all experience implicates the imagination. Actively engaging the imagination in order to experience the world as an enchanted place is a practice that pays off over and over again. It yields beauty, insights, truth, meaning, and love. The skylark sings in all of us.

3

The Truth of Nature

Welcoming in the Stranger

Nature Is Full of Bugs

Camping isn't for everybody. Neither is hiking for that matter, or even just spending a day at the park. Some people don't feel a kinship with nature. "It's full of bugs," they say, or "it's dirty." And the truth is, nature *is* full of bugs and dirt. There are actually a lot of good, six-legged reasons not to want to go outside. I understand why some people don't want to "go out" into nature. But there is another side of nature too, or shall we say, "Nature," (with a capital "N"). This side of Nature can enliven, enrich, and invoke in us an experience of enchantment. This Nature is a deeper nature, one that lies below or goes beyond our immediate experience of the outdoors as an uncomfortable place, full of creepy crawlies. It has less to do with the inconveniences of going outside and more to do with the discoveries of what's inside—of us, others, and the world. At least, that's the Romantic view on things, and it's worth considering because when viewed this way Nature becomes a powerful source of enchantment, an antidote to our modern, disenchanted lives.

For the Romantics, the truth of Nature is the truth of life itself, "a motion and a spirit, that impels," as William Wordsworth called it. It's "out there," in the mountains or at the ocean, but it's also nearby, in your yard, garden, or suburban neighborhood. The truth of Nature is elusive. It can be said in many ways. And it takes a certain kind of hospitality to welcome it in, to really hear it and embrace it.

At first glance, the Romantic idea of Nature can sound a little esoteric. But that isn't necessarily the case. Romantic references to Nature are usually indirect references, poetic or philosophical references, because, as we will see, Nature is a saturating experience. It exceeds or overflows the categories or words we bring to it. Moreover, for the Romantics, our experiences of Nature are embodied experiences. Nature speaks to us in and through our flesh, eyes, ears, and heart. We *feel* it, quite literally. It speaks to our imaginations too, which, after all, is housed *in our bodies*. Part of our aversion to thinking about Nature in such poetic and epistemological terms has to do with our modern assumptions about what nature actually is. We tend to think of nature as a network of intricately interconnected plants and animals and minerals (i.e., an ecosystem), a bunch of stuff "out there," outside of my house or beyond the freeway. It's "the environment." It's the physical and material universe, which is governed by the natural laws of physics. While this materialist view of nature isn't inaccurate, it is incomplete. And of course, living in the modern age as we do, it's our default position. It's the basic way we view "nature" in a secular world. Let's begin with a brief summary of what this view entails before going on to see how an alternative view of Nature might be a source of enchantment.

There are four different ways we view nature in our secular materialist worldview. They're all related to each other, but each one highlights a different aspect of our relationship with nature. The first, as I've mentioned, is the view of nature as the place "out there," outside my house or office, or at the edge of town, where the grass starts to grow, or in the mountains or out in the woods, or wherever. Nature is all of the places not included in the word "civilization." It's wild animals and wild trees and wild landscapes. This idea of nature comes to us from many ancient sources. It's an old idea that's stuck around for a long, long time. It's part of the mythology of Western thought, in fact. The first nomadic peoples that setup a permanent village probably looked at the surrounding landscape and saw an "us and them" sort of relationship, which might naturally take the form of civilized vs. uncivilized, order vs. chaos, safety vs. threat, and so on. Nature as the outdoors became a place to conquer, a source of fear we needed to overcome. Great explorers ventured off into the wilderness to discover new lands. Fairy tales warn us not to veer off the path (of civilization) and get lost in the wilds (of nature). All of these ideas find a commonality in the view that nature is the organic, untamed environment, and it exists *apart* from where we spend most of our time. It's out there, "wild and free," as the American philosopher Henry David Thoreau put it.

Another, related view of nature is that it amounts to The Great Big Ecosystem. This is the view of the natural sciences like biology, geology, botany, etc. A variation on the first idea holds that by "nature" we mean the material world of living organisms, geological processes, weather, soil, etc., all of which work together to form a vast and interrelated whole. Sometimes we refer to this whole as "the environment." We even have terms for people who view nature this way: natural scientists, environmentalists, or more pejoratively, "tree-huggers" or "granola-types." To varying degrees, these folks see nature as a big, beautiful place precisely because of its scientific intricacy, its vast and dizzying variety, it's mesmerizing complexity, and it's really neat permutations. They are justifiably awed by nature's genius and ingenuity. "Isn't it amazing," they say, "that the anglerfish developed a natural lure made of bioluminescent bacteria in order to entice it's deep-sea prey with an irresistible beacon, just before pouncing on them for lunch? Isn't that just awesome?" The fact of The Great Big Ecosystem *really is* amazing when you think about it. But the point here is that at the core of the idea is the view that nature is an amalgamation of the material universe. It's a beautiful one, and it's the one we have here on earth, but there are literally billions of other variations on other planets and they all amount to the staggering variety of ways matter and energy take form and arrange themselves. Nature is The Great Big Ecosystem, and we can study it, classify its residents, and be awed by its complexity. And, at the end of the day, we can come to *know* it.

This last idea—that we can know nature—marks an important move in our relationship to nature, especially in the modern era. The idea that nature is "out there," wild and free, but also knowable through scientific inquiry has had a lot of (unintended?) consequences. After all, "knowledge is power," as the staunch scientist Francis Bacon famously said, and to be able to classify, tame, and understand nature according to scientific laws allows us to manipulate it to human ends. It means that we can *use* nature by mastering it with our knowledge. This brings us to our third view: we see nature as a vast store of resources. It's tempting to say this view is always dangerous and degrades nature by converting it into a commodity, and maybe that's true, but humans have been harvesting from nature since the dawn of humankind and the relationship hasn't always been viral. It has at times also been symbiotic. The point here is that regardless of whether we use nature's resources responsibly or irresponsibly, we still see nature as something we can *use*. It's a resource for human consumption. This view often comes with its own vocabulary. It's lumber, not wood. Ore, not mountainside. Cattle, not cows. On this view, nature's value is in its utility, not its mesmerizing variety, or alluring wildness. But like the other two views of nature, this view of nature as a vast store of resources is predicated on the idea that nature is a place or amalgam of things that are made up of matter that can be manipulated to our benefit or used to keep us safe.

A final variation on the modern view of nature is that nature is where you go to get away, to reset, to vacation. Unlike the first and last views, which saw nature's wildness as potentially threatening or something to overcome, on this view, nature is a place with a healing potential, a sanctuary from the hustle and bustle of everyday life. Sometimes you'll hear people say, "Nature is my church," or something like that. Here, nature is calming (we watch the ocean waves roll in), thrilling (we watch a waterfall pour over a cliff), or touching (we watch a doe care for her fawn). It is a place that reminds us of our connection to the world, out "likeness" with the other creatures that inhabit the earth, or our ancestral bond with the land.

Sometimes it reminds us of the insignificance of our lives. This can have a paradoxical effect: rather than making us feel worthless, it gives us an empowering perspective and suggests we need not take ourselves or our daily dramas too seriously. There are larger forces at play, and that's oddly comforting. Pleasure accompanies the realization that you're puny when you stand before a grand mountain vista. This idea—that nature is a source of healing—has Romantic roots, as we will see, but it has also been appropriated by the materialist view of nature, and can be turned back on us using the language of science. In doing so, the poetic or philosophical truth of nature is converted into a biological truth, and can lose its luster. It becomes disenchanted. For example, many (though not all) of us feel an intuitive connection with nature. When we go into nature and then return to our daily lives, we feel renewed, attentive, and connected in a way we didn't before we left. In the hands of a disenchanted discourse, this experience of nature is explained in terms of biology. A recent BBC news article entitled, "How Staying Indoors Affects Your Immune System," discusses the benefits of going outside as it relates to bolstering your defenses against viral infections and normalizing cortisol secretion, which in turn helps you manage stress. And you know that "refreshed feeling" you have after going to the beach? Attention restoration theory explains that: "the ability to concentrate may be restored by exposure to natural environments" due to its "aesthetic advantage" which can have an important effect on attention restoration as determined by such measures as "digit span forward," "digit span backward," and "Trail Marking Test B."[1] This account is not wrong, but it's weird. For those who've had a transformative encounter with nature, this sort of empirical explanation doesn't get at the *lived experience* of Nature; it only explains the observable impact of nature on our brains. It's interesting, but I've never heard anyone say they're going into nature to normalize their cortisol secretions or improve their digit span

1. Ohly, "Attention Restoration Theory," 305.

forward performance. There's something else at play when we go outside, something more than what science can tell us.

The difficulty in putting our finger on the difference between what we experience when we go outside and what science tells us we are experiencing lies in what we mean when we say the word "truth." According to the four views of nature we've just discussed, "truth" is something that corresponds to "reality," and "reality" is material, as we have already seen. To say something true about the world is to explain it in terms of scientific observation. With nature in particular, a statement is true if it accurately describes nature in terms of its material processes and its physical properties (again, as it "really is," according to science).

In philosophy, we call this a correspondence theory of truth because it's a view of truth that assumes that a statement is true if what it says corresponds to the state of affairs in the world, to what's really going on "out there." Consider the sentence "the forest is dark." On a correspondence theory, this sentence is true if, well, the sun has set and its light rays no longer fall onto the dense collection of trees over there so that they're covered in relatively obscure shadow. Then, it's true that "the forest is (actually) dark." That may sound simple, but it's a very complicated idea. Think about it for a moment: to claim that a sentence is true if it corresponds to a state of affairs "out there" in the world assumes that there is indeed a world "out there" that exists independently from us and that we can access somehow. The big assumption cooked into correspondence theory is that there is, in fact, an objective, independent, external world that we can experience and know and against which we can weigh a statement's veracity. But in the last chapter we saw that, according to Kant, the human mind in general and the imagination in particular play a fundamental role in constituting the world, in forming our experience of what's "out there." The very reason we can have experiences of "reality" in the first places is because as humans we're hardwired with the capacity to have them. Our minds come pre-loaded with the right software, so to speak (e.g., the ability to categorize things according to time and space, count quantities, distinguish between existence and nonexistence, etc.), and this software is necessary to "take it all in" and to create a unified whole. Once our minds do their work on what comes in through perception, we assemble a unified whole and call it "the external world." That raises a big question: is there really a reality "out there," independent of us, as correspondence theory assumes? I know: that's deep.

Once you start to wrap your head around this idea (called transcendental idealism" in the history of philosophy), it's hard to justify the claim that there is an "out there" independent of human experience, and even if there is, how would we ever access it except through our minds? It seems like whatever "reality" is, it is in some very important way always formed *by us* in the confluence of the human capacity to *have experiences* and *what gives itself to us* in experience. Here's the upshot: there's more to the story of truth than a simple one-to-one correspondence between what's just been said and what's going on out there in the world. Figuring our what nature is takes more than simply observing it, measuring it, testing it, and then writing up your findings in a journal.

Let's look at another example that will bring us closer to a Romantic sense of truth. Consider the sentence "Nature is a source of healing." On a correspondence theory of truth, that sentence is true if we can show that it corresponds to "reality." We might say that the sentence is true if we can show that there are biological processes induced in a human person exposed to natural environments that cause in her the release of hormones that reduce or eliminate physical or psychological discomfort. In that way, it would be true that "nature is a source of healing." That's a secular materialist account of the truth of nature.

But we know that when someone says "Nature is a source of healing," they mean something more than that, something less empirical and more experiential. They want to say something like *there is a kind of lived-encounter one can have with Nature that transforms you on a philosophical or existential level, not just on a biological or psychological level.* They're saying something about the tension-filled experience of being a human person and the joy of relief one can experience when you find solace and perspective in the quiet pulse of lapping lake waters along a shoreline. They're saying something about all of the pressures, anxieties, and worries that come with being alive, worries that are often intensified by the confines and structured oppression of domesticity or suburban life. They're saying something about the rejuvenating *je ne sais quoi* you experience when you step into a quiet meadow and confront the sheer beauty of existence. To experience Nature as a source of healing is to marvel at the profound fact that *there is something rather than nothing.* (Think about that for a minute. That's mind blowing.) So you see? The sentence "Nature is a source of healing" is more than "true," at least in the correspondence way of thinking about it. It's true in a poetic, existential, and philosophical way. Maybe even in a religious way. Nature is indeed a source of healing. Now we can see that's true in a number of ways.

I don't want to overstate the case though. The correspondence theory of truth is not bad. It's not the enemy. Quite the contrary. It's useful, and it has it's place in the grand enterprise of knowledge production. But as we can see, correspondence theory doesn't give us a complete picture. Existence is just too big to fit in any one, single theory of truth.

In order to avoid disenchantment, we must be on guard against over-committing to any one theory of truth and reducing everything to that model. All truth theories reveal as much as they conceal. To experience enchantment, we need to be open to different, non-empirical theories of truth. These theories of truth are not grounded in linguistic correspondence to the material world but instead try to account for the way we as humans experience ourselves *as existing in the world*, as meaning-making beings that always exist within a milieu of values, relationships, language, symbols, etc. We are born into a pre-existing "nest" of meanings, a nest that is woven together in a sometimes-tight and sometimes-loose confederation of values. We can draw from this nest to make new meanings, and to get at the truth of Nature. The Greeks had many different words for truth. One word, *aletheia*, was of particular importance to them and is helpful in understanding this "lived truth" versus "observable truth" distinction I'm trying to make. *Aletheia* means "disclosure," or "unconcealedness." The term was revived by a twentieth-century philosopher named Martin Heidegger, who was himself influenced by the Romantics. The Greek origin of the word suggests a concern with truth as a sort of *revealing*, an opening-up onto something. *Aletheia* points to what "shows up" when you make space for truth's arrival without determining beforehand what that truth is. *Aletheia* is truth in the lived-reality sense of the word, not the empirical sense. It is in this sense that the Romantics spoke of the truth of Nature.

The Truth of Nature

In 1819, the English poet John Keats wrote these lines:

> There was an awful rainbow once in heaven:
> We know her woof, her texture; she is given
> In the dull catalogue of common things.
> Philosophy will clip an Angel's wings,
> Conquer all mysteries by rule and line,
> Empty the haunted air, and gnomed mine—
> Unweave a rainbow[.][2]

Keats uses the word "philosophy" here as a stand-in for any analytical approach to nature that tries to explain it away in terms of categories ("dull catalogues") and "common things." He is criticizing the sort of reductive approaches to nature that we've already described, ones that try to "conquer all mysteries" through empirical explanations. He is especially keen to the

2. Keats, "Lamia," 161.

power dynamics at play between knowledge and nature, which according to secular materialism implies that knowledge of nature is a form of dominance over it, giving us an ability to control it, use it, and extract things from it. What's also interesting about Keats's lines are his overt references to an enchanted experience of Nature. He speaks of an "awful rainbow" (by which he means awe-inspiring), "angel's wings," "mysteries," "haunted air," and (my favorite) "gnomed mine[s]." He says that empiricism would "unweave a rainbow," implying that the rainbow is first given to us as an enchanted "something": an intricate tapestry of color, a marvel of natural entwinement. The rainbow appears magically, an ethereal presence, shimmering, brilliant. In Keats's lines we see that for the Romantics, nature and Nature are not the same thing. Capital "N" Nature is a "motion and a spirit, that impels," the flux of becoming that is always revealing itself around us, making itself manifest in a flower's unfolding or a red robin's hop. Small "n" nature is nature according to a materialist view of things. Small "n" nature refers to nature as a physical phenomenon, a combination of the four modern views of nature we discussed above, which can disenchant. But for the Romantics, the truth of Nature was a kind of *aletheia*, an unveiling or unconcealment of a deeper, more poetic truth at play in the cosmos.

Novalis made a similar point in his poem "When Numbers and Figures":

> When numbers and figures
> Are no longer the keys to all creatures,
> When they who sing, or kiss
> Know more than the deeply learned,
> When the world itself reverts again
> To free life and to a (free) world,
> When light and shadow too
> Are wed again unto true clarity,
> And one recognizes in fairy-tales and poems
> The (ancient) true histories of the world,
> Then, there flies away before a single secret word
> This entire inverted existence.[3]

Like Keats, Novalis is arguing that the scientific gaze at best conceals the truth of Nature (the "deeply educated" scientist knows less than "those who sing, or kiss"), and at worst produces an "inverted existence." But Novalis goes on to emphasize the other side of nature; that is, Nature, and what it has to offer us as a source of enchantment. Once we let go of the idea that "numbers and figures"—think of the scientific classification tables in your

3. Novalis, *Schriften*, 675.

high school biology textbook—are the "keys to all creatures" and recognize that symbolic sources of wisdom like "fairy-tales and poems" give us access to Nature's truth in a way that science cannot, then we will be able to hear the "single secret word" of Nature. And notice how many times Novalis employs the language of "truth" and "falsity" to describe what this more poetic orientation to Nature reveals. This is an epistemological poem: it examines the way in which knowledge discloses itself first as science, and then later and more fully as Nature and poetry. For Novalis and Keats, the tools of empiricism, observation, categorization, accounting, dissection, etc., can occlude our ability to see the magic of Nature. They are animated by a desire to control, not revel. Unlike Nature itself, they are analytic, not creative.

These two examples illustrate a broader Romantic skepticism toward viewing science as a one-size-fits-all method for discovering the truth. But, as always, it is important not to overstate the point. The Romantics were not anti-science. They did not see it as an enemy to truth. They simply thought that we must be aware of its *limits*. This caveat is extremely important and worth coming back to again and again: we don't need to pit enchantment against science or symbolic thinking against empirical investigation. They can co-exist. The problem of disenchantment arises when we *privilege empiricism above all other forms of knowing*, as we have seen. This is a fault of scientism, not science. To drive the point home, all we need to do is look at the Romantics themselves. Most of them had a deep and abiding interest in empirical ways of knowing. Samuel Taylor Coleridge was fascinated by chemistry. He attended numerous lectures by his close friend and chemist, Humphry Davy. Novalis studied geology at The Mining Academy of Freiburg. Goethe developed an intricate theory of color. Keats was trained as a surgeon and apothecary. Mary Shelley's *Frankenstein* takes the relationship between humanity and science as one of its central themes, and she demonstrates throughout the novel a deep curiosity of electricity and physics. The Romantics were not against science, but they were against scientific *reductionism*.

So what is "the truth of Nature," exactly? Well, for the Romantics, it's not something we can say "exactly." In other words, it's not the sort of truth that scientific exactness can capture. It's a delicate truth, a shadowed truth, an obscure truth that defies categorization. The truth of Nature is something we have to approach from an angle, through poetry, philosophy, and aesthetic observation. It's not something we can measure or pin down, like Goethe's butterfly.

To understand the truth of Nature is to *experience* it. To know it is to encounter it in symbols and metaphors. Philosophy gives us some tools to talk about the truth of Nature, but even philosophical language only gets us so far. Philosophically speaking, the truth of Nature is the sheer fact of life itself. It is the eternal unfolding of existence, the rich tapestry of becoming that is expressed in an unyielding act of love, a never-ending act of giving that repeats, over and over again. It is the Mystery of Being revealing itself in every moment of being. It is there, in the mouse's squeak, the flower's bloom, or the skidding cloud sliding across the sky.

Love is the appropriate word here because in its *agapic* form the word "love" invokes the structure of a *gift*, and that is what the truth of Nature is like. It is something *given* without expectation of reciprocity, a generosity that flows freely and shatters the bounds of economy. Nature is. It unfolds with no intended recipient and with no clear giver. One might say it is the gift itself, or that the truth of Nature is the truth of *Love*. The truth of Nature is the silent stillness and the mighty roar, concomitant of all existence. It is excess, surplus, saturation. Perhaps the most profound philosophical insight of all is literally right under our noses: the truth of Nature is the thrilling fact that there is something rather than nothing. Consider for a moment: there is something. There is a world. *This* world. It's a marvel, some might even say a mystery. The Great Mystery of Being: that there is something; that we are here; a world exists. The deep sense of gratitude that comes with a recognition of the miracle of existence is another way to say "the truth of Nature." The fact of existence, it's dizzying variety, it's penetrating beauty, its subtle depth, these are all different expressions of the truth of Nature. Opening yourself up to that truth can be deeply enchanting. But despite philosophy's best efforts, the Romantic notion of the truth of Nature is best left to direct experience and poetic expression. Let's look then at how the Romantics experienced and expressed the truth of Nature to get to our second strategy for enchantment.

A Forest Clearing: Making Way for Nature's Unfolding

The Romantics wrote a lot of poems about Nature. As you might expect, many of their encounters with its truth occurred out there, in the wilderness, during a ramble in the woods, a trek up a mountain, or sailing on the ocean. Percy Shelley was notorious for his meanderings through the Italian countryside. William Wordsworth "wandered lonely as a cloud" through the English Lake District. Like many of us today, the Romantics often encountered Nature outside the confines of city walls or suburban sidewalks. But not all Romantic encounters with Nature happened outside. Some happened inside too, while sitting in a carriage or a living room. The Romantics were not extreme survivalists, or even avid campers, really. They enjoyed life's comforts just like the rest of us. But that didn't keep them from discovering Nature's truth (and it won't stop you, either). According to the Romantics, you don't have to love bugs and dirt in order to experience Nature. The key is to *welcome Nature in*. Let's see how they do it.

Going Out to Go In

John "Warwick" Smith, *Tintern Abbey by Moonlight*, c. 1789, graphite and watercolor with scratching out.

William Wordsworth described the truth of Nature in "Lines Written a Few Miles Above Tintern Abbey." It's one of the most beautiful accounts of Nature's enchanting power ever written. The poem still resonates with us today partly because it's clear and accessible, and partly because, well, it's just good. It gets as the lived experience of it all. Here are a few lines from the poem:

> And I have felt
> A presence that disturbs me with the joy
> Of elevated thoughts; a sense sublime
> Of something far more deeply interfused,
> Whose dwelling is the light of setting suns,
> And the round ocean and the living air,
> And the blue sky, and in the mind of man:
> A motion and a spirit, that impels
> All thinking things, all objects of all thought,
> And rolls through all things. Therefore am I still

A lover of the meadows and the woods
And mountains; and of all that we behold
From this green earth[.][4]

As the poem's title suggests, Wordsworth composed these lines somewhere in the Welsh countryside, deep in the Wye River Valley. It's nice to
imagine him overlooking the ruins of the old gothic abbey, overgrown with
crawling vines and gnarled tree roots (although recent scholarship suggests
it may have been home to squatters and quite polluted. But no matter.)
Wordsworth was most definitely outdoors when he was inspired to write
"Tintern Abbey." And these are some great lines, some of the best in all of
English poetry. They go a long way toward capturing with words the uncap-
turable truth of Nature, which of course is at the end of the day, impossible.

This is our first dose of the Romantic take on the truth of Nature. So
what's it like? How did Wordsworth come to experience it? How can we?

Notice how Wordsworth first describes the truth of Nature as a "presence." It's really *there*. It's something that is "really real" and that is moving
through him and the world around him. It's not measurable, of course. You
can't take a scoop of it to a laboratory and dissect it. But it's undeniably
there, and he *knows* this to be true, though in a non-empirical way. He
feels this presence with his body. It nudges or "disturbs" him into "elevated
thoughts," thoughts that go beyond the mundane trivialities of everyday
existence. This might remind you of the paradox of Nature we discussed
earlier, where when standing before a sheer cliff face or watching a thunder-
storm roll in we feel puny, but we also take pleasure in the perspective that
it brings, directing our minds away from our pedestrian dramas and toward
things eternal like love, friendship, and beauty. He goes on to describe the
truth of Nature as filling him with a "sense sublime," and of "something
far more deeply interfused." In the philosophical register we used earlier to
describe the truth of Nature, this is Wordsworth's version of the animating
principle of life itself, eternal becoming, Nature unfolding forever and taking up its dwelling in "the light of setting suns," the "round ocean," and "the
living air." These images suggest a circle: death in the setting sun; pregnancy,
gestation, and birth in the round ocean; and life, movement, and change in
the living air. The truth of Nature moves even within "the mind of man" (or
humankind), which is not separate from Nature, but part of it, "interfused"
with it. We are not standalones, living inside of our own tiny, skull-sized
kingdoms. Our minds and our bodies are porous, and Nature moves within
us as a "motion and a spirit" impelling "all thinking things" and "roll[ing]
through all things." He ends these lines appropriately, with a reference to

4. Wordsworth, *The Major Works*, 134.

love. Wordsworth acknowledges that he is "still a lover of the meadows and the woods and the mountains." On one level, all he means by this is that he really likes being outside. But on another, more penetrating and poetic level, he means that he is and always has been an active participant in the truth of Nature itself. He *is* Nature. His love of the meadows and the woods joins him with them as he too unfolds in selfless becoming. Both he and Nature are always in a poetic act of creative revelation, expressing themselves in the unyielding gift of life. That is what it's like to experience the truth of Nature.

Now that we get the gist of his meaning, let's look at *how* Wordsworth came to have this experience. What did he do—practically speaking—to encounter this truth? Well, for starters, he went outside. Although, as we said, you don't have to go outside to encounter the truth of Nature, for Wordsworth, it helped. One of his main strategies for encountering the truth of Nature was to go out into it. He was not afraid of dirt and bugs. But he wasn't granola either. He lived in a comfy cottage in the little English village of Grasmere. He took tea and socialized and shopped and slept in a soft bed and sat by a fire when the English winter rolled through. He didn't live off the grid, or even raise chickens. In that regard, he wasn't very different from the rest of us.

But what he did do was *open himself up*. He created a space for Nature's truth to reveal itself to him. He went on a walk in the woods, alone, and looked around, and listened, and waited. For what? For the truth to emerge. According to Wordsworth, to experience the truth of Nature and to be enchanted by it you have to take on what we might call a "disposition of hospitality." You have to be open to welcoming in the unexpected guest that is Nature. The unexpected guest is the one who arrives unannounced, the one who surprises and delights with her unforeseen friendship. All great religions celebrate hospitality as a way of welcoming in truth. Hestia, one of the great Greek Goddesses, reigned over the hearth and kept warm the home in case of the stranger's arrival. Jesus in Matthew 25:34–40 tells us that all those who welcome the stranger welcome the Divine. In Hinduism, it is often said that "the guest is God" (अतिथिदेवो भव). This orientation of welcoming, this hospitable disposition is key to encountering the truth of Nature. Like Wordsworth, we have to put ourselves in a position to invite Nature in. We have to leave the door open, so to speak. We have to intentionally place ourselves in a forest clearing (which doesn't have to be a literal clearing, but simply a space of open invitation). We'll have more to say about that below, but for now, let's just note that Wordsworth's first step toward experiencing Nature's enchantment has less to do with camping and more to do with a sense of welcoming.

Standing at the Threshold

J. C. Stadler, *View of Westminster Bridge including Westminster Hall and the Abbey*, c. 1790, aquatint with etching, colored.

In another poem, a sonnet entitled, "Composed upon Westminster Bridge," Wordsworth shows us how to open ourselves to Nature without hiking around the Welsh countryside. In "Westminster Bridge," Wordsworth encounters the truth of Nature in an in-between space: in a horse-drawn carriage (the automobile of his day). He was inspired to write these lines while driving through London, which in the nineteenth century was not exactly a lush pastoral landscape. And yet, Nature revealed itself to him:

> Earth has not any thing to shew more fair:
> Dull would he be of soul who could pass by
> A sight so touching in its majesty:
> This City now doth like a garment wear
> The beauty of the morning; silent, bare,
> Ships, towers, domes, theatres, and temples lie
> Open unto the fields, and to the sky;
> All bright and glittering in the smokeless air.
> Never did sun more beautifully steep
> In his first splendor, valley, rock, or hill;
> Ne'er saw I, never felt, a calm so deep!
> The river glideth at his own sweet will:
> Dear God! the very houses seem asleep;

And all that mighty heart is lying still![5]

We happen to know the exact details of Wordsworth's inspiration for this poem. He and his sister Dorothy describe it in their correspondence. The two were setting out from London to Dover en route to Calais, on the northern coast of France. They were going to meet Wordsworth's daughter for the first time. As they rode across London, they noticed something striking about the way the slumbering city appeared to them in the magic of the morning hours. Imagine them clopping along, the streets silent, the warm air wrapping around them, the sun's soft rays massaging the cityscape as they rode through it. They were enchanted.

That's when the poetry kicked in. Ever-attune to the truth of Nature, Wordsworth described London's vast and sprawling neighborhoods with rich and symbolic language, he noticed the way the "beauty of the morning" lay on them "like a garment," and how the "ships, towers, domes, theatres, and temples" were "bright and glittering" all around. They were both struck by the sheer splendor of it all, as well as the sense that the entire city, though "asleep" was very much alive even as its "mighty heart is lying still!"

This last bit about the "mighty heart" of the city might sound familiar. It beckons back to "a motion and a spirit that impels," which Wordsworth mentions in "Tintern Abbey." This "motion and spirit" is another way of naming the truth of Nature. In "Tintern Abbey," it impels "[a]ll thinking things[.]" But in "Westminster Bridge," it is not only "thinking things" that are impelled by the truth of Nature: even the buildings in the city seem to have a certain vivacity and ability to participate in the power of life itself, the same power that makes the "river glideth at his own sweet will."

So far, so good. But there's another thing. Look at *where* Dorothy and William are when they encounter the truth of Nature. They're in a horse-drawn carriage. They're comfortable, cozy, and protected. They're not traipsing around in the woods. They're not even strolling through a city park. They're somewhere in-between the stone buildings of London and the open wildness of the English countryside. They're in what we might call a "liminal space," a borderland betwixt the "inside" and the "outside." This liminal space has some interesting features in the way it captures two experiences at once, and yet captures neither fully. The carriage functions something like an RV, though it's more open, moving, and exposed to the elements. And yet, it's not completely exposed. The carriage does shelter them from the natural environment. If it rained, it wouldn't fall on them. Being in the carriage, being in-between, puts Dorothy and William *in* their natural environment, and sets them *apart* from it. The space is both new

5. Wordsworth, *The Major Works*, 285.

and familiar. It is neither "here" nor "there." It signals outward and inward. It is in this space that Dorothy and William experience the enchanting truth of Nature.

Why? What allows that to happen? It happens because these liminal spaces are disruptive openings, they're cracks in the fortress of mundane life. They're like a clearing in a forest that forces you to pause and look up and go, "Ah, here I am." Liminal spaces break us free from the monotony of life and draw our attention to the fact that we're here, embedded in a constructed world, one run by fabricated rules, norms, and expectations. They call into question the hypnotic rhythm of the everyday and make us *notice it*, like a fish might notice the water in which she's swimming. Liminal spaces create the opportunity for Nature's truth to reveal itself.

But it's not just being in the space that does the trick. You can't just hop in a carriage and expect to encounter Nature every time. When Dorothy and William enter their liminal space they also take on a certain orientation toward the world, a certain disposition concerning their place in it. They *open themselves up* to something new, to something unforeseen, to something "coming in" and showing itself there. We might say they welcome in the Stranger, not knowing who or what she might be, or if she will even arrive in the first place. They enter the space, and wait, and see. You don't have to go outside to let Nature in.

Indoor Nature

Some Romantics encountered Nature without stepping foot outside. Wordsworth's long-time friend and co-author of *Lyrical Ballads*, Samuel Taylor Coleridge, describes in his poem "Frost at Midnight" how the truth of Nature enters into our homes, and how it can be enjoyed while sitting next to a fireplace or a sleeping child. Let's look at a couple of passages from that poem to see how Coleridge invites the Stranger in and takes joy in her enchanting company from the comfort of his own home.

"Frost at Midnight" begins with a thrilling first line: "The frost performs its secret ministry / Unhelped by any wind."[6] What better way to describe the truth of Nature than as a "secret ministry," a sacred teaching whispered in the frost as it creeps across a winter window? It's enchanting, really. Next, he describes the setting and the other people in the room: "The inmates of my cottage, all at rest," which include his "cradled infant" who "slumbers peacefully" beside him. Everything is calm, still, and warm. Notice that Coleridge, the great Nature lover, is not out trudging through the

6. Coleridge, "Frost at Midnight," 645.

snow looking for "the real outdoors." *He's not even outside.* That's important. This poem shows us how we can experience the truth of Nature from the comfort of our living rooms.

It's a still, winter's night. Everything is peaceful. Very peaceful. *Too* peaceful, even. Something strange happens. The peace that Coleridge experiences actually becomes *unpeaceful*. It becomes unsettling. Its odd intensity is both calming and exhilarating. Coleridge finds himself in-between, both/ and, tranquil and unnerved. He enters a liminal space. He's in the borderland between the sanctuary of his home and the icy world just beyond his window. The fact of Being presses in on his quietude, calling it into question as an unseen—but wholly felt—presence. The Stranger arrives. Coleridge uses the same word Wordsworth uses in "Tintern Abbey" to describe this event. The radical calmness of Being "disturbs" him, "vexing" his meditation with an "extreme silentness."[7] The quietude of Being, the absence of sound and activity and movement, is itself a kind of presence that demands contemplation and forces an encounter. Coleridge is aware. He knows something is here, something has entered in. But what? The rest of the poem is an attempt to answer that question. But we already know the answer: it is the Stranger.

Coleridge stares into the fire, going deeper into poetic reflection. His imagination kicks in. He describes the fire as "low-burnt," putting off only a "thin blue flame." A film of ash "flutter[s] on the grate." This little slice of ash clinging to the grate is a key to the entire poem. In English folklore, this film was called "a stranger" and foretold the arrival of an unexpected guest.[8] It was an omen, so to speak, but also a remnant. In the following stanzas, the ash takes on extended signification. It reminds Coleridge of his childhood, when he saw the ash in other fires, and watched "that fluttering stranger" as it beckoned him in anticipation of "things to come." His memories take him to a moment when as a young school boy he would be lulled into daydreaming from his boring lessons but always kept an eye on "the door half opened" where he would "snatch[] a hasty glance," hoping "to see the stranger's face" should someone enter into the room.[9] Like Wordsworth in "Westminster Bridge," Coleridge is describing an orientation of invitation, a general sense of hospitality toward what could come. Whether inside his cottage or inside his schoolroom, he is open to the truth of Nature' appearing. He leaves the door half open, metaphorically speaking, so that the Stranger—who is the truth of Nature—may enter when she pleases. The key is the disposition of hospitality, the welcoming-in that presages the unexpected guest.

7. Coleridge, "Frost at Midnight," 645.
8. Robinson, "Samuel Taylor Coleridge: 'Frost at Midnight.'"
9. Coleridge, "Frost at Midnight," 647.

Towards the end of the poem Coleridge imagines his child having a more Wordsworthian relationship to Nature, "wander[ing] like a breeze / By lakes and sandy shores, beneath the crags / Of ancient mountains."[10] So again, like Wordsworth, Coleridge acknowledges the value of literally going outside to encounter Nature, but the setting of "Frost at Midnight" proves that while going outside may be helpful, it is not necessary. A coalescence of memory, attention, hospitality, and stillness can create the conditions for Nature's arrival almost anywhere. Coleridge ends the poem by describing how his son will have the chance to explore the natural landscape of the Lake District and enjoy all that Nature has to offer, but he then goes on to note that the "eternal language" which "God Utters" through Nature is taught "in all, and all things in himself."[11] Coleridge's reference to God here should not be taken too literally, and certainly not as an expression of twenty-first-century Christian theology. Coleridge's religious views were not always orthodox (at least for a time). We might instead read Coleridge's reference to "God" here in line with the tenor of the entire poem, which is a meditation on the way Nature reveals its truth to us in subtle and profound ways. Thus, the "eternal language" which "God" speaks is the truth of Nature disclosing itself to us. Coleridge completes the stanza on a prophetic note by suggesting that the more we commune with Nature, the more we wish to invite it in: the "Great universal teacher" will "mould / Thy spirit, and by giving make it ask." What a beautiful line, "by giving make it ask." When we are open to the truth of Nature it will arrive like an unexpected guest, teach us its wisdom, and then provoke us into a more open, curious, and invitational way of being. The truth of Nature will leave us enchanted.

Enchantment Strategy #2: Encountering the Truth of Nature

If you're feeling like the idea of the truth of Nature is still a bit vague, and you're not really sure what it actually *is*, that's good. Remember, the truth of Nature is not the sort of truth you can pin down. It's not a cognitive truth or a scientific truth. It has to be sensed, experienced, explored, and interpreted. The truth of Nature is always a partial truth, a partial disclosure.

This is one of the many reasons why poetry rather than empirical observation is a better tool for "getting at" the truth of Nature: poetry signals towards things by drawing unexpected connections between ideas, objects, feelings, and thoughts. It's a sort of indirect route to the truth. Poetic

10. Coleridge, "Frost at Midnight," 647.
11. Coleridge, "Frost at Midnight," 649.

connections illuminate or invoke a *sense* of something rather than flat out describing it. Poetic expression does not express *knowledge,* but *understanding.* To "know" something is to encapsulate it, to be able to explain or describe it fundamentally. We know for certain that 2 + 2 = 4 and that George Washington was the first president of the United States, and with that knowledge comes a completeness that foreclose any alternatives. Because we know George Washington was the first president, it can never be said that John Adams was, or Thomas Jefferson. As we saw earlier, knowledge in this sense is based on a correspondence theory of truth, which has its value, but is inappropriate for describing non-empirical truths, truths like the truth of Nature.

The truth of Nature is not knowable in a correspondence sense. It cannot be grasped and reduced. Instead, it must be "understood," where "understanding" means a process of ongoing exploration and interpretation. Understanding is always partial and provisional. It seeks illuminations, not finality. It is a perpetual project of invention and re-invention, interpretation and re-interpretation, aimed at revealing insights rather than reducing things into discreet pieces of knowledge. The value of these insights is that they give us a new perspective on the meaning of life, or a moment of wisdom about what it means to be a human person. Understanding is about enrichment, not information. So, if you're feeling like the truth of Nature is a bit vague, that's because it *is,* at least in terms of scientific modes of knowing. But if you try to *understand* the truth of Nature rather than *know* it, you'll discover that *parts of it* can become clear, and that it has a wealth of insight to offer. It can add a beautiful texture to your life, unlike anything else.

So how do you encounter the truth of Nature? At one level, you've already encountered it, at least vicariously, through the philosophical explanations and poetic examples we've just discussed. Let's summarize them: philosophically, the truth of Nature is the astounding fact that there is something, and that all that is is expressed in an unyielding movement, unfolding, becoming, and animation. The truth of Nature is the gift of existence, in which we participate and which participates in us. Poetically, the truth of Nature is the Stranger who appears when the door is left cracked open. It is "a motion and a spirit that impels." It is the quiet guest who arrives at night and discloses to us an insight about our relationship to the world, and to each other. It is the invitation to understand, but never to know. Like Jack Frost, who in English folklore is said to paint in repeating detail and patterns the window with frost while we sleep, the truth of Nature discloses itself as an intricate interlacing of beauty, loveliness, subtlety, rhythm, and awe, everywhere we look. The truth of Nature is the "presence that disturbs" when we venture off into the woods, or when we sit in silence in our living rooms. It is "the mighty heart" of a sleeping city. It is the "secret ministry" of all that is.

The best way to encounter the truth of Nature is to do so directly, not vicariously or even intellectually. No philosophical discussion will ever do it justice. You have to feel it for yourself. And for a lot of people, this can be difficult. There are really three types of people when it comes to those who do and do not experience the truth of Nature. First, there are those who seem to have been born in tune with Nature. They don't need any help at all to experience its truth. Perhaps they were raised by hippies or spent summer vacations in Yellowstone, or grew up on a lake. But for whatever reason, Nature speaks to them. They probably don't need to go on reading this chapter. Then there are those who have never heard the truth of Nature, and maybe never will. These are folks who have for some reason or another never developed an affinity for the outdoors or an attention to the magical side of life, and they're simply not interested in doing so. For them, all of this talk of the truth of Nature amounts to pseudo-religious diatribe. They're not interested. To them I say: fair enough. Nature isn't for everyone, and you don't have to experience its truth to experience an enchanted world, but it is one way to do so. Finally, and most importantly, there are a huge number of people in-between these two poles. This third, largest group of people is made up of folks who are intrigued by the possibility of hearing Nature's truth but don't know how to experience it. They need help. It's to them that this enchantment strategy is directed. My hope is that this strategy, imparted to us by the Romantics, can help those who with just a little nudge might hear Nature's enchanting truth.

Step 1: Get a Guide

If you were to go fly fishing or backcountry camping (Bugs! Dirt! Yuck!) you might consider hiring someone to lead you through the brambles and take you to all the sweet spots: that perfect bend in the river where the water slows and the trout are chomping at the bit, or that perfect mountain view campsite that only a handful of people know about. You'd need someone who has been there before, who has gone on ahead of you and can show you the way. You could stumble upon these places by yourself, of course, but a guide can take you there straight away leaving you with more time to soak up the experience.

It can help to get a guide when you're looking for the truth of Nature. Your guide may be a friend who's sensitive to his surroundings, who seems to pay attention to the small and beautiful things. Or, it may be a book (like this one) or an article written by someone interested in philosophical insights and living them out. It may even be a stranger—someone you've only just met—who speaks Nature's truth and captures your attention with her perceptive commentary. Spend time with these guides. If you listen and ask questions, they can share with you their experiences and strategies for encountering Nature's truth. They can tell you what they've discovered, and how you can discover it too. They can put you in the best position to have the experience you're looking for because they've had the experience themselves.

Some people are born open to Nature's truth. They just have a knack for encountering it. They can be the typical outdoorsy-types (you know them when you see them), but sometimes they're not. Sometimes they're quite unassuming, just regular old people you'd never peg as "outdoorsy." My mother is a Midwestern, lower middle-class, blue-collar nurse. She and my father raised us in a townhome in a southern Ohio suburb. In most ways, she's about as normal as you can be. Given the option, she'd choose potato chips over granola bars, every time. But she has an astounding attunement to the truth of Nature. It's a marvel to watch her marvel at it, and when I go with her somewhere quiet (a mountain glen, a forest clearing, a backyard vegetable garden), she always has something beautiful to say about the Mystery of Being unfolding. She loves to comment on the way a moon-flower's leaves curl out of its shell early in the spring, or the way tomato plants hang a tangy scent in the air as they begin to swell with life in late summer. She makes a wonderful guide. Find people like her. Invite them to walk with you and explain how it is they open themselves to Nature. I use the word "walk" here rather than "hike" because I want to stress the fact that you don't need to go out into the wilderness to encounter Nature. It's right here. Just take a walk through your neighborhood with your guide and listen to them explain the beauty they see, and how they come to see it. Be patient. Be attentive. Let your mind be open to things you may never have thought before. It can be fun. Note the practices, attitudes, or ways-of-being that this person engages in when they listen for the truth of Nature. There is an art to openness, and a guide can teach you the subtleties of the invitation. Go ahead. Take a walk with them.

If you don't have a friend that can serve as your guide, consider a philosophical or poetic guide (or use all three!). If you're more a contemplative than a conversationalist, you might prefer a philosophical or poetic guide over a flesh-and-blood friend anyway, and that's just fine. Sometimes quiet reflection is a better way to open yourself to Nature (and sometimes it's not). If you want to go it alone bring with you a short poem or philosophical essay or selection from a larger text that resonate with you. Read through the material either before you take your walk, while you're on it, or just after it (But don't wait too long. You want Nature to be fresh in your imagination). Consider the way the poet or philosopher describes the truth of Nature, and try and see whether you can see what they see while on your walk, try and get a feel for what they're getting at.

I remember the first time I read John Keats's "To Autumn." It was late fall, and my life was in transition. I was getting ready to leave a job that had made me unhappy for quite a long time, and I was gearing up for a new form of life that was full of uncertainty. My day-to-day had fallen into a rhythm that was not particularly fruitful for me, intellectually or spiritually. I was in a dry spell, to say the least. I was disenchanted. Something needed to change. I needed something to point me toward the beauty of things, toward the sense of possibility that always accompanies endings. I've always been drawn to the turning of the seasons, and so I chose to contemplate John Keats's "To Autumn." It seemed fitting, given the time of year.

After reading the poem, I took a walk through my neighborhood. I noticed an apple tree in my neighbor's front yard. I'd see it before. It wasn't anything new. But this time, I stood and stared at the tree. I was struck by the swollen fruits dangling from a thread on the over-laden limbs. I recited to myself a few lines from the poem. Keats was my guide. I understood then what he meant when he said that the season and the sun were "conspiring" to "load and bless with fruit the vines that round the thatch-eaves run." I marveled at how, in this life-filled moment just before winter's arrival, the power of autumn could "bend with apples the moss'd cottage trees," creating a grace and curvature no artist can capture. Like the fruit in Keats's poem and the apple tree before me, I was "filled . . . with ripeness to the core." I saw in the meat of an apple bursting forth in sweetness the truth of Nature unfolding, a truth of which I too was an expression. I remembered that, like the apples and the buzzing bees and the plump hazel shells, there is a delicious fullness, an almost outrageous ripeness and richness to life. The Stranger had arrived, and I let her in.

Keats got me there. He was my guide. Through his poetic description I was able to "look, and see," and I could open myself up to the truth of Nature. If you're not into Keats, you might read Wordsworth's "Lines Written in Early Spring," or "I Wandered Lonely as a Cloud" before going out. Focus on a specific image the poet invokes, or a theme that expresses your feelings. Maybe even memorize a line or two. Then, when you're amidst Nature, recite those lines to yourself, look around, and wait for the Stranger to appear. Rest in silence and the invitation; quietude and hospitality. They will make enchantment possible. And when the truth speaks, listen.

Step 2: Cross a Threshold

One thing you may have noticed about my examples so far is that they all involve going outside, in some degree. I know what you're thinking: "But you said we didn't have to go outside to experience the truth of Nature." And you don't. For the Romantics, however, there does seem to be something important about crossing a threshold, about moving from one space to another in order to encounter Nature. There's a kind of transition from the mundane to the sacred. Let's look closely at that in order to figure out how the Romantics teach us to "go outside" without getting dirty.

Wordsworth, Coleridge, and a host of others all point us to the idea that to encounter Nature we must cross a threshold. You have to move from one mode of consciousness to another, or from one way-of-being to another. That's what I mean by "crossing a threshold." There needs to be an intentional "going out" or "going over" where you (re)move yourself from the rhythm and rolling lull of your everyday life and enter into a space of newness, freshness, and invitation. One philosopher, Edmund Husserl, called this moving away from "the natural attitude" and adopting the "phenomenological attitude," an attitude that observes closely the way the world appears before you, at its most fundamental level. You don't have to trek into the wilderness, but you do have to somehow get outside of your daily routine. Now, this is easily done by literally taking your body and moving it from one place to another, by going outside, from your living room to the front porch, or from the front porch to a park. In some ways I think this is what the Romantics recommend. It may sound trite, but recognize that moving your body from one place to another moves your mind too. We feel a shift in our mental focus when we move from one environment to another. But crossing the threshold doesn't need to be dramatic. Recall that Wordsworth did it by simply going for a carriage ride. He left his house—but not the city—and got into a cart, and opened himself to Nature. You might try that too. Jump in your car and take a drive to a local nature preserve or picnic ground. Or just roll down the windows and cruise through a neighborhood one evening, letting the twilight air run its fingers along your cheeks. The point is to cross over into a new place and to adopt an orientation of hospitality. Thresholds are themselves openings, spaces we go *through* to transition from one form of life, one disposition, to another. To experience the truth of Nature you must in some way cross over.

In "Frost at Midnight," Coleridge doesn't cross any literal threshold. He stays inside, seated by a low burning fire, just relaxing and contemplating. He remains so during the entirety of the poem. But an attentive reader will see that the frost of which he speaks is creeping up on the *outside* of the window. Coleridge must look *through* the window to see the frost, despite its closeness to him. And when he does look, his attitude changes. He notices, responds, and imagines. The window itself is a threshold, and Coleridge crosses over it, or rather through it, to see the frost on the other side of the glass. You see? Crossing over can be as subtle as a glance. It can be a look out the window, but it is this "looking out" to another place, across a threshold, your eyes moving from within to without, that reveals the secret ministry of the frost. That's another example of how one might cross a threshold without leaving the living room.

Step 3: Issue an Invitation

In all three poems, "Tintern Abbey," "Westminster Bridge," and "Frost at Midnight," the poets invoke a tone of invitation. They welcome something in. This attitude of invitation is critical if you want to encounter the truth of Nature, if you want to be enchanted by it. As we've seen, the word "Stranger" is appropriate here because the truth of Nature arrives like an unexpected guest. When we move across a threshold into a new space, a space that is foreign or different from our everyday routine, and open ourselves to what's possible, we make room for the Stranger to arrive. The Stranger has a hard time entering our lives when the door is shut, when our daily routines, rigid patterns, and comfortable ways-of-being close us off to what's possible, to what's unforeseen and surprising. That's why the Romantics recommend crossing a threshold in the spirit of invitation: the newness of the space on the other side of the threshold heightens our awareness to what else is out there and makes us ready to receive something we may not have expected. When, like the Romantics, we enter a new space and adopt an invitational spirit we increase the odds of encountering something novel, some previously unseen truth, some insight into the life of things. We welcome the Stranger in.

Wordsworth and Coleridge were masters of showing us how to open ourselves to Nature. Their poetry teaches how to attune yourself to the Stranger's voice and adopt a disposition of hospitality toward it. Coleridge does so with exquisite sensitivity in "Frost at Midnight," and in another poem we've already discussed, "This Lime-Tree Bower My Prison." Recall that the poem begins with Coleridge lamenting the fact that because of an injury (his wife accidentally spilled scalding milk on his foot) he could not go on a hike with his friends. Instead of traipsing through the woods with them, he was stuck at home, waiting for them to return under the shade of a lime tree. He was disappointed. He was in a funk, feeling like he was missing

out on Nature's truth. But then, as in "Frost at Midnight," Coleridge starts
to pay attention, he starts to look out at the world right in front of him. He
leaves the confines of his own, tiny, skull-sized kingdom (symbolized as the
prison bower of the lime tree) and crosses over into the limitless expanse of
Nature, the Mystery of Being unfolding in front of him, in the tiniest insect
and simplest flower. He invites the Stranger in. He welcomes the truth of
Nature to show itself underneath the humdrum lime tree. And it does. It's
arrives from out of nowhere, and is everywhere: in the "shadow of the leaf
and stem above / Dappling its sunshine" and in the "solitary humble-bee"
who "Sings in the bean-flower!"[12] The Stranger arrives, and her presence is
enchanting. What's notable here is that after Coleridge crosses the threshold
of his own ego and enters into the space of Nature's vast and infinite unfolding, he takes on a disposition of hospitality and invites a new experience.
The invitation is not simply a change in attitude, or just choosing to look at
something from a different perspective. It's clearing a space for something
outside of you to come in, for something in the world to arrive and impress
itself upon you. The Stranger—if she comes—comes from *without*. This is
an important point. Nature *transcends* the individual person. It is you, but
it is more than you too. When the Stranger arrives for Coleridge, she sets
him free from his prison. He realizes that he is able to enjoy the enchanting
company of Nature, that indeed, "nature ne'er deserts the wise and pure – /
No scene so narrow but may well employ / Each faculty of sense, and keep
the heart / Awake to love and beauty!"[13]

The Romantics tell us that with a little practice we can come to see
the world as symbolic, poetic, and joyous. When we adopt a disposition
of hospitality and welcome in the truth of Nature we are welcomed home
ourselves. We experience the world as a meaningful place rather than an
empty space. Romantics of all stripes used this same strategy to encounter
Nature's truth. Percy Shelley, as we have seen, rambled through the woods to
find Nature and invited it in to provoke and catalyze his imagination. John
Keats in "To Autumn" personifies the fall and follows her through cyclical
evolutions of maturation, ripeness, and decay. What these Romantics are
telling us is that part of the key to hearing the secret ministry of Nature is to
leave the door half-open, cross a threshold, and welcome in the unexpected
guest. The next time you're taking a walk through your neighborhood, having a cup of coffee on the porch, or gazing out the window, leave the door
cracked. You never know, the Stranger may arrive, and if she does, you'll
almost certainly be glad to see her.

12. Coleridge, "This Lime-Tree Bower My Prison," 637.

13. Coleridge, "This Lime-Tree Bower My Prison," 637.

Step 4: Listen to What the Stranger Has to Say

Now that you have a guide, you've crossed a threshold, and you've opened yourself to Nature, you need to listen to what Nature has to say. And I mean really *listen*. Listening is an art. It's more than paying attention. It's more than just hearing. Listening happens when we calm ourselves and settle down, when we don't feel the need to exert our own ego against what's coming in. We tend to reside too completely in our own subjectivity, lording over our skull-sized kingdoms. We feel an almost innate need to defend against other views, opinions, perspectives, or experiences. This shielded position can muffle what we are able to hear, our ability to listen. How many times have you been in a conversation with someone and gotten the sense that they're just waiting for you to stop talking so that they can tell their story? *Are they even listening?* you ask yourself. To listen, you must in some way put yourself aside, or step outside of yourself, or exceed yourself (all metaphors, of course) in order to make space for the unexpected, to welcome it in properly.

Listening is not passive, though. It's not non-action, or some form of empty mind meditation. Listening is *active reception*. A good listener is taking in what's coming at them and ruminating on it, taking it seriously, and contemplating what it might mean in relation to other things the listener might know or be thinking about at the time. Good listening is not judgmental, at least not in the dismissive sense. It's not weighing the merits of what's being said and then judging its veracity and looking for points with which to disagree, things to argue about. Instead, good listeners are curious, inquisitive, and conversational. They want to know more (the Greeks called this impulse *eros*). They actively receive and wrestle with what they hear, but in a spirit of charity, of hospitality. It's funny, when you meet a good listener, you know it. Their whole body sings with curiosity. They are engaged. They lean in. They focus. They have a stillness and a calmness about them that can be disarming, and yet they have an energy that excites. The good listener is able to be both generously receptive and actively inquisitive, still and yet full of motion. They silently make connections and contribute to the richness of the conversation. Good listeners are a joy to be around. They themselves can be enchanting.

Coleridge gives us some examples of what listening to Nature looks like, as does Wordsworth. Both exhibit the qualities of a good listener. Coleridge begins "Frost at Midnight" with a double nod to the subtle art of listening. The poem begins almost *in medias res*, with Coleridge listening to the frost "perform its secret ministry," followed immediately by the "owlet's cry," which is echoed in the diction and sound of the words he uses to describe it. He even listens to the "extreme silentness" of his cottage. The poem is full of examples like this. Notice what Coleridge is doing when he's listening, notice his behaviors: the poem takes place at midnight, an hour that seems outside normal time (a temporal threshold). He is quiet, but attentive. He is observant. He is still, but his mind is actively engaging in the world as it appears to him. Each of the images he describes in the opening of the poem—the frost, the owl's hoot, the low-burning fire—have a softness to them, an imperceptibility, and yet because of his attentiveness and ability to listen to them he can hear what they have to say. Their message comes "loud as before," it strikes him with an insight and a deep sense of truth about the life of things. The next time you're listening to Nature, think of Coleridge, sitting in his cottage listening to what's around him. Remind yourself of the way he paid attention to something as forgettable as winter frost on a windowpane or a film of ash on a fire grate. And then remember how much was actually there, how much he was able to hear or see when he quieted himself enough to listen. One of the nice signs about this strategy is that the kind of active and charitable reception that is good listening can allow you to hear Nature's truth in not only your surroundings, but in other people too. More on that in the next chapter, though. For now, in order to experience the enchanting truth of Nature, just practice listening to its "eternal language." Take a walk down the street this springtime and note the way your neighbor's daffodils "toss their heads in sprightly dance," and the secret playfulness, joy, and becoming that their pirouettes reveal.

Step 5: Remember, Repeat, Renew

The final step in this enchantment strategy is to be able to call up the truth of Nature when it's not actively speaking to you. Remember it. Whenever that vague, existential melancholy the French call *ennui* creeps into your life, recall the sound, the feel, and the smell of Nature's ministry. In times like these we can imaginatively conjure the truth of Nature we once encountered and in doing so repeat it to ourselves. There is renewal in this repetition. William Wordsworth was a master at this. He wrote extensively about the power of memory, recollection, and renewal in his poetry. In perhaps his most famous example, he wrote: "For oft when on my couch I lie / In vacant or in pensive mood, / They flash upon that inward eye / Which is the bliss of solitude, / And then my heart with pleasure fills, / And dances with the Daffodils."[14] In remembering the truth of Nature you are recalling and repeating a truth once spoken. And in this recollection, there is pleasure

14 Wordsworth, *The Major Works*, 304.

and solace. You may find your spirit momentarily refreshed by the simple memory of a morning sunrise, a twilight evening, or a round, full moon. Our time with the Stranger can give twice.

In the previous chapter, we discussed the mistaken belief that imagining amounts to fancy or make-believe. But the imagination is much more than that. The imagination is a dynamic mental faculty that synthesizes the world for us and imbues it with meaning. Remembering and imagining are not the same thing, but they have in common the quality of creative activity, which can bring forth a past impression and make meaning of it. Use your imagination in remembering, but then let the memory of Nature speak for itself. Let it invoke in you again the feeling that came with its wisdom the day you encountered it. The memory of the striking truth of Nature is sufficient to deliver the joy that came with your initial rendezvous. Remember, repeat, renew: that is how you remain open to the truth of Nature and continue to experience its enduring enchantment. The next time you're in a long and laborious committee meeting, or on your seventh Zoom call of the day, or if you're locked up in a house full of kids, or worse a cubicle, recall a moment in which Nature spoke to you, let that moment "flash upon" your "inward eye," and be reminded of the enchanting truth of Nature.

Concluding Thoughts

Nature to the Romantics was not "God" in the all-mighty, Alpha Male, King-of-the-Mountain, Divine Ruler sense, but it was to them deeply "religious." Nature directs or draws us toward the transcendent, towards things eternal. It reveals to us both a dynamic unfolding and a moral sense, an intuition into the order of things. Paradoxically, it says that existence is indeed vast and expansive, but it is also small and intimate. It tells us that our presence in insignificant and yet, because we are indeed present, we too participate in the Great Mystery of Being: that there is something rather than nothing. For that fact alone, our existence is significant, and our lives take on a deeper sense of meaning because of it. That meaning has a moral inflection. The truth of Nature reveals to us that we are not adrift in space, we are not cosmic orphans, wandering the desert without a home. We have a place. There is a joy and an ethic in the pattern of the deer's path, in its graceful glide through a forest thicket (even if that forest abuts a suburban backyard). There is no need to reconcile these different aspects of Nature's truth. They're not contradictions. They're inflections, each suggesting another way of conceiving of Nature as something other than "the outdoors," or "the environment," or simply a storehouse of resources. Nature according

to the Romantics is a source of life-giving wisdom, and to express that ultimately inexpressible wisdom we need a different language than science and
empiricism. For many, only the language of religion or poetry can describe
the truth of Nature.

And Nature *is* telling us something. It *is* whispering its secret ministry.
When we learn to experience the truth of Nature our lives are imbued with
a magic, a texture, and a depth. Nature enchants because it reveals to us an
abiding connection to the world around us, a connection that runs deeper
than the mere "fact" of the natural world and our place in it as highly evolved
animals. The truth of Nature reveals beauty, belonging, and a moral sense of
life. It celebrates the miracle of existence itself, and at times calls us to join
in the celebration. The truth of Nature is like a Stranger or an unexpected
guest who arrives and with his company brings surprise and pleasure. We
spend the evening talking with him, laughing together, and enjoying the
gift of friendship. He tells us things we never knew, things that surprise and
delight us, beautiful things. Because of his company we no longer feel the
need to reduce the world to matter, or to explain it away in scientific terms.
We are able to rest in the space in-between, in the space of Keats's "negative
capability" and to find ourselves at home.

4

Sincerity over Snark

Reclaiming the Sacredness of Human Expression

Snark, Cynicism, and the Problem
of Postmodern Speech

It's fascinating to pay attention not only to *what* people say, but *how* they say it. After all, how you say something is also how you talk to someone. And how you talk to someone shapes your relationship with them. There's a lot at stake in how you say something. What's equally fascinating is how different structures impact how you say something; that is, how the space in which you speak makes you speak a certain way. Take Twitter, for example: 280 characters. That's it. That's the limit to what you can say. (The average tweet is about thirty-three characters.) What kind of speech does this produce? How does it make you talk to other people? Lots of ways, of course, but one way is for certain: it makes you *brief*. By design, Twitter (and other short form media like TikTok, TedTalks, Snapchat, etc.) want you to say something snappy, grab their attention. Get in, and get out. That's what matters. "Enlighten us, but make it quick."[1] In these forums, you shouldn't expect slow deliberation.

What should you expect? What kinds of speech do social media spaces produce? Provocative speech. Argumentative speech. Controversial speech. Polemical speech. Snarky speech. Speech that is irreverent and ironic. Speech that makes you smirk or sneer. There's no questioning the ubiquity of social media in our culture, so it's hard to overstate the influence these

1. This the actual slogan of Ignite Talks, TedTalk's competitor.

kinds of speech have on the way we talk to one another, the shape of our relationships, and the values of our society.

So there's a lot at stake in how we talk to each other. In this chapter, I want to examine the habits of speech we derive from social media-type spaces, and see how they produce and reinforce a kind of disenchanting, postmodern cynicism. Cynicism and snark make demands on us. They say, be critical, be witty, no matter the cost. The trouble is, these modes of speech erode the human capacity for connection, and that leaves us at odds with what we *hope for* out of human expression, and how we *would like* to talk to one another.

To really understand how disenchanting postmodern cynicism can be, let's look at the underlying philosophical ideas that animate it. Then we'll turn to the Romantic alternative: sincerity. Contrary to modern norms, the Romantics thought we could reclaim the sacredness of human expression through sincere speech, by reaching beyond ourselves in an act of poetic yearning and imaginative performance. (More on that to come.) But let me be clear from the start: cynicism, irony, parody, and other related forms of speech are not in themselves anathema to generative human discourse. They have a place. As we examine our modern speech habits, I'll point out where they have an important role to play in how we talk to one another. (I can't say the same for snark, though.) But because this is a book about enchantment, I'm going to focus more on how structures like social media over-emphasize certain modes of speech, cheapening their effectiveness and using them to produce a disenchanting *mood*, one that seems to haunt almost all of our modern relationships.

In chapter 1, we surveyed three forces of disenchantment: scientism, capitalism, and deconstruction. These three forces swirl about the modern milieu of life and make up a large part of the water we're swimming in. All three impact the way we talk to one another. But deconstruction is especially important with regard to the question of human speech because it takes as its central concern the nature of language, which is, of course, the key ingredient for speaking.

Deconstruction is a philosophical program developed by French philosopher Jacques Derrida in the mid to late twentieth century. Deconstructive analysis focuses on revealing the inherent instability of concepts, narratives, languages, and meaning. Derrida argued that language is a never-ending web of meanings that constantly defer to one another, and that language is always at play with itself. The upshot of this observation is that the meaning of a linguistic expression is never settled. It is always fraying at the seams, so to speak, and the ideas and narratives we construct using words carry within them this same, inherent instability. We live in a restless world, a world of reference-after-reference, where meaning is mirrored back and out, a reflection of a reflection. Like a phantom, meaning becomes an ephemeral wisp, constantly undoing itself as soon as it is said. Language is always deconstructing itself.

Philosophically speaking, Derrida's observations are brilliant. He's turned out to be one of the most influential philosophers of the twentieth century. But as deconstruction left the Ivory Tower and trickled down into popular culture, mass market capitalism appropriated its methods and monetized them in short-form media. The once thoughtful critiques of culture issued by deconstructive thinkers have now become predictable and banal. Deconstruction is repackaged and sold back to us in the form of snarky quips, perpetual critique, and the fetishization of power dynamics. Much of our online speech is made up of bitesize bits of nothing, a little sarcastic laughter here (meme), a vapid moral claim there (#virtuesignal), but little else by way of earnest self-expression makes its way into our public forums. In its absorption into postmodern culture, deconstruction has become a formulaic and unproductive way to critique something (queue the smart-aleck comment) without ever committing to anything (I'm too wise to believe in anything). It's had a chilling effect on sincere speech, and cut off our ability to connect with one another.

One more important point about the history of deconstruction: when Derrida's insights were expanded into what we now call "postmodern" philosophy, it adopted a more ambitious agenda than Derrida originally imagined. Postmodern criticism took on a more overtly political approach, with its goal being to reveal the provisional, contingent, constructed, unstable, power-laden nature, of, well, *just about everything*. In this sense, postmodern critique has become formulaic. Pop culture postmodern critics claim there is no Archimedean point from which to judge a norm because we all speak from a certain historical, cultural, and experiential position. That idea isn't too controversial, actually. Like most people, I agree with it. But they then go on to use this knowledge of our positionality to delegitimize any position, which ends up delegitimizing all positions. In privileging the fact of provisionality, even well-intentioned conversations end up in the quagmire of perpetual deconstruction (which was not Derrida's aim). We participate in a "gotcha-style" form of cultural critique, where a person's contribution to a conversation reaches its zenith when she pulls back the curtain on another's position and says, "That's exactly what a [fill-in-the-blank-identity] would say! More bias! More oppression!" Analyzing the substance of a position takes a back seat to exposing the power dynamics at play in the speaker's positionality. That's pop postmodernism. Sincere expression isn't even on our radar. Reaching out toward another person is no longer the point of human speech. The goal is to unmask the speaker and expose his bias: contextualize, historicize, and dismiss.

I want to make one thing clear. I'm not anti-Derrida, or even anti-postmodern. Deconstruction and postmodernism have their place in our broader cultural discourse. At their best, they make us acutely aware of the power dynamics and dangers of oppression at play in our worldviews, and in what we say, and how we say it. History shows that blindness to these dynamics leads to ignorance, dogma, violence, and death. But taken too far, the postmodern concern with speech bias and positionality can become itself oppressive. If your sole focus is on uncovering biases and pointing out positionality, that's all you'll ever see. Your own perspective becomes predictable and trite. You see bias everywhere. You read oppression into everything. Conversation ceases because no one wants to talk to you for fear they'll be dismissed out of hand, simply because they come from a position (as we all do). And the minute human conversation ends, the moment speech is no longer a viable tool we can use to reach out toward one another, that's the moment human relationships become disenchanted.

This slide from postmodern critique to disenchanted cynicism can be subtle. It sneaks up on you. Like Twitter, it has a set structure that forms the shape your speech can take. It goes like this: at first, the project of rooting out biases and power dynamics is exciting. You feel like you're uncovering sources of injustice, and often you are. It's thrilling to notice them, and to call them out. But then, after a while, you notice something peculiar. You keep seeing the same oppressive structures everywhere, underneath the surface of just about anything anyone says. This happens because, in many cases, those structures really are there, but also because *that's all you're looking for.* You start to become jaded. *How can everyone be so blind to their own biases?* you ask yourself. *How can anyone not know that what they're saying is tainted by the way they look, how they grew-up, how they were raised, where they went to school, etc.?*

You tire of other people's ignorance. Your analysis shifts from a thirst for justice to a taste for snark. You want to mock this ignorance, and all these stupid people that you just can't believe voted for so-and-so. You start to appreciate the satisfaction of the "call out" more than the veracity of the critique. That's natural. We all grow tired of righting the same wrong, time and time again. So you assume an air of superiority, arrogance, even. You see yourself as one of the few who have awoken to the truth, while most others remain asleep, unaware of their own contributions to oppression. "Oh," you say, "Here comes another un-reflective bigot." You stop considering the possibility that the person in front of you might have something intelligent to say, regardless of her race, gender, age, nationality, socioeconomic class, or any other identity marker. You've had enough. Conversation becomes parody. You no longer engage in thoughtful discourse and instead resort to snarky comments about the Other on social media. Queue the "dumb liberal" meme, the "racist Republican" hashtag, or whatever. Sincerity dies. Snark reigns.

Once we all start doing this (and sharing it on social media), post-modern cynicism becomes not just a method, but *a mood*. It shapes our culture. It pervades almost all of our inter-personal communication. The most coveted position in a public conversation is the position that critiques all positions, that takes no position. It jeers, chastises, and revels in its own revealing. It fixates on unmasking the other and avoids vulnerability by eschewing any commitment itself. The postmodern "critic" (if he is even worthy of the name) shield's himself from criticism by engaging *only in* criticism. He puts nothing forward. He does not offer anything nourishing, anything redemptive. The result is an endless cycle of smirks, gotchas, snide comments, and dismissiveness.

The result is short-form social media. Cynicism needs an outlet. It needs a forum for expression. Social media is the postmodernist's play-ground, his platform, and his pedestal. It's the place where he goes to combat everyone and everything, to say everything, and nothing. Adjudicating between postmodern positions no longer makes sense because, according to the postmodern program itself, *there are no realities*, there are just different views bolstered by different sets of "facts" (everyone has their own alternative facts). We come to accept and then revel in the fact that everything is unstable. Everything is fraying. Everything is coming undone.

David Foster Wallace diagnosed this problem back in the 1990s, well before the rise of social media. Were he still alive, he would have much to say about social media's thirst for derision, cynicism, and mockery. He'd note (I'm sure) the paradoxical way in which The Great Connectors end up cutting us off from one another. And he'd offer thoughtful commentary on the way Facebook, Instagram, and Twitter (in a truly dizzying double move) both reward us for saying something pithy (gather up your likes, retweets, and views, etc.) and insist upon our perpetual participation in the "cycle of saying" (you too must click, like, comment, etc.). And he'd tell us to choose another path. At the end of "E Unibus Pluriam," Wallace envisions the next "real literary 'rebels' in this country," emerging as "some weird bunch of 'anti-rebels,' born oglers who dare to back away from ironic watching, who have the childish gall to actually endorse single-entendre values. Who treat old, untrendy human troubles and emotions in U.S. life with reverence and conviction."[2] Of course, these rebels will be met with postmodern yawns,

2. Wallace, "E Unibus Pluram," 192–93.

eye rolls, and too-cool smirks.[3] But that is the wager the rebel must make. That is the risk of sincerity, the path to an enchanted discourse, and the way to reclaim the sacredness of speech.

The Romantics understood this, in their own way. Although it would be anachronistic to say they contemplated postmodern snark, you could say they understood sincerity, and what's at stake when the structures governing public and private discourse do not allow for it. The Romantics remind us that, despite the dismay we experience in a culture saturated with cynicism, we do not have to give ourselves over to its sad sibling, nihilism. The powerful drive of the human spirit to reach beyond itself is still here. There are alternatives to postmodern snark, methods beyond deconstruction. There are ways to reach out toward the Other, to bear witness to the complex beauty that emerges when two human souls encounter one another, and speak sincerely.

Who Am I, Anyway?
The Sincere Self in Romantic Thought

For the Romantics, sincerity is more than just letting your feelings out, or laying bare your heart to someone. Romantic sincerity is a way to commune with the swirling, expressive power of life itself. That's quite different from how we see it today. We tend to view sincerity with suspicion. We sometimes see it as a weakness, or sentimentalism. We value shrewdness and clear-eyed rationality. To us, a sincere person is a pleading person, someone who wants you to know he *really* means what he says, in an almost pathetic, puppy dog kind of way. But just like Wallace, the Romantics saw sincerity as an act of rebellion. It was a form of speech that pushed back against the stultifying and sterile discourse of Enlightenment rationalism. It affirmed the value of human conviction, viewing it as a manifestation of the creative forces at play throughout the universe. That's a lot to take in, I know. So let's take it one step at a time. We'll begin with a comparison between two forms of communication—one modern, and one Romantic—using it as an entry point into how sincerity can contribute to an enchanted life.

What's the difference between an epitaph and a tweet? One we read on a gravestone, the other on an iPhone. One we take to be an earnest reflection on life (or death), the other is a rapid fire text, usually about the day's news. One seems solemn, the other not-so-serious. Both use short form to get the job done. Both try to catch the eye of the passerby, to get them to pay attention to the little insight they offer. But there's a big difference between

3. Wallace, "E Unibus Pluram," 193.

the way we experience those insights. A tweet compels us to roll our eyes, or smirk and swipe. But an epitaph compels us to sit, to ponder, and to reflect. Wondering about the difference between an epitaph and a tweet might seem a bit odd, but it's an updated version of the question William Wordsworth asked back in 1810, in his "Essays upon Epitaphs." There, Wordsworth analyzed how it was that epitaphs produced their powerful effect on us, how they grip us using just a few short words (that I bet averaged less than 280 characters). He asks, "What's going on in an epitaph that moves us so deeply?" What he discovered, was *sincerity*.

Returning to our version of the question, then, the answer might seem simple: epitaphs are about death—a somber subject—and tweets are about less serious stuff. But we know that isn't true. Especially over the last few years, as we've seen Twitter become a public platform for presidents, politicians, and policy leaders to comment on the day's events or push their agenda. People use Twitter to comment on international politics, race, class struggle, and any number of serious topics.

You might be tempted to explain the difference in terms of genre. Genre is the set of expectations you bring to what you're reading. For example, when you pick up a romance you expect to get a bunch of swash-buckling adventures. Likewise, if you read a gravestone you'd expect to get some genuine expression of lament, because well, death is sad and that's what epitaphs tend to be about. It seems natural that you'd sit and ponder an epitaph because of the expectations about its subject matter that you bring to it. Contemplation is part of the genre, so to speak. But with Twitter, you're only going to spend nanoseconds on what's written because that's the expec-tation the genre sets for you in its character limit.

Like Wordsworth, I think there's more to it than that. According to him, well-written epitaphs move us because of their sincerity. Epitaphs give expression to our deepest human concerns about mortality and the mean-ing of life. They are particular instances of more universal experiences that we all share. Everyone must die. That is a cause for mourning. Epitaphs draw our attention to these troubling truths and reveal something about them. But *how* they produce these sincerity effects is what interests Wordsworth.[4] For him, a sincere epitaph is one that genuinely testifies to the essence of the person who has died through an appeal to "the common or universal feeling of humanity" and "a distinct and clear conception" of the individual.[5] Epi-taphs pull this off through a poetic mixture of colloquial diction, informal

4. For an excellent and thorough analysis of different "sincerity effects" in Word-sworth's poetry, see Forbes, *Sincerity's Shadow*, 1–46.

5. Forbes, *Sincerity's Shadow*, 15.

syntax, a natural or psychologically probable movement of thought, and strong passion.[6] What's interesting for our purposes is not whether Wordsworth is right about all of this, but his more radical, underlying idea that sincerity is and should be a normative ideal for human expression, that a *good* epitaph is a *sincere* one.

In many ways, this is the most Romantic of Romantic thoughts. Wordsworth seems to be saying that because self-expression is the external communication of a deeply felt truth experienced somewhere within the speaker, it should be taken seriously as a creative and revelatory act, it should be seen as an act of transcendence, not just idle chatter. Self-expression is at its best a revelation of the innermost self, and that self which participates in the Great Mystery of Being. To express one's self, then, is to utter with conviction, to make accessible to the outside the truth that is on the inside. Sincerity is a courageous act of disclosure, one that demands honesty and requires a great deal of vulnerability. It *shows* us something. It reveals what is concealed in our hearts. It brings to light the otherwise hidden aspects of what it means to be human. For perhaps the first time in Western thought, Wordsworth's "Essays on Epitaphs" articulated a theory of sincerity that places at its center genuine humanness. For Wordsworth, sincerity is the standard by which we should judge the value of each other's speech.

Consider that idea in light of the commonplace kinds of communication you see on social media, or just in everyday life. You can begin to feel the force of the Wordsworth's point about sincerity: we should be thoughtful, delicate, deliberate, and courageous in our self-expression because it reveals the moving depth inside each of us. It calls for care, not critique. Honesty, not irony. Being on either the "giving" or "receiving" side of self-expression puts us in a place of trust and hope, both of which are enchanting experiences because they put us in touch with some of the deepest mysteries of human existence. When was the last time you saw (or said?) something sincere? I ask the question not to chastise but to show how foreign the idea of sincerity seems to us now, in a postmodern world dominated by pithy one-liners, quick comments, and irreverent observations. We put no premium on sincerity. We certainly don't value it as much as the Romantics did. But maybe we should.

In his seminal work, *Sincerity and Authenticity* (1972), literary critic Lionel Trilling traced the historical development of two forms of human genuineness in Western thought. Sincerity, or, the "congruence of avowal and actual feeling," developed according to Trilling as a kind of normative ideal that sanctioned the human desire to articulate one's inner convictions

6. Perkins, *Wordsworth and the Poetry of Sincerity*, 41.

so as not to deceive others. For Trilling, the heart of sincerity was the idea
that speaking plainly to others means exactly that: speaking *to others*. Sincerity constituted the struggle to reconcile the self with society. The willingness to "put it out there" meant that others could trust you, rely on you, and
believe you. No dissembling, no deceit. And why is this important? Because
sincerity is about taking what happens in the human heart seriously. It is a
form of expression that in its very articulation manifests a truth. As we saw
in chapters 2 and 3, on the Romantic view truth is less about correspondence to states of affairs in the world and more about the ineffable mystery
existence. It's about Nature unfolding and the way in which we participate
in it, the way in which we are expressions of it. By sincerely revealing our
inner lives to others we are able to connect with them in ways that solipsism
and ironic critique cannot because sincerity is fundamentally about reaching out, not protecting what's within. Under the rubric of Wordsworthian
sincerity, when we directly confront our inner experiences and speak them
to another person we bravely give ourselves over to truth, and tussle with
the tension of being a self in society with others. To do otherwise, to dis-
semble, dupe, or deceive, is to craftily avoid the open space of vulnerability
that is required for deep human connection. *In*sincerity is "not of the lion,
but of the fox," as Dante puts it.

The idea of sincerity has a long history, but our concern is with sincerity in the hands of the Romantics, and what it means for enchantment.
Trilling's distinction between sincerity and the more modern value of authenticity is a nice bridge into specific Romantic notions of sincerity. I'll
summarize it here. Authenticity is the idea that come hell or high-water we
will speak those truths that accord with our genuine selves. Where sincerity
has a fundamentally social inflection (viewing truthfulness as a means to an
end), authenticity takes on a more self-oriented focus (viewing truthfulness
as an end in itself). The difference is subtle, but important. Moving from
other-directed expression to self-directed attestation marks a seismic shift
in what we think is the purpose of inter-personal communication. The Romantic idea of sincerity emerged as a way to give life and expression to the
deep human desire to reach beyond ourselves toward another, to somehow
get outside of our tiny, skull-sized kingdoms and reveal something moving
and share it with another person. Authenticity, on the other hand, rests in
the idea that truth lies *inside* the tiny, skull-sized kingdom, and the goal of
expression is to honor it, to defend it, despite its public reception or society's appetite for it. Indeed, authenticity seems to ring loudest when it goes
against the social grain. This should sound familiar because, as we've already
discussed, authenticity is the other sort of speech (in addition to snark and
cynicism) that characterizes our modern speech habits.

The Romantics were about sincerity, not authenticity. But as they explored the idea in their paintings, poetry, and prose they began to sense a tension. As it turns out, the inner self is a lot more elusive than it seems. Romantics like Lord Byron and John Keats began to see that "the self"—that is, the underlying, real "me" that is hidden somewhere deep within—is actually hard to find. These Romantics began to suspect that "the self" is perhaps better understood as a more mercurial sort of thing (if it is a "thing" at all) and that exploring "who I am" might require I try on different masks or personae, that I might at one moment feel one thing, and then at another moment something quite different. Indeed, I might even feel multiple, conflicting things all at once. Which of these feelings are the feelings of my true self? It's a good question. Even Wordsworth, the great champion of Romantic sincerity, was aware of its delicate relationship with the self and the way the self seems to always be on the move, turning and churning and morphing and changing. In light of all of this, what does it even mean to engage in sincere self-expression?

Romantic Sincerity in Three Keys: Wordsworth, Byron, Keats

There is no single Romantic view on sincerity, but most Romantics shared in common the idea that sincere discourse is enchanting (my word, not theirs) because it gives self-expression a kind of force, it opens up onto a space of self-transcendence, reaching beyond the self and toward the Other. Sincerity also requires a risk, a wager. How will the other person receive me? Will she reject me? Will she critique me, or belittle? Or will she welcome me with grace? Will she make a space for me?

Because speaking according to the Romantics is essentially a creative act, we must take it seriously. But that does not mean that all sincere speech is serious speech. Sincere speech can be funny, too. (Byron had a great sense of humor.) Even when sincere speech is humorous speech, however, the Romantics viewed it as something sacred. Moreover, sincere speech requires a certain amount of deliberation and reflection in order to *come off* as sincere. Thus, there is also a performative aspect to sincerity. It's an effect that must be achieved. In the end, the Romantics considered sincerity as essentially paradoxical: in reaching inward, sincerity allows us to reach outward, and what we discover when we reach inward is that there may not be a "me" in there in the first place. Like language, the self is unraveling. The dynamic nature of the self creates some interesting tensions in Romantic literature. We'll explore them in the next section. But for now, understand that the

Romantic idea of "reaching out" was the primary goal of sincere expression (and what distinguishes it from authenticity). Romantic sincerity is a longing: for community, for human kinship, and for belonging. It gives voice to the strong pull we feel to be *with* other people, to be understood by them, even if only through a glass darkly. Where postmodern cynicism might do a great job exposing power dynamics and positionality, Romantic sincerity wants to go beyond the self, and to connect one person with another in a way that does not deconstruct, but in a way that nourishes, and sustains.

Sincerity as the Pause before the Poem

Most scholars agree that William Wordsworth was "the first poet to cultivate sincerity as a poetic value."[7] Wordsworth defined poetry as "the spontaneous overflow of powerful feelings: it takes its origin from emotion recollected in tranquility," but as we have already seen in his "Essays upon Epitaphs," he adds to this definition the idea that sincere expression articulates through particular human experience something that implicates a universal human concern. In other words, sincerity strives to point us toward moments when eternity pierces the veil of time. While for Wordsworth, the yearning for sincere self-expression emerges from "powerful feelings," it is not reducible to those feelings, nor is it a matter of mere sentimentality. It's more complicated than that, and more interesting. Sincerity is not about being "naive, and goo-prone," as David Foster Wallace puts it, but about what happens when we *reflect* on the overflow of powerful feelings, when we "recollect them in tranquility." For Wordsworth, sincerity implicates a pause. And the pause makes all the difference. Sincerity is not just impassioned pleading, or saying what you mean, really, really earnestly. It's not baying at the feet of your crush. For Wordsworth, it's the effect of an imaginative act and creative articulation of a past experience of powerful feelings upon which you've contemplated.

7. Angela Esterhammer, "The Scandal of Sincerity," 104.

Benjamin Robert Haydon, *William Wordsworth*, 1842, oil on canvas.

There's a lot buried in that last point, but it's an important one. It goes to the core of what is at stake in Wordsworth's idea of sincerity. Romantics are often criticized for prioritizing the heart over the head. You'll some-times hear people say Romantics are too, well, "romantic." What they mean by this is that Romantics were too passionate, too emotional. They were a wishy-washy group of feeling-junkies who were taken up with the power of their emotions, over logic and reason. But that's a caricature. It's not what they were really about. Wordsworth's idea of sincerity is a case in point. For Wordsworth, sincerity is a poetic mix of art and heart and mind. It is an effect that occurs when through the creative use of language, the poet explores the original impulse of the heart that gave rise to the poetic motivation, but he does so through a conscious reflection on how his creative mind "makes sense" of that moment. In other words, sincerity is an expression of a powerful experience and a *reflection upon that experience*. So sincerity requires both thinking and feeling. But what's most interesting is that for Wordsworth, there is a pause built into the structure of sincerity. That's the big point. This moment of self-reflection in which the poet thinks deeply and imaginatively about the spontaneous overflow of powerful feelings and brings those thoughts and feelings into words is the key to sincere expression. Sincerity requires a breath, a moment of silence that precedes the moment of creation (i.e., the moment of speech). This pause or breath isn't just about slowing down, or meditating, or calming one's passions, or getting your composure. It's about aesthetic reflection on what moved you: the way it felt, the way you received it, what it did to you, how you compared it to other experiences, what symbols or images it evoked, how it resonated with your soul, etc. In short, *what it meant to you*. For Wordsworth, the pause is a condition for the possibility of sincerity. And it's the birthplace of poetry.

Once the poet pauses, she then has a space to creatively engage the moment, recalling it and allowing it to "flash upon that inward eye." She works with language to articulate its meaning. She gives it shape and texture. The expression that emerges from this cocktail of experience and aesthetic reflection is sincere when it delivers to the reader a kind of poetic knowledge that is birthed out of a "pitch of concentration and feeling."[8] That's where the magic of Wordsworthian sincerity happens. The heart is moved, and then, after attentive observation of that movement, one is able to speak sincerely about it. Now, not all reflective self-expression is sincere self-expression. For Wordsworth, there is an art to sincerity. In order for sincerity to "happen" there also needs to be the kind of "generalizing up," in which the poet is able to see the universal in the particular. To achieve sincerity the expression must interrogate a specific instance in life (a child's death, a beaming moon, a field of daffodils, etc.) and discover in it something important about humankind in general.[9] Moreover, the expression must take on a certain style. It should use everyday language (it can't be too pedantic), rely on informal sentence structures (it can't be too highfalutin), give voice to a "natural" or "typical" movement of thought (it can't be too weird), and it must invoke strong passion (it can't be banal). All of these

8. Ball, "Sincerity: The Rise and Fall of a Critical Term," 10.
9. Forbes, *Sincerity's Shadow*, 15.

things swirl together in a confluence of poetic creativity that, according to Wordsworth, generate sincerity.

What's this got to do with enchantment? Keep in mind the contrasts between postmodern forms of expression (cynicism, irony, irreverence, etc.) and Romantic sincerity. Wordsworth's theory of sincerity points us toward enchantment in a number of ways. First, there is a clear distinction between Romantic sincerity and modern authenticity as demonstrated by the "direction" in which the two types of expression face. Sincere expression for Wordsworth is *outward facing*. It moves towards another person. It lays bare one's inner life in order to reveal to another person its truth. This "laying bare" breaks us out of the cage of the ego by pointing us toward a universal human concern. Remember: for Wordsworth sincerity draws on a particular experience in order to connect us to a more pervasive or general human truth. Authenticity on the other hand is about self-expression for its own sake. It's less about reaching out and more about testifying to one's "inner truth." It's therefore *inward facing*, and justifies its articulation by the fact that it gives voice to a "true" inner state.

Sincerity and authenticity have different purposes. Wordsworthian sincerity is about human connection. It sees other people as a chance for transcendence: the Other is a space for the possibility of reception, hope, and trust. It speaks with a hope that I might be received despite or even because of my earnest giving of myself, which in turn reveals a truth that resonates with us both. It trusts that the Other will hear me, and may be moved by what I say. For Wordsworth, sincerity speaks with conviction out of the dangerous hope that my soul will be accepted by another person with gentleness, sympathy, and welcome. And that in my sincere expression we may both discover something universal, something that is true for both of us, for all of us. There is for Wordsworth a dynamism to the structure of sincerity, a complex interplay of experience, reflection, articulation, reception, trust, hope, and risk that opens onto the possibility of self-transcendence.

Wordsworthian sincerity enchants in other ways, too. Because sincerity's aim is to convey the universal truth grounded in a particular experience, it is inherently connective; that is, it looks for the commonalities between us, not the stark differences. This concern with commonality feeds human connection and nourishes community. And in community, you have the chance of belonging. Sincere self-expression can help you overcome the alienation of individualism. Sincerity builds bonds of sympathy, common ground, and care between you and another person. It compels you to leave the isolation of your own mind, to shove off from what Herman Melville in *Moby-Dick* called the "one, insular Tahiti" inside each of us. It beckons you to brave the open seas of otherness. Where cynicism defends against criticism by battening down the hatches against inter-personal vulnerability, sincerity opens them up.

Finally, Wordsworthian sincerity enchants by directing us to deep and abiding human concerns. It doesn't let us rest in superficialities or to take shelter in shallow things. Sincerity is serious, in this regard. It is unsatisfied with talk about the weather, trite observations, stale clichés, or manufactured opinions. Sincerity gives the everyday an existential charge because it finds the eternal in mundane, human activities. Life is a sincere expression of existence, and is therefore ripe with opportunities to encounter these eternal truths. In his simple poem, "She dwelt among th'untrodden ways," Wordsworth recounts the story of a forgettable country girl who simply was, and is no more. "She lived unknown, and few could know / when Lucy ceased to be; / But she is in her grave, and oh! / The difference to me."[10] Her death made all the difference because in it he felt the universality of grief and of loss. Sincerity requires that we pause and consider, that we reflect on our powerful feelings, and that we search them for shared, common experiences of truth.

Sincerity as Playful Performance

With all this talk about death and eternity, you might be feeling like sincere folks are all a bit too serious. There's no sense of humor. That's partly true, actually. Sincere speech always has something serious to convey, and so there is always a serious angle to what is said. But the Romantics loved to laugh. They were hilarious, in fact. Many of them were masters of irony, critique, parody, and so on. But unlike postmodern forms of speech, even the funniest Romantics were never concerned with maintaining the so-called "critical distance" privileged by cynicism and snark, the kind of distance that guards against vulnerability. No, the Romantics were all in. They fully embraced their humanness, with all its quirks, foibles, and idiosyncrasies. And sometimes that made them laugh.

One particular form of sincere speech that emerged in the second wave of Romantics (Keats, Byron, the Shelleys, etc.) was Romantic irony. The idea that irony can play a role in enchantment may seem to contradict what we've been saying so far, but stick with me. There is a certain kind of irony—Byronic irony, to be exact—that goes deeper than postmodern irony in its attempt to get at what it means to be human. With Lord Byron at the helm, these second-wave Romantics began to explore the tensions latent in earlier forms of Romantic sincerity. They challenged some of Wordsworth's assumptions about the "inner life," but they also enriched his ideas,

10. Wordsworth, *The Major Works*, 147–48.

pushing them further than perhaps he was willing to go. They interrogated this "inner/outer" distinction, and called into question the "metaphysics of the self"—that is, the reality of the self we think we're expressing when we engage in sincere speech. Like a Zen koan, they asked, "What is this 'self' that expresses itself?"

Thomas Phillips, *Lord Byron in Albanian Dress,* 1835, oil on canvas.

Byron in particular sensed a tension in Wordsworth. If sincerity is rooted in self-revelation; that is, if sincere expression depends on an underlying self to be expressed, what—or where—is this self? *Is there even such a thing?* "Who am I?" is an age-old question. The earliest philosophers grappled with it, and we still do today. On the one hand, the answer seems obvious. I am me, I am my body, experiences, and thoughts. What else is there? But on the other hand, after just a little critical reflection, we see that each of these things is more mercurial, more elusive than they seem at first. What is my body? What makes up my experiences? Where are my thoughts? The answers aren't so clear.

Take your body, for example. Is that what makes you, you? Imagine a boat about to set sail. The captain and crew are ready to go. The ship is brand new, fully outfitted with what it needs for the long journey. The boat embarks. It's not long before it starts to leak a little, take on some damage, and just experience the normal wear-and-tear of being out to sea. The crew makes repairs, swapping out planks in the hull, changing and repairing the rigging, etc. Over the course of the journey, plank-by-plank, rope-by-rope, nail-by-nail, every piece of the ship is replaced. When the ship reaches harbor, is it the same boat? What makes the ship, *the* ship? Isn't your body like that? You're born into a body and over time it changes. Every cell dies and is replaced over the course of your life. In fact, according to biologists, your body "replaces" itself *multiple times* throughout your life. If the answer to "Who am I?" is "my body" that would mean there is no durable "you," there is no "you" that's been there all along. According to this logic, who you are today is someone *fundamentally different* than who you were when you were ten, or two. But that doesn't seem right. So who are you?

We could go on with the other theories like this, but I don't want to belabor the point. The Romantics understood the problem of personal identity, and they understood the implications of a self that cannot be pinned down. Even Wordsworth appreciated the slippery nature of the self. In fact, it is precisely *because* of his sensitivity to the self's slitherings that he preferred poetry over prose. As we have seen, poetry allows for a surplus of meanings, symbolic excess, and indirect references. The advantage of poetry is that it does not seek to know the rainbow by unweaving it. Instead, it tries to provoke or express the *experience* of the rainbow itself through the creative use of language. Given the elusive nature of the self, poetic expressions that attend to the ever-changing nature of life seem more appropriate than precise, analytical forms of expression.

In this sense Lord Byron was similar to Wordsworth in his method, but he took a very different angle in his style. For Byron, sincerity is about the play of selflessness, the performance of the self, not it's revelation. According to Byron, we experience ourselves always in flux, always changing, and lacking any metaphysical substance. Sincerity is about how we live in this mercurial space. It's about how we thrive in it, how we come to be by *performing* the self, and how we use language, gesture, and other figurative speech—including irony—to express the various ways the self can appear. In other words, where Wordsworth saw sincerity as a means to dig deep into one's experiences and connect them to universal human concerns, Byron saw it as a way to explore the evanescent nature of the self as a changing and performative social activity.

Lord Byron was known for his flamboyance and revolutionary flair. His one-time lover, Lady Caroline Lamb, described him as "mad, bad, and dangerous to know." He routinely flouted social norms, dressed in wild attire, and wrote polemical poetry that provoked scandals and called into question any static sense of who he was. Byron once quipped that should he be asked who he was he might reply that he had "no character at all." His comic masterpiece *Don Juan* (1819–24) constantly shifts its tone from sentimental to silly to serious to cynical. At times the hero broods and laments, at others he laughs and belittles. Like Byron himself, he is hard to pin down. But throughout the poem Byron seems to have complete control of the hero, as well as the language and style that he marshals. He moves and shift and changes but never slips into chaos. That in itself testifies to the depth of his understanding of the paradox of selfhood: we are ceaselessly changing and yet in some way we also have a bit of control. Byron engages in satire and self-mockery, but never snark. His irreverence has a point. It's serious, and funny. Unlike postmodern irony, Byron's use of irony aims to reveal something true about life, not simply to show how he is "in on the joke" or to buffer himself against criticism. Even in his more comedic moments Byron somehow never loses sight of the fact that he is doing something important; that he is trying to get at a deeper truth about human existence. Most if not all of Byron's poetry (indeed, his life) is about the self-as-a-performance; that is, the myriad ways in which we give our selves to others through a variety of appearances and personae.

Here's an example of playful, Byronic sincerity. It's a lovely little poem called, "So we'll go no more a-roving":

> So, we'll go no more a-roving,
> So late into the night,
> Though the heart be still as loving,
> And the moon be still as bright.
>
> For the sword outwears its sheath,
> And the soul wears out the breast,
> And the heart must pause to breathe,
> And love itself have rest.
>
> Though the night was made for loving,
> And the day returns too soon,

> Yet we'll go no more a-roving,
>   By the light of the moon.[11]

This is what Romantic scholar Willard Spiegelman calls "a classic hangover poem." It's funny, its insightful, and its serious. The poet's lamenting the fact that he can't go out drinking and partying with his friends anymore, so he writes a beautiful poem about it. Why? The poem doesn't say exactly, but we know from Byron's letters that he wrote this poem during Lent, a time of fasting and contemplation which follows the rollicking indulgence of Carnival. He was twenty-nine when he penned it: old enough to know better than to spend the night binge drinking but young enough to still enjoy it. Byron playfully directs our attention to the sense of overindulgence and the pains that follow as he recollects his time with his band of itinerant friends as they shared in drunkenness and friendship. It's easy to imagine them wandering from bar to bar or party to party, laughing, singing, teasing, and just generally "a-roving." The only observer to this playful chumminess is the moon. The poem takes place at night, a time of blurred and shifting borders an experience not unlike Bacchus worship. The night is a time when distinctions are blended. Byron notes that even though there are more opportunities for fellowship and fun ("the heart be still as loving" and "the moon be still as bright") he must forgo them for a time (forever?) in order to "pause," "breathe," and "rest." In the last stanza Byron leaves open the possibility that, indeed, he may never again go a-roving.

This all seems fairly straightforward. The point is that the party's over, and that's sad. But on a closer read we can see Byron's performative sense of sincerity at play, and his use of humor and irony to express it. The poem has a deeper significance when we read it as commentary on the joy of life itself, which is a kind of magical roving but a roving that will one day end. The playful poem takes on a somber air. Like Byron, we see that we must learn to revel in life's illuminating glow, just like he and his friends soak up the light of the moon. We should be grateful that life can be so intoxicating, so full of joy and companionship and beauty and fun that it can at times take our breath away. The night (which can be read as life) was in fact "made" for loving, for union, for richness, for joy, for celebration. And yet, the day—which here in a clever reversal means death—returns "too soon," forestalling our joys and cutting life off before we've had our fill. The poem is indeed a tragic one. And that is its brilliance: it is both comedic and tragic, both joyous and lamenting, both playful and serious. Through the poem the poet weaves together what seem to be polar opposites. He pays homage to the fact that in life, and as changing selves, we are full of contradictions, shifts,

11. Byron, "So we'll go no more a-roving," 958.

tensions, and changes. We are joy and sorrow. Day to us is death. Night is life. Drunken roving is sober seriousness. Whimsy is contemplation. When we read the poem this way, we get a taste of Byron's sincere expression made as playful performance, and we are invited to consider how, like the poem, we too are full of paradox, full of shifts and changes. We too are a tumbling cluster of inversions.

In another of his poems, *Don Juan* (1819–24), Byron more explicitly takes up the question of sincerity and its relationship to the effervescent and mercurial self. Toward the end of the poem, the hero Don Juan describes an improvisational performer named Lady Adeline Amundeville as she puts on a show for her audience. In Canto 16.97, he writes:

> So well she acted, all and every part
>   By turns—with that vivacious versatility,
> Which many people take for want of heart.
>   They err—'tis merely what is called mobility,
> A thing of temperament and not of art,
>   Though seeming so, from its supposed facility;
> And false—though true; for surely they're sincerest,
> Who are strongly acted on by what is nearest.[12]

This is an interesting passage for those of us interested in Byronic sincerity. First, note what's going on in the scene: Lady Adeline is a *performer*. She knows that she is putting on a show. But for Byron that does not undermine her sincerity, though it does call into question the Wordsworthian idea of sincerity as revealing one's self without recourse to dissembling. Second, she has "mobility." "Mobility" according to Byron is an "excessive susceptibility of immediate impressions—at the same time without *losing* the past."[13] Mobile people are sincere people. They are in touch with "what is nearest," that is, their own embodied experience as a living, breathing, expressing, shifting, and changing person. They are able to maintain a close proximity to what they're feeling, and are able to express it convincingly to others. But they don't get hung up on how they feel or what they're conveying. They can move from one feeling to the next without clinging to the previous one. To some, this may come off as fickle or capricious (taken for "want of heart"), but for the mobile person this fluidity is a sort of serious play, testifying to the self as an ever-changing confluence of feelings and states. Adeline's performance is sincere insofar as it embodies these mercurial dynamics. And finally, Byron suggests that the sincere, mobile person is "strongly acted

---

12. Byron, *Don Juan*, 547.

13. Estherhammer, "The Scandal of Sincerity," 111 (citing Byron's prose annotation on *Don Juan*).

on" by that which calls her to self-expression. She does not have full mastery over her feelings and states (and body?). Instead, her feelings have a kind of agency, they act on her, compelling her to communicate them, and through her performance reach out toward others.

Notice how different this view of sincerity is to Wordsworth's. Unlike Wordsworth, Byron emphasizes sincerity as a production. He sees virtue in Adeline's ability to move and shift and shape her self-expression "on the fly," so to speak, presenting to her audience a whole range of feelings. Wordsworth, on the other hand, focuses on sincerity as the outward expression of a universal truth embedded in a particular instance. For Byron the emphasis is on the performative testimony of the changing nature of the human heart. For Wordsworth, it's on the aesthetic use of certain kinds of speech to convey a human truth. You might say that the fact that "the self is always changing" is the universal truth Byron wants to articulate in Adeline's performance—and that does seem to be the case—but Byron's way of conveying that truth is different from Wordsworth's. There is a certain seriousness to Wordsworth. But Byron shows us how playfulness, irony, coyness, revelation, and concealment are also tools for sincere expression.

Think about it. It's easy to imagine Adeline having fun, isn't it? It's easy to imagine her enjoying her own performance. She draws upon her fickle "temperament," which is not "of art" but still requires "heart." She is "false— though true" in her expressions. She takes pleasure in toggling through her emotions, stringing the audience along as she does. She has a "vivacious versatility" that is almost mesmerizing. Whether she is indeed trying to express what she really feels, or to create a sincerity effect for the audience remains an open question.

Here is Byronic irony at its best. Lady Adeline uses performance to say something true. A performer is someone who is *not* speaking for herself, but speaking as a character. But Byron intimates that it is precisely in this "speaking for another" that we "speak for ourselves." We are the activity of taking on personae. We are truest when we are acting. We show our real face each time we don a mask. Because there is no static, underlying self which we can reveal through spontaneous self-expression (*à la* Wordsworth) the self that is worth expressing is the self that takes different forms, the variegated self of multiplicity: now honest, now dissembling; now courageous, now a coward; now self-assured, now weak and unsure. Each aspect is a shimmering moment of ephemeral truth that appears and then becomes something else. The irony is that Lady Adeline shows us that we can only *have* a character when we *play* a character. Otherwise, we have no character at all.

This is a use of irony that goes far beyond postmodern snark. Where for us irony is essentially a defense mechanism against critique, a way to avoid vulnerability and guard against judgement, in the hands of Byron irony becomes a powerful literary tool to depict the deeper truth that who we are is always in question, that the answer to the question "Who am I?" is at once both "everyone" and "no-one." Byron leaves us with a statement that comes off more like an inquiry: Is what Lady Adeline is attempting to convey her true feelings, such that what is "sincerest" is actually "what is nearest"? Or is it that there is a disjunction between the "inner Adeline," which remains elusive (even to her?), and the "outer Adeline," who is always given to others through the mediation of language, body, gestures, etc.? Can she ever know herself enough to show herself to others? *Is there even a self to show?*

Sincerity as Emptiness

We now turn to a final example of Romantic sincerity: John Keats's emptiness. In many ways, Keats took the idea of sincerity to its limits. Despite his young age and tragic death (he died of tuberculosis at twenty-five), Keats left an indelible mark on the Romantic movement, and on the history of English poetry. His keen sense of sympathy for others—including people, animals, and even objects—allowed him to see into the life of things. Few Romantics rival his artistic abilities.

What was sincerity to Keats? To answer that question, we first need to consider his idea of "negative capability." For Keats, the problem with modes of knowledge like scientism, empiricism, and in some cases even philosophy, is that they privilege cognitive understanding over poetic mystery. They seek complete explanations, full accountings, and rational descriptions. Vagueness vexes them. Ambiguity annoys them. They are "incapable of remaining content in half knowledge." According to Keats, this obsession with explanation blinds us to the beautiful. Rather than neurotically pursuing absolute knowledge (which is code word for "mastery" or "control"), we must develop in ourselves an openness to a variety of truths. We must cultivate a receptive posture that becomes a "thoroughfare for all thoughts."

In a letter to his brothers, on December 22, 1818, Keats defined negative capability as "when a man is capable of being in uncertainties, mysteries, doubts, without any irritable reaching after fact and reason." Negative capability provides a space for beauty to "obliterate all consideration." In a posture of negative capability, we learn to live in the "Mist," as he calls it in another letter. We are able to explore the "dark passages" of our lives. We do not thirst for a higher-order truth or answers to the mysteries of existence. Instead, we develop a sensitivity and even love for the ever-changing, always partial appearances that we call "reality." We learn to see the world "through a glass darkly," as it were (the apostle Paul's words, not Keats's, but both pointing towards a similar truth).

Keats explored this idea of negative capability throughout his poetry. Like Byron, Keats was suspicious of the self. He had strong doubts that any metaphysical "thing" lay "underneath it all." Given the impossibility of pinning down the self, Keats adopted a position of negative capability toward it. He did not see the project of sincerity as the project of laying bare one's soul, but of observing one's reaction to compelling encounters with the world. Although a great admirer of Wordsworth, Keats came to see that even Wordsworth privileged the privacy of his own mind over reaching out beyond himself, toward the other. Given Keats's suspicions of the idea of an actual self, it is natural that he would turn to negative capability as a more poetic orientation. After all, "if it is impossible to grasp the self with a consistency that indicates truth has been obtained, then perhaps one could achieve greater self-understanding by abandoning the effort of grasping altogether."[14] This approach to sincerity goes beyond even Byron's embrace of the self-as-performance. For Keats, if there is no self with which we must align our avowals in order to speak sincerely, then we should open ourselves completely to the world, allowing it to enter into us and speak its truth through us. This, in essence, is his idea of *sincerity as self-emptiness.*

"A Poet is the most unpoetical of any thing in existence," wrote Keats, "because he has no Identity—he is continually in for—and filling some other body."[15] The poet is a "chameleon."[16] Keats distinguishes his idea of the protean poet from the poet of "the Wordsworthian or egotistical sublime," who takes as his point of departure for sincere expression the spontaneous overflow of powerful feelings; that is, the activity of the self as a confluence of feelings and inner-life.[17] The Keatsian poet is "not itself—it has no self—it is everything and nothing—It has no character."[18] We hear echoes of Byron in Keats's words here, and that's no coincidence. They were contemporaries, and read each other's works (although they were not fans of each other). But Keats goes further than Byron in his insistence that the self should empty itself in order to achieve sincerity. For Keats, to be sincere is to lose the self in observation, to extend one's sympathetic bonds toward the other, and then to articulate the insights that emerge in

14. Forbes, *Sincerity's Shadow*, 151.

15. Keats, "Letter from John Keats to Richard Woodhouse, 27 October 1818," 1424–25.

16. Keats, "Letter from John Keats to Richard Woodhouse, 27 October 1818," 1424.

17. Keats, "Letter from John Keats to Richard Woodhouse, 27 October 1818," 1424.

18. Keats, "Letter from John Keats to Richard Woodhouse, 27 October 1818," 1424.

poetic (i.e., beautiful) form. The result: knowledge and beauty; or better, the marriage of knowledge and beauty.

"What the imagination seizes as beauty must be truth," Keats writes.[19] It is through the clear perception of a thing's beauty that one comes to know it. It is not so much that Keats denies the activity of the inner life or the possibility of a certain kind of sincerity rooted in personal feelings, but that he is more concerned with the kind of sincerity that emerges out of our experience of *other things* and *other people*. This is outward-directed sincerity through-and-through. For Keats, sincerity requires that we pay attention to the other, that we quiet our soul and give it over to the sensitive observation of another person's way of being, or another object's appearance in the world. From this position of sensitive observer, we are able to open ourselves to the world, to let it flow into us and fill us. We can efface ourselves and come to know the world's truth in and through its beautiful appearances. There's a lot going on here, I know. But the key is to appreciate the idea that unlike Wordsworth and Byron, Keats sees as a condition for the possibility of sincerity a kind of self-emptying or self-suspension that draws our attention *outside* of ourselves, to the world of concrete things, rather than inward, to the world of personal feelings or even performance. Out of this emptying we are able to speak sincerely about what we have encountered because we have developed a sensitivity to the world that is not overly reliant upon our own inner convictions.

19. Keats, "Letter from John Keats to Richard Woodhouse, 27 October 1818," 1403.

John Keats, *Tracing of an Engraving of the Sosibios Vase,* c. 1819.

In "Ode on a Grecian Urn," Keats shows us how to achieve sincerity through emptiness. He walks us through a series of observations he makes about an old, decorated, Greek pot. That's an important point. Keats's whole focus in the poem is on a concrete thing, a mundane thing, even. His focus is not on his feelings (Wordsworth), or their mercurial nature (Byron). It's just about an old pot. Importantly, however, the urn is *an object in the world.* It is a material thing. And because it is a thing-in-the-world, it is, according to Keats, an opportunity for sincere expression because through the act of poetic emptying, the poet can come to identify with it, and in doing so speak for it, giving voice its eternal truth/beauty.

Keats describes the urn. It's painted. Around it flows beautifully drawn characters, decorative vines, dancing gods and goddesses, and nymphs and lovers. Everyone is in a state of ecstasy. It's clear that throughout the poem the pot is right there, right in front of Keats. He's looking at it with us, walking us through his observations. The poem has a kind of immediacy. It's as if we're with Keats at the Louvre, circumambulating the urn, leaning in with him to look closely at its details, to scrutinize its depictions, and notice everything it has to show us. Then something funny happens. As you're reading the poem and walking around the urn with Keats, you realize that Keats is observing *two* things, actually: the urn, and us observing the urn. He's watching us watch the pot, so to speak. The poem is a live-action production of what it looks like to think through, in, and around a concrete object. It's a depiction of the poet's (and our) orbit around a thing as he looks for ways to enter into it, to identify with it, and to give it voice.

To achieve this state, Keats invokes the art of negative capability. He does not claim to fully know what's happening. He's not itching to *explain* the urn in scientific terms (e.g., "The Sosibios Vase is a Neo-attic marble krater from the Hellenistic period, standing 78 cm in height, depicting a scene of. . .") but he does strive to *articulate* it. Like the pot, the self that observes remains elusive, fleeting, absent and present, persistent but vague. A tension arises, but Keats does not try to resolve it. Instead, he rests in it. He does not know what the urn and its images mean, and he does not seek after certainty about their meaning. He doesn't run to the information desk and get a pamphlet explaining who the people are. He resides in beauty without feeling the need to explain it away, to conquer it by knowing it.

Remember when Keats mentioned living in the Mist?[20] That's what's going on here, that's what he's showing us how to do. It is in the Mist we find Beauty. And Keats is a master of the Mist. He wraps us in it. His poem works on us, luring us into a state of negative capability. The words and phrases loop around the vase. He takes our hand and we walk around it together. We probe and question and never settle. We share in a series of "look at that!" moments without resolving exactly what it is we see. In this orbital pattern of poetic reflection, almost like a mage or wizard, Keats calls forth the Mist. He chants a series of unanswerable questions that, like us, seem to swirl around the object:

> What leaf-fringed legend haunts about thy shape
> Of deities or mortals, or of both,

20. See p. 130 above.

> In Tempe or the dales of Arcady?
>   What men or gods are these? What maidens loath?
> What mad pursuit? What struggle to escape?
>   What pipes and timbrels? What wild ecstasy?[21]

This is what sincerity-as-emptiness looks like. It means to observe, to face, and take in the always-partial appearances of the world. It means to stand in negative capability. And that includes facing the always-partial appearance of ourselves *as selves*. We are never "completely here," we have never fully arrived. There is no static, settled self. We cannot achieve sincerity as a congruence between feeling and avowal because there is no sturdy, one-to-one relationship between what we say and what we feel. Rather, we are always in a state of becoming. We are a milieu of body, emotion, thought, perception, imagination, etc. The urn "tease[s] us out of thought," and draws us toward sensitive and quiet observation of ourselves and the world. In its silence it compels us to listen. "Heard melodies are sweet," Keats writes, "but unheard are sweeter."[22] Again, we are to look, to listen, to see, to observe, and to rest in the Mist.

This last point is perhaps Keats's most penetrating when it comes to his sense of sincerity. What is the result of living in the Mist? What happens when we embrace negative capability? The answer for him is *silence*. We notice, we marvel, and we are quieted. Indeed, we are enchanted. There is no more appropriate response to the irreducible mystery of the urn, which is the mystery of life, than to be silent before it. The "silent form" of the urn refuses to be reduced by our desires for explanation. The unknowability of the urn persists as both beauty and truth, and these two will *always* persist so long as we look for them:

> When old age shall this generation waste,
>   Thou shalt remain, in midst of other woe
> Than ours, a friend to man, to whom thou say'st,
>   "Beauty is truth, truth beauty—that is all
> Ye know on earth, and all ye need to know.[23]

There is here yet another irony: Keats explains to us this silence through the written word, through his poem, which is a kind of saying, not silence. But like Byron, this irony is of the playful, insightful sort. There's no trace of snark here. He is well aware of the paradox of poetry: that it attempts to say the unsayable. And so, we are left with an artist's rendition of

21. Keats, "Ode on a Grecian Urn," 1466–67.

22. Keats, "Ode on a Grecian Urn," 1467.

23. Keats, "Ode on a Grecian Urn," 1468.

a moment of truth, which is a truth that is never fully revealed. It is a truth about the self-as-overflow, self-as-performance, and self-as-emptiness. It is a truth about a way of speaking to others about these truths without falling into cynicism. For the Romantics, the evanescent nature of the self is not a cause for perpetual deconstruction. It is not a reason to point out at every opportunity the self's constructed nature, its positionality, and provisionality. Romantics want more, they want to plunge the depths of the self (to see if there is one). They want to play on its surfaces. They want to attest to its complexity, give voice to its beauty, and celebrate its creative and imaginative potentials. They see in its ever-changing nature a full range of creative possibility and exploration. You see? This is not romantic sentimentality, nor is it bleeding heart emotionalism. Romantic sincerity reclaims self-expression as sacred, and sees the self-as-sacred insofar as it is always coming into itself. By expressing, revealing, performing, and emptying the self we participate in The Great Unfolding that is human existence. Sincerity is a genuine attempt to reach within ourselves in order to reach outside of ourselves. We yearn for sincerity not because being "true to one's self" (i.e., authenticity) is inherently valuable, but because *in being sincere we stretch beyond ourselves*—we reach out toward the Other—and this reaching out opens onto transcendence.

Enchantment Strategy #3: Speak Sincerely

We've covered a lot of ground in this chapter. If you're feeling like things have gotten dense, that's because they have. Some of this may seem a bit technical, a bit philosophical, but getting into the weeds will prove important for drawing out the practical implications of Romantic sincerity and living the enchanted life.

Romantic sincerity presents a manner of speaking and self-expression that is truly revolutionary. Sincerity is out of vogue because we live in an empire of snark. Postmodern cynicism—obsessed with the fact that everything is fracturing—insists that conviction and earnest expression are cheesy and that vulnerability is for the birds. But as we have seen, they aren't. The Romantics give us sacred self-expression without slipping into emotionalism, a way to re-enchant our speech that's not lost in the quagmire of critique and repetition. Sincere speech requires some bravery, trust, and hope to pull off, but the payoff is enormous: it offers real human connection, real self-expression, and real transcendence. By drawing on the rich tradition of Romantic sincerity we can breathe new life into their ideas and see their transformative potential in our world today, a world that seems so void of genuine speech and meaningful, interpersonal engagement.

Step 1: Be on Guard against Snark

To learn to speak sincerely, the first thing you'll need to do is be on guard against snark. Now, this doesn't mean that you should always avoid snark or that you can never say something cynical. You can. It's life, after all. But it does mean that you should resist the temptation to view everything in a cynical light. The more you let snark in, the more you'll be tempted to use it yourself. Don't adopt it as your primary form of speech. Don't let yourself get caught up in thoughts like "Oh, that's exactly what someone like you *would* say," or "Ugh [eye roll], that's so cheesy," or "Who cares? It's all a joke anyway."

Snark can take lots of forms. It's ubiquitous in our culture. Any expression aimed solely at critique, condescension, and dismissal is usually made of snark. The primary places you'll find snark will come as no surprise: memes, tweets, social media, flippant remarks made in conversation, infotainment (what we used to call "news"), the comments section of a blog or article, almost any political discussion. Just look (briefly) and you'll see these places are loaded with predictable, pithy one-liners parroting the postmodern obsession with provisionality. It's all there, in almost every forum of modern communication. Snark rules the day.

The good news is, it's easy to sniff it out. It follows a formula: it's something said (a) in a tone of critique (b) intending to deface, mock, or criticize, an otherwise heartfelt expression (c) to show that the speaker is "in on a joke," and (d) to create a critical distance between the snarky speaker and the subject matter in discussion. Snark is usually a defense mechanism masquerading as insight. It almost always relies on the typical techniques of irreverence, self-referentiality, and irony to create a sense of "this doesn't affect me, I see things as they are: broken." Snarky folks usually describe themselves as "realists," as opposed to romantic "idealists." They won't be duped, and revel in their ability to point out the absurdity in anything. These patterns of thought become poisonous when they snuff out the possibility of sincere self-expression before it ever has a chance to come forward.

If you find yourself locked into a conversation with a snarky cynic, things can get difficult. You only have a couple of choices to guard against it, and the disenchantment it portends. You'll have to either remove yourself from the conversation, convince them of the value of other forms of speech, or just rebel against it by saying something sincere. But that last thing is an enormous risk. Not everyone is up for it, understandably. While I'd urge you to try sincerity before walking away, I also know that can be tough. The cynic wants it to be tough. He thrives on pushing down your impulse to sincerity through the glorification of his own cleverness. So other than just saying something sincere, the best thing you can do is to cultivate within yourself a sincere disposition and to develop a sensitivity to the disenchanting effects of cynicism. You're the average of the five people you spend the most time with, so the old adage goes. If that's true, fraternizing with cynics will make you one. Avoid it. If you give too much mental space to them they may begin to bleed into you. They tend to exert undue influence on us by presenting themselves as "in on the joke," and who wants to be the person who doesn't get the joke? You risk becoming the joke yourself. Surrounded by cynics, you begin to fear that if you speak sincerely you will reveal yourself to be a fool. But you aren't a fool, and your inner life is full of mystery, truths, and beauty. As sincere speakers, we are indeed rebels, pushing back against the culture of critique that wants to foreclose any chance of the enchanted life. Don't let that happen.

Step 2: Feel, Pause, Say

Once you've curtailed the cynic, the next move is to get in tune with your own inner life. The difficulty here is that "normal life"—the life of your job, the economy, social media, the twenty-four-hour news cycle, etc.—doesn't value the ruminating nature of the inner life. They are structures that cut into the time it takes to pay attention to what's going on inside of us. External life rushes at us, leaving little time for self-reflection. That's part of the reason why we have to be so protective about where we direct our mental energies. Remember what David Foster Wallace said, critical thinking isn't just about being able to analyze something, it's about being choosey about *what it is you think about.*

Once you clear a space for sincerity (by moving cynicism out), you have to fill that space with moments of thoughtful self-reflection. That's what Wordsworth teaches us. We have to pause and look. We have to pay attention to our experience of ourselves in order to engage in sincere self-expression. Now, there's a bit of a paradox here because, as Wordsworth also noted, there is something spontaneous about sincerity too. There is a kind of ebb and flow of our consciousness that does not lend itself to being pinned down, observed, and then articulated. That's something like what he was getting at when he said that poetry is the "spontaneous overflow of powerful feelings," but as we have seen this too involves a pause, a breath, a moment of reflection—even if only a short one—that calls our attention to our inner life and considers it with nuance and sensitivity. When the overflow of powerful feeling arrives, we have to stop and notice it.

We can learn a lot from Wordsworth's pause. On his account, sincere self-expression requires a moment of creative reflection *before* expression. Consider what it takes to carve an epitaph into a tombstone: time, deliberation, forethought, artistry. That's exactly what Wordsworth is telling us is required for sincerity. It's not that we need to be poets, or that we have to say things with majesty and eloquence. In fact, what Wordsworth loved about epitaphs was their earnest simplicity, their everyday diction, and their straightforward grammar. What it takes is to allow yourself to feel deeply, spontaneously, and truly. And then to *pause*. To breathe. To notice. To reflect. What do you see? Who is this person who has these feelings? What is the nature of your internal life? What's going on in there? What are its contours, inflections, or character precisely at this moment of powerful feeling? It's all there, in the pause.

According to Wordsworth, what you will discover is that your inner life is a complex milieu, rich, at times tumultuous, but always revealing. It will show you something true about life, which like you is always vacillating, unfolding, churning, and moving, like "earth's diurnal course," as he says. Inside of you, in the moment of the pause, you will witness the turning of Nature. You will find in your own particular and idiosyncratic experience something universal. You will see that you are participating in life's ebb and flow, and you will be compelled to say something about it, to bring that truth into being for others to hear and see. You will wonder whether they hear it too. You'll want to reach out and go beyond yourself.

And here is where the first "saying" happens, the first moment of sincere self-expression. This is the moment of bravery, when you must be the lion and not the fox. This moment is also a wager. You are taking a gamble. I can't promise you'll be well-received. To speak sincerely you must express yourself in trusting hope that the other person will receive you with compassion, not cynicism. That she will welcome you, not because she "agrees" with you, but because she recognizes in your sincerity a vulnerability and a truth that must be cared for, else it will be wiped away. You must hope beyond hope that you will be received with love, hospitality, and grace. You must trust—even when there is no reason to do so—that the truth of your inner life will resonate in some way with the other person, that it will say something universal, even if the content of what you express does not align with the other's "beliefs." You see, sincerity is not about agreement and disagreement. It's not about beliefs. It's not about whether what you say aligns with what I think. And it's certainly not about weighing and evaluating the veracity of someone's expression, as though it were a truth claim about the way the world is, scientific or otherwise. No. Sincere expression is about reaching out toward the other. It is a leap of faith, a jump out of the safe and alienating confines of your own mind and into the unknown and unpredictable world of other people. It's about the hope that we need not live alone. When someone speaks sincerely, they are extending to you a hand—a vulnerable, woundable hand—a hand that comes out of the darkness of separation and loneliness and reaches toward you *in order to connect with you*, in order to forge some kind of common ground, some community, that goes beyond their skull-sized kingdom. Sincerity risks rejection but hopes for charity. That's the wager. The sincere person is a rebellious person: she takes an irrational risk, hoping, trusting, and believing that she will be received with grace and kindness by the other. There is bravery in that, and truth.

Step 3: Mind the Gap

Earlier in this chapter, we got into the weeds a bit about different ideas of Romantic sincerity and the self (Who am I? What is the "self," anyway? etc.). Well that's about to pay off. Recall that the second wave of Romantics started to think that there may not be any underlying "self" revealed in sincerity; that is, there is no essential self "in there" that express itself through a congruence between its own attestations and inner feelings. It's not that there's *nothing* there, it's just that what the self is . . . is unclear.

Byron loved this idea. He reveled in the gap between the "who I am" and the "what I say." For him, this is a playful place, a place to explore the mercurial nature of the human person. This gap complicates the idea of sincerity because if we can't put our finger on the self that we're trying to express, and all expression is mediated by language, signs, and symbols interpreted by an audience (other people), then sincerity becomes a kind of performance, one in which we try to attest to our "selves" before an audience that at the same time is trying to make sense of what we're putting out there. There's a dialectical nature to sincerity, a back-and-forth between self and society that impacts whether or not the expression appears as sincere. We can try and manipulate the message but it's somewhat out of our control because it has to be interpreted by another person *as sincerity* in order to come off as sincere. And because who we "are" is always changing—because we're all mobile—any sincere expression seems to lag behind the feeling it conveys. A second gap emerges. For Byron, these "gaps"—between who we are and what we say, and what is said and when it's said—become a place to explore ourselves, and our relationship with others. These gaps are an open landscape, blank canvases. Byron encourages us to try on different masks, different personae, different forms of expression in order to explore and express our sense-of-self at any given time, and in doing so come to understand something true about who we are, even as a fleeting thing.

In order to harness the enchanting effects of Byronic sincerity you have to embrace your incomplete self, your evanescent self, your self that is never fully present but that is always coming into presence and dissolving into absence. The big lesson Byron has to teach us is that *sincerity doesn't mean seriousness.* You can have fun being sincere. You can be playful. Heck, you can even be ironic so long as your irony doesn't serve only to critique or mock others but instead reveals a truth. Don't hold on too tightly to "who you are." That's the purview of authenticity, not sincerity. Byronic sincerity gives us permission to feel one thing one moment and then to feel another thing another moment.

My wife and I often say to each other, "Don't hold me to this, I might change my mind in five minutes," and then go on to say what we think or feel. That's not being flighty. It's taking sincere expression as a kind of pro-viso, an acknowledgment that the "underlying" thing that makes me "me" is variegated and that while there is something consistent about me there is also something inconsistent too. Again, its trusting in the grace of the other person to accept that truth, and to acknowledge it, maybe even discover it about themselves. This acceptance allows for sincerity to emerge, and then to flourish. Like Byron's Don Juan or Lady Adeline, don't be afraid to per-form a little. Don't be afraid to try on different ways of saying who you are or whatever it is you're trying to express. Give to others the grace you hope to receive. What you'll notice is that in doing so, your conversations become light and airy without compromising a sense of seriousness or genuineness. You'll find yourself invested in what you're saying—even if its playful—and invested in what others are saying because you know it's coming from an earnest and brave attempt to reach out to you. This sort of discourse is ex-actly the opposite of postmodern irony. It restores the enchantment of a good conversation, and it revives the charity of a good listener. It can be quite beautiful.

Step 4: Be Silent, Be Gracious

There is a final lesson to learn from Keats: *embrace sincerity's silence.* Some-times the sincerest thing you can do is allow for the sincerity of *another person* to come out. You can be the charitable guest, the loving recipient of the rebel's cry. Rather than feeling compelled to lay bare your own soul, you can see the beauty in bearing witness to another's.

According to the philosopher Emmanuel Levinas, there is something quite unique about another person. Not "unique" in the popular sense of everyone is a unique individual, like a snowflake or a fingerprint. Of course, they are, but that's not his point. Levinas is saying something more radical than that. He's saying that fundamentally, another person is *unknowable*, that unlike a coffee mug or a Camaro, you can never fully know someone. With the possible exception of animals, there is no other "thing" in the world that appears this way. People are unique in their unknowability.

There's a certain intuitive quality to Levinas's point here. It's not so much an analytical conclusion as it is an experiential observation. Think about it. Who do you know, completely, without any hidden corners or mysteries left to explore? Other people are in a way fundamentally inaccessible. They're not "objects" in the same way that, say, a car is an object. You can never open up the hood of another person and identify all its parts, and figure out how it works, and what makes it hum. You can know their body as an organ, but that's not the same as knowing *them*, is it? Another person, or "the Other," as Levinas calls it, always appears as an excess, a surplus of meanings and possibilities and experiences and feelings. The inner life of the Other always remains hidden. Sure, you can become familiar with someone's patterns of behavior, their quirks and preferences, even their typical thoughts and emotional reactions. But you can never *know* them, you cannot have a complete understanding of them as an object in the world. You can never master them. If you wrote someone's biography, there would never be a point at which you put down the last period and say, "There, that's it, my friends. That's everything there is to know about so-and-so."

Consider this fact in light of Keats's idea of negative capability and sincere listening, or sincerity as emptiness. Given that the Other always appears as an unknowable excess, then, according to Keats, we ought to take on a posture of negative capability with regard to him. We ought not itch over the fact that we cannot know the Other. We should not find it irritating that the Other eludes us, or that his expressions are at one time playful and at another time serious, or that he portrays one persona on Tuesday, and another on Wednesday. We must not strive to master the Other, but to remain in his mystery. We must rest in the Mist. According to Keats, the proper response to the Mist is not yearning to know, but attention to it. The Other is not a problem to be solved, but an excess to enjoy, a surplus to receive. The final task of the sincere person is to rest in the Mist of the Other, and listen.

Think of Keats, quietly circumambulating the Grecian urn, paying fierce attention to its curves, carvings, and characters, noting every detail, from its whimsical edges to its tiny, decorative designs. Keats was a valiant listener, a keen observer. He graciously opened himself up to the world. Other *people* call for this kind of radical attention too, more so actually, than even the urn (beautiful though it is) because, unlike the urn, people appear not as an object, but as an excess, as an infinity. People are different than objects. They cannot be catalogued. They cannot be reduced. Keats's sincerity was a sincerity of silence, one that teaches us that the sincerest act is the one that allows the self to slip away, and to be filled with the truth and beauty of another person. This is sincere listening, not sincere expression. Sincere listening is an invitation to the Other to express himself to you, and through you, to use you as a vehicle for his self-revelation. By being silent you become a chalice of love and hospitality to another person. You are a safe harbor, a home. You reverse the isolation of existence expressed as post-modern irony and you validate the worth of the Other's leap of faith. You say "yes" to the trusting hope that another person expresses when they speak sincerely. This is a sacred yes. A holy yes. You recognize and honor the risk the Other has taken. You commend their bravery, and you make a space for them, a place of refuge in a world otherwise full of loneliness and alienation.

There is something deeply moving, deeply enchanting about sincere listening. The compassionate reception of another's sincere expression, saying yes to their yearning to connect, to go beyond themselves, creates a moment of joy. It's difficult to describe, but when you have the courage to speak sincerely and then encounter the grace of another person who handles you with delicacy and care, you feel imbued with a new energy, a new sense of promise, a feeling that you are not resigned to a life of quiet desperation, alone in the vast emptiness of your own subjectivity. In sincerity you find transcendence and the gift.

Concluding Thoughts

Of all the enchantment strategies in this book, sincere self-expression may be the most challenging to live out, but it may also be the most rewarding. It comes with risks: the risk of rejection, the risk of sentimentality, the risk of muddling your meaning and being misunderstood, the risk of encountering the cynic, the risk of self-expression becoming self-obsession, and the risk of being mocked for having the audacity to make yourself vulnerable to an Other. To make matters worse, we live in an empire of snark, a world inhospitable to sincere self-expression. To be sincere is to be courageous, foolhardy, even, at times.

But the reward of taking this risk is the possibility of enchanted human relationships. It is the chance to overcome your innate sense of alienation and bridge the gap between yourself and the Other. It is the chance to form community, connection, and a common bond with other people. And it is an opportunity to engage in forms of speech that are life-giving, nourishing, and soul-feeding, forms of speech that can redeem us. David Foster Wallace was right: today's rebels must be a weird bunch, odd balls willing to risk it all for a moment of enchanted human interaction. Such is the way of things.

So if you decide to take the wager and try your hand at sincere expression, understand that it comes with some pains, some discomfort, perhaps even some insults. It's not easy to be the only one in the room who cares about sincerity. There may be someone there who's more committed to saying something funny, something snarky, or something cynical. They may take aim at you. But that is the risk of being a rebel. And don't forget, as Byron showed us, being sincere doesn't mean being somber. It doesn't even mean being serious. Sincere people can be playful, fun, and light-hearted. They can be the life of the party, not its buzzkill. At her best, because she appreciates the sacredness of self-expression, the sincere speaker enlivens others. People find her insights genuine and interesting, her vulnerability refreshing, and her wit somehow redemptive. Rather than being just a "bleeding heart" she becomes the source of enchantment for others.

5

Life in Symbols

The Art of Poetic Contemplation

The World Is Flat

One of the most powerful ways in which the modern, materialist worldview disenchants is in its attempt to reduce everything to one meaning, to identify what "it" really means. The "it" here can be almost anything: a book, a movie, something someone said, the blueness of the ocean, happiness, etc. Rather than seeing things we encounter in life as ripe with many meanings, we try to explain them in terms of what they "actually mean." We flatten things out. For example, we might say a book about a little boy and his honey-loving stuffed bear is "really" about the author's sense of abandonment, or his mommy-issues. Or the movie about the zombie apocalypse is "really" about the catastrophe of climate change. Or the blueness of the ocean is "really" just the water's absorption and scattering of light wavelengths. We want to sort out the puzzle, to make something make sense, and to put our finger on "it." We get a strange sense of joy in "figuring it out." It's as though the material world is the way it "really is" and everything else is just an add-on. If you can give a material explanation for something, then you've really gotten to the bottom of it.

Underneath this impulse is an assumption about the nature of truth; namely, that something is true to the degree that it is explainable, to the degree that we can line up what's said with what's actually going on in the material world. But symbols aren't like that. They don't lend themselves to empirical explanation. When the Romantic poet Novalis said he was searching for a blue flower, he's wasn't just telling us about the time he wandered through a meadow looking for a delphinium. He was telling us something about his human experience of life itself, about a feeling of longing for what is not here, about presence and absence, home and estrangement, oneness, and what it means to return. "Huh?" you might say. That's my point. We find symbols confusing, annoying even. *We want to know what it really means.*

We disenchanted folks have hard time figuring out what to do with symbols, especially those that point toward non-empirical truths or truths that defy empirical explanation. Our tendency is to reduce, not to open up. Now, symbols are really complex, and in a lot of ways we don't get to choose whether or not we're thinking symbolically. In fact, someone might (rightly) argue that language itself is a system of symbols, and by virtue of the fact that we're all born into a language, we automatically think in terms of symbols. We can't *but* think symbolically, this line of argument would suggest, and so all this stuff about being disenchanted because we don't like symbols is just plain false. On one level, I agree with that. In fact, I'd take the argument further. We're swimming in a sea of symbols: red means stop, swoosh means Nike, tie means classy, Tesla means money, books mean smart, etc. The entire world presents itself to us through symbols. Everything we see, hear, touch, taste or smell, invokes a vast array of references. You might even go so far as to say humans are the kinds of beings that experience the world symbolically, from the ground, up. So what do I mean when I say that as secular materialists we're uncomfortable with symbols? Let me try and explain.

It's not so much that we can't or don't *think* symbolically as it is that we *interpret* reductively. What I want to examine is a somewhat subtle relationship between secularism and symbols, one that causes us to struggle with things that don't comport with our underlying notion of truth and reality, a notion based in scientific materialism. I want to look at how we approach symbols that resist scientific or secular reductionism, or how we tend to spin symbolic meaning toward a materialist explanation. What do we do with symbols that resist that spin? How do we treat them? And how does this treatment lead to disenchantment?

As we've said, our modern, secular world is dominated by a reductive scientism (which is different from science). Scientism privileges scientific truth over all other forms of truth. It interprets all experience in terms of strict scientific materialism. According to scientism, for something to be true and meaningful it must comport with scientific modes of thought. Scientism works with secularism to insist that any references to non-empirical truths (e.g., mythology, poetry, religion) are either make-believe or subordinate to scientific knowledge because of some epistemological deficiency (i.e. they express something that can't be measured, replicated, verified through experimentation, etc.) This preference for perception, our almost unspoken belief that only things we can experience with our senses are *real* truths, permeates our thinking, and it fundamentally shapes our relationship to symbols. It makes us want to reduce a symbol's meaning to something concrete; or worse, to jettison a symbol altogether if we find it's not *literally* true.

This move is deeply disenchanting. It eschews poetic contemplation in favor of empirical perception. It trivializes our human habit of seeing the world as a brilliant web of meanings, a confluence of values, feelings, drives, and desires. It says to us that unless we can anchor a symbol's meaning in some literal truth, some perceptible fact, some historical event, the symbol is at best deficient and at worst deception. That's what I mean when I way we're uncomfortable with symbols, or that we no longer think symbolically: we have in our secular age this strong, almost unnoticed tendency to read the world in terms of materiality, empiricism, and perception. We don't know how to think symbolically, with a richness and an excess. We cannot stand in the face of a symbol without feeling a little irritated, without wanting to determine, finally, "what it means." Here are two examples.

I once had a conversation with some friends about the unreality of Santa Claus. The big issue was whether or not it's cruel to tell children Santa is real, only to tell them later that he's not. A lot of parents struggle with this sort of dilemma, especially with younger children. They don't want to "lie" to their kids, understandably so. They don't want to tell them one thing, even if its pleasurable to believe it, only to pull the rug out from underneath them a few years later. The child's inevitable disappointment is too much to bear, and the whole thing feels like a cruel betrayal. The fact that Santa Claus is not *literally* real means to these parents that he is not *in any sense* real, and so it's not fair to tell a child there is an actual, snow-loving elf up there in the North Pole when, *in fact*, there isn't. Instead, they adopt a milquetoast disposition to the whole thing, choosing to sort of ignore Santa, just letting his presence play out in the background of Christmas culture while deflecting questions about him from their children until the kids are (finally!) old enough to understand he's "just a story." While I think this approach is misguided, I understand it. I'm even a little sympathetic to it. At the most basic level, I would agree that telling a child something is real and then later telling her that it's not seems cruel. But there's more to it than that.

You see, the problem here isn't that Santa is not literally real, it's that we don't know how to think of him as *symbolically* real. Symbolic realism is just as important as literal realism, perhaps more important. What a child must discover is the truth of Santa as a symbol. His reality is not diminished by his non-existence as a flesh-and-blood person in the North Pole. His reality is enriched and enhanced when one understands his symbolic reality, when one understands that the truth of Santa Claus runs deeper than his literal truth. Santa is much, much more than a literally true or untrue story. He is generosity, the gift, mystery, the magic of the night, warmth in a time of cold, time, impossibility, an invitation into the realm of enchantment. His frock is holly-berry red, a red that refuses to wither, even in the depths of winter. Thus, he is life itself. He is the human aspiration to kindness, the altruism that breaks the economy of transaction and opens onto the possibility of the gift, which is the possibility of love. You see? Santa's truth is truer than literal truth because it speaks with a multiplicity of truths. There is more truth in him than empirical truth can provide. His deepest reality is ineffable, and so it must be said in a symbol. It can only be spoken through myth, gesture, gift-giving, and shared traditions. This is not a deficient form of truth, but a *deepened* one. The task for parents who struggle with Santa's (literal) unreality is to shepherd their children into the next, deeper reality of Santa-as-symbol. The "big reveal" for children is that Santa is *more real* because he is not *literally* real. What he stands for, what he engenders in us, is a truer truth than the literal truth of his non-existence.

Here's another example. It's a controversial one. Consider God. Whether you grew up religious or not, when you're young you usually think of God as The Big Wizard in the Sky. There he is, flowing grey beard, sitting on his throne or floating around in the clouds, orchestrating things below with his Almighty Power. He (yes, "he") is the master of the universe, loving, but with an angry streak. He's a big, magical being, the Big Being, but a being nonetheless. I'm not saying you believed any of this by the way. Maybe you did, maybe you didn't. I'm also not saying everyone grew up in a religious home. Of course, they didn't. What I am saying is that, regardless of whether you grew up religious or not, you were almost certainly handed this picture of God in one form or another. It's the default, Western image of God. At some point in your life you probably questioned whether this idea made any sense. Perhaps you were young and got suspicious about the story not adding up, or perhaps in your teenage years you rebelled against it because it felt oppressive. Or perhaps something tragic happened to you or someone else, something quite serious, and the idea of an Alpha God orchestrating things from above no longer serves as a meaningful concept in light of this tragedy. For some, it does, and for others, it doesn't. Some people grow into a rich tradition and religious life thinking about God as the Great Being, and some people leave religion and opt for secular humanism, scientific atheism, or Buddhism, or some other not-God-as-Wizard view on things. That's the way it typically goes in the Western world, at least for most of us.

What's interesting about these two trajectories is that in either case, the question we ask ourselves is the same question: "What to do with the

Big Wizard?" What do you do with the idea of God as the Great Being-in-the-Sky once you've recognized that it's impossible for you to believe in it? What happens to this model of God when you realize that even *trying* to believe in it so violates your innate sense of rationality and flies in the face of things you *know* to be real (like the presence of evil in the world, e.g., the Holocaust, child sex trafficking, etc.) that you find it borderline insulting someone would even suggest you "just have faith"?

Now, you might say that for you none of this is an issue because, well, you just don't believe in any of that nonsense. You're over it. It's not a *struggle* for you. God doesn't exist and that's just the way it is. But I want to push back on that a bit. Sure, the problem of the Big Wizard may not be a struggle for you in the sense that you don't feel torn about believing in this model of God or not believing in it, but it *is* a struggle in the sense that you don't know what to *do* with the idea of God once you've decided it's "wrong" (other than simply dismiss it). You may not even feel like you need to do anything with it. You just ignore it, stop thinking about it, and pass some mild judgement on others whenever you hear them mention the word. For many people who've jettisoned this idea of God there is an unspoken assumption that they've just accepted things for how they *actually* are—the world exists, there is no God—and that's all there is to it. They've moved on.

But God has a funny way of sticking around, even for those who've told him to go away. You may have replaced God-as-Wizard with one of the following: belief in a Higher Power or a ubiquitous Energy, the promise of Scientific Progress, the possibility of Human Flourishing, or the personal satisfaction of your own Spirituality (but definitely *not* religion). The thing to which the word "God" points persists, even after you've let go of the model of God as the Great Being in the Sky. And that's because there's *more* to the idea of God than that. As St. Augustine says it, our hearts yearn for more. They are restless. We as humans always seem to desire the yet-to-come, a future or a vision that is in some way better than what we have now, here, before us. This desire is not a bad thing. It is productive, and generative, and life-giving. But it can also provoke anxiety and dis-ease if it does not find some form of expression that gives it voice. Even after the "death" of God, the desire for God endures. So what do we do with this desire?

The trouble is, in our modern, materialist age, we don't have the tools to think about something other than—or more than—a literal truth, for example, the truth of this desire (which is, after all, a desire for truth). We think, "If God isn't real, get rid of him." But you see, this approach fails to appreciate the symbolic, poetic, metaphorical, literary, and mythological truth of God, and talk about God. It eschews references to God because they don't conform to scientific materialism (or because Christians you've met over the course of your life have left a bad taste in your mouth). But what's lost is recourse to a broad and deep body of symbolic thought, a rich and profound history of real people, in real places, wrestling with the meaning of their own existence and trying to find ways to express and make sense of what it is to be human. Sometimes they use words like God to get at that experience, and sometimes (as in Ecclesiastes 1:2–4), they call everything into question, including God-talk ("Fleeting mist of fleeting breath. All is mist and vapor").

Let me make two things clear before we go on. First, for the religiously minded reader, I'm *not* saying God is just a symbol. I'm not making a theological argument here about the nature of God. That's up to you to decide for yourself. I'm using the idea of God as an example to illustrate how a failure to appreciate the symbolic leads us to throw away rich and meaningful symbols, ones that regardless of their metaphysical status can give us an insight into human life. So please, don't stop reading on the mistaken belief that I'm arguing God is just a symbol. That's not my point. Second, for the secularly minded reader, I'm *not* saying you should be a Christian or believe in God-the-Wizard. I'm not. My point is that you don't have to turn your back on all religious language—which is rich in symbol and wisdom—simply because you don't believe in the God-as-Wizard idea. That's a form of overcorrection that comes out of secular scientism. My bigger, more important point in all of this is that whether we're talking about Santa Claus or God or some other cluster of rich and poetic symbols, we in the secular world fail to appreciate the wealth of insight and wisdom we can glean from thinking symbolically, from encountering the world in and through symbols.

The struggle with symbolic meaning is based on a bad premise. It presumes a false dichotomy. That is, it presupposes the idea that we have to choose between literal and non-literal truths, that one is "really" true and the other is just "pretend true." But we don't have to accept this choice. We don't have to agree that there is even a choice here to make. What's difficult is that the secular water we're swimming in makes us feel as though we do have to see things this way, pitting literal and non-literal truths against each other. We feel like we have to decide: either the Wizard exists and I submit to him, or the Wizard is made-up and I ignore him. Either Santa Claus is real and I tell my kids the story, or he's not and I spare them the lie. But there is a whole range of options in between these two opposites. My point is that setting the question up as having "two opposites" is misguided because it creates an unnecessary and too-narrow conflict between kinds of truths. If we deny and then dismantle the idea that literal truth and non-literal truth are the limits of our choices, we can begin to see how there is a deeper and more complex world of truths available for use to explore, and out of which to make meaning. This is the possibility that symbolism opens-up.

Once we dismantle the false dichotomy, we are free to move fluidly between *truths*: literal truth, metaphorical truth, allegorical truth, symbolic truth, poetic truth, existential truth, experiential truth, etc. The question is no longer "Wizard or no-Wizard?" Instead, it is, "What is the meaning of the Wizard?" "What does it reveal?" "What is it pointing us toward?" The beauty of a symbol is that it is always an *excess*. Its meanings overflow, so to speak. They express more than they signify, but they also contain a bit of the thing to which they're referring as well. For example, a red breasted robin symbolizes spring in at least two ways. First, he makes his initial appearance at the start of spring and in that way actually contains a bit of spring within himself, but he also goes beyond the signification of the season alone insofar as he "comes out of nowhere," like *all life* seems to do in some mysterious way. Thus, the robin-as-symbol-of-spring both carries a bit of spring in him but also suggests more-than-spring in his appearance.

Encountering a symbol requires that you take the symbol seriously as an instantiation of the thing to which it refers while at the same time recognizing that the symbol's referent goes beyond the symbol, it is always *more* than the symbol. That's precisely why we use symbols in the first place: the thing to which we're trying to refer escapes reduction, explanation, and precision. What is a gift? What is generosity? What is love? These things can only be "gotten at" indirectly, through the use of symbols, which is why we have an almost infinite number of poems, stories, paintings, and songs about all of these topics. They are fundamentally irreducible. When it comes to God, the question isn't whether the Wizard exists (or at least, that's only the threshold question). The question is what does it *mean* to envision God-as-Wizard? And then: what's *beyond* the Wizard? What's on the edges of the Wizard-as-symbol? What is the word "God" pointing to? What is it we're striving toward when we say that we love God? And what is it we're struggling with when we say that there is no God? You see? These are *symbolic* questions, not scientific ones. But our insistence on scientific truth as the *only* legitimate kind of truth means we end up banishing these questions to the (supposed) backwaters of religion, or writing them off as mere superstition or immature belief. We end up dismissing all of these questions as some variation on the theme of nonsense. That's a disenchanting shame.

Poetic Contemplation in Romantic Thought

Romantics take a lot of flak for making things seem magical when (according to some people) they're really just mundane. Whenever you say someone's a "romantic" you mean they're a bit naïve, that they look at the world through rose-tinted glasses. This criticism of Romanticism is a bit shallow, but it's not entirely false. The Romantics did view the world as enchanted. There's no doubt the Romantics "Romanticized" the world, but what does that mean?

As we saw in chapter 2 with Novalis and Shelley, one way to understand Romanticization is as a kind of "upward force," casting the ordinary in extraordinary terms. By invoking the creative-responsive power of the imagination, Novalis and Shelley experienced the everyday world with fresh eyes and ears, making poetic associations and connections and imbuing mundane life with an aesthetic richness. The skylark's song is not *just* a skylark's song. But remember that Romanticizing runs the other way too: it has a "downward force" in which the Romantic renders the extraordinary, ordinary. This version of Romanticizing can reveal how things we might experience as foreign, grandiose, fantastic, bizarre, or otherworldly actually speak a common truth shared between all human hearts. They remind us of our shared humanity.

Consider for a moment Percy Bysshe Shelley's poem "Ozymandias." In it, Shelley Romanticizes down, taking an exotic scene and using it to comment on the everyday fact of human finitude. He writes of an "antique land," somewhere far off in the desert, blasted by sand and wind and heat. Scattered across the dusty dunes lay "[t]wo vast and trunkless legs of stone," the ruins of a great statue—a king—his broken limbs protruding out of the dirt that covers him. "Half sunk," his "shattered visage lies." The crumbling body parts are weathered, worn, forgotten. The narrator marvels at the now-defunct figure, reciting to us the inscription on its pedestal: "Look on my works, ye Mighty, and despair!" Here, Shelley is Romanticizing down, using elements of the foreign, the strange, and the fantastic to tap into our common, everyday experience of mortality and impermanence. We know everything is fleeting. We see the bananas turn brown. Everything comes to an end. It doesn't matter if you're a far-off king or an average Joe working in IT. "Time and tide wait for no man," as Geoffrey Chaucer put it. Death comes for us all. We are destined to decay. Ozymandias (which is the Greek name for the Egyptian Pharaoh Ramesses II) may seem otherworldly, he may claim to be impervious to time, but his fate is the same as yours and mine. His life is our life. His land is afar. His name is foreign. But his truth is our truth. In his sunken visage we see our own.

And this brings us back to symbolic thinking. "Romanticizing up" and "Romanticizing down" are two ways to use symbols (skylarks, moons, statues, sand) to gesture toward truths that are felt, not measured. They're non-empirical truths, although our senses play a vital part in how we come to know them. The truths we discover in Romanticizing are truths *only discoverable through the use of symbols.*

In a minute, we'll see more of how the Romantics Romanticize, but there's one other point I want to draw out here about the Romantic use of symbols. Symbols serve another function: they open a space for poetic contemplation. Symbols create clearings, and in these clearings, we are invited to pause, to stop, and to consider the nature of values and their relationship to our life's meaning. The clearing is an opening, an opportunity to reflect upon and imagine what life is really about, what concerns us most. In some cases, this sort of contemplation directs us to the deepest of human truths. One example is right under your nose: Being itself. Through the use of symbols, the Romantics draw our attention to the stunning fact that there is something at all, that the world exists. Think about it: *there is something.* That really is a striking fact. It's easy to become numb to it because we're so saturated by it, but it's always there. We go on about our lives, day in and day out, caring for our children, doing our jobs, eating our meals, visiting with loved ones, saving, retiring, vacationing, etc., without giving the majesty of existence a *single* thought, let alone a *second* thought. But that's what the clearing is for. That's what symbols provide: the space for the second thought. One of the great tragedies of modern, secular life is that we take life itself for granted. I don't mean *your* life. I don't mean that you don't ever think about dying, or that you don't in some way appreciate the fact that "you only live once." That's not what I'm talking about. I'm talking about *life itself.* I'm talking about The Mystery of Being. *That there is something.* The Romantic drive to Romanticize the world is in large part a drive to shake us out of our own existential blindness, to reveal the magic of Being that is literally right there, right in front of you. In fact, your existence testifies to The Mystery of Being. It's an instantiation of it. At their best, the Romantics show us how in a crumbling statue, an old Greek pot, a moss-covered abbey, or a frosty windowpane we experience the Mystery of Being. In any other number of forgettable moments, the miracle of existence is there, shining before us. That's a big part of what it means to Romanticize the world, and to be enchanted by it.

According to the historian Isaiah Berlin, the Romantic use of symbolism was in large part an attempt to wrestle with and participate in "[t]he brute fact" that the universe "is not fully expressible, it is not fully exhaustible."[1] You simply cannot capture The Mystery of Being with a single word, a single theory, or a single explanation. Try as we might, we can't do it. It doesn't matter whether you're using science, religion, or some other mode of inquiry. No one method suffices. That's why we need symbols. For the Romantics, symbols express what can *only* be expressed symbolically. They manifest and gesture toward truths we cannot access purely through rational means. They are poetic and invitational.

Not all symbols operate on this level, of course. As we've seen, some conventional symbols express a simple, clear-cut message: red light means stop. But other, more meaning-charged symbols operate in a different register. These "deep" symbols—e.g., a country's flag, a cathedral, a ring—say the unsayable. They express a multitude of meanings. They speak with an excess of meanings, a surplus of significations. Continuing with the Christmas example from above, we might consider the Christmas tree. Every year we all go around picking the perfect conifer, dragging it into our homes, and decorating it with all sorts of ornaments and knickknacks. Why? What does the tree *mean*? It's a symbol, so it's impossible to say with any finality. And that's the beauty of it. You can try to make a list of references, of course. The evergreen stands for eternal life. The lights stand for the stars, which in turn stand for hope. The ornaments call to mind memories, or loved ones, or themes related to the tree itself, like charity, love, or joy. You might even go deeper: the woody smell of the tree perfuming our houses reminds us that nature is never far off, that we are indeed both spiritual and material beings. The conical shape directs our attention to the top, to the starry firmament, invoking both a sense of groundedness and airy contemplation (I know it may sound like a stretch, but just think of all the people who stare up at a Christmas tree). No matter what meaning we assign to the tree, each meaning must end with ellipses. There is always another way to say what it means, another angle to highlight. There is *always more to say about it*. That's the beauty of a symbol: it says all these things without saying anything. The symbol doesn't "capture" a truth, it invokes a plurality of truths. It invites interpretations. It gives us a glimpse of the truth it conveys while at the same time gesturing beyond itself, to the truth-as-irreducible, as always resisting complete explanation.

Enchanting symbolism is everywhere. You don't have to wait until Christmas to encounter it. You're surrounded by it, actually. Thanks to our long and rich Western tradition, we have a vast inventory of symbols from which we can draw and make meaning. Many of them are familiar to you,

1. Berlin, *The Roots of Romanticism*, 61.

but others are more obscure: an apple is both temptation and the sweetness of life. A candle is hope: small and fragile, but full of warmth and promise. Incense is elevated thought, the human longing for a future yet-to-come. A cup of bitter drink is the sorrows of life from which we all must sip. All these symbols speak with many voices.

But don't be fooled. Despite the plurality of meanings, symbols don't just mean *anything*. For example, what is bread? I'll bet you can draw symbolic associations from it almost without trying. Go ahead, what comes to mind? Bread is food. It sustains. Bread is life. Bread is the mouth-watering smell of sustenance baked in the heat of care and concern. It is the gift of the field. It is labor and effort. Given as a gift, it is generosity. Broken between two people, it becomes friendship. It means many things. But there are some things it does not mean. Shame, for example, or jealousy. Bread does not symbolize these things. Why? Because over time, over ages and ages of writing, and thinking, referencing, and, well, *eating*, we (in the West) have developed these more generative and nourishing associations with bread, and also because it is a material thing—it is food, after all—so it carries its own, objective assumptions and value. Do you see? Bread means a lot of things but its meaning is *not arbitrary*. There is a long history of associations from which we can draw and innovate when we encounter a symbol. Symbols arrive always already embedded in a tradition that precedes them. This is a good thing. It's what gives symbols the ability to both express an idea, and to challenge it. Symbolic meaning can morph, but it is never completely unmoored from its culture. Symbols are anchored by things like tradition, but given flight by things like the imagination. Both are at your disposal should you wish to become enchanted.

The Blue Flower, the Albatross, and the Tiger: Romantic Symbols in Action

The Romantics had some techniques to develop their own symbolic thinking, methods to cultivate the skill of poetic contemplation. In some ways, symbolic thinking comes naturally to us as human beings because—as humans—we are the kinds of creatures that think symbolically, that have the capacity to interpret the world around us through the use of symbols. But in other ways, symbolic thinking can seem foreign, or at least it can take some effort (initially). This is in large part because we're out of practice. When it comes to meaning-making, our mass culture almost always opts for the least common denominator; that is, the most commonly held associations, the ones easiest to make. We are not routinely pushed to see things anew, to forge new meanings. Rather, we're routinely fed the same old stuff, repackaged as a sequel, or a version 2.0, of the thing that preceded it. But poetic contemplation requires that we recognize both the old and the new, that we draw upon the inventory of meanings that we already find ourselves swimming in, and that at the same time we move toward the horizon of other possibilities, of new meanings that have yet to emerge. Let's look at three examples of this sort of symbolic thinking in Romantic poetry, and then we'll distill from them our next strategy for a re-enchanted life: the art of poetic contemplation.

The Blue Flower and the "Problem" of Meaning

Novalis loved to talk about a blue flower. In his partially completed novel, *Heinrich von Ofterdingen* (killer name, I know!), Novalis tells the tale of a young man who goes in search of this elusive, azure flora. The book opens with all the hallmarks a great Romantic story: it's night, the wind is howling, the moon is shimmering, our hero is lost in the throes of a visionary dream, an unnamed stranger arrives, etc.:

> The parents have gone to bed and are asleep, the clock on the stairs ticks monotonously, the windows rattle with the wind, the chamber is lit up now and again with fitful gleams of moonlight.
>
> The boy lay tossing on his bed, and thought of the stranger and his talk. "It is not the treasures," he said to himself, "that have stirred in me such an unspeakable longing; I care not for wealth and riches. But that blue flower I do long to see; it haunts me and I can think and dream of nothing else. I never felt so before; it seems as if my past life had been a dream, or as though I had passed in sleep into another world, for in the world that I used to know who would have troubled himself about a flower? Indeed, I never heard tell of such a strange passion for a flower.[2]

Heinrich is basically a Romantic travel log. It's about a young man in medieval times who goes on a journey and along the way grows and matures into poetic wisdom. It's a story about enchantment, really. We first meet Henry at home, in his bed, where he has this mysterious dream and a vision of a blue flower. Henry and his mother set off to visit his grandfather. Along the way, they run into a whole host of people, places, and images that capture Henry's attention and ignite his imagination, initiating him into a

---

2. Heine, *Travel-Pictures*, 282. This is Francis Storr's English translation of Heinrich Heine's German quotation of the opening to Novalis's *Heinrich von Ofterdingen*. I like it best, but there are other translations of Novalis's words, of course.

life of mystical insight. He meets a group of medieval merchants who chat endlessly about poetry and art. Later, he meets a miner, a hermit, a musician, and a sage, all of whom reveal to him the secrets of their craft, and teach him ways to access the unity of existence by overcoming the limits of space, time, and individualism (big stuff, I know). It's an interesting and meandering read, a fun mix of the weird, the philosophical, and the poetic. It's full of fairy tales too, and allusions, metaphors, and long asides. It's not a "normal" book, that's for sure.

But for all its weirdness, there is a plot, and a central conflict: the one thing that always pulls at Henry, that never lets him go, is his desire for the blue flower. The entire novel is "irradiated with [its] light and fragrance."[3] Like any good symbol, the blue flower both gestures and lures, it expresses and points beyond itself. Henry meets a woman, Mathilde. They fall in love, and just as he seems about to find happiness with her, she drowns in a river. She is lost, or so it seems. Henry continues on a series of short adventures: he meets another maiden, explores a magical cave, and visits a haunted monastery (seriously, it's good stuff). Like Henry's life, the book wanders. In some ways, that's the point. But despite its esoteric themes, the novel stays rooted in a quest; that is, it's always about Henry's pursuit of the blue flower. He never loses sight of it. It shows up again and again, sometimes as blue flame, and other times in less direct forms. As the Romantic critic Boyesen writes, "the presence of this wondrous flower is felt on every page, and quite unawares one may catch a glimpse of its fragile chalice."[4] Novalis died at the age of twenty-nine, before completing the second part of the novel. According to his friend, Ludwig Tieck, Novalis planned that in the end, Henry would pluck the blue flower and be untied with Mathilde. But we'll never know for sure. Like the blue flower, the ending evades us.

What's so important about a random, half-written Romantic novel about a blue flower? What's this got to do with symbolic thinking, and with re-enchantment? Lots of things, I think, but what's particularly important for our purposes is that in *Heinrich*, Novalis demonstrates for us how to think symbolically, how to experience the world as a surplus of enchanting meanings. We have to ask ourselves: *what does the blue flower mean?* A lot of ink has been spilled over that question, not only by niche Romantic scholars like myself, but also by mainstream bloggers, singers, movie directors, novelists, and other, less pedantic types. For example, the book *The Blue Flower*, by Penelope Fitzgerald, was a critical hit and tapped into Novalis's biography to try and wrestle with the blue flower's meaning. There's a short,

---

3. Heine, *Travel-Pictures*, 282.
4. Boyesen, *Essays on German Literature*, 324.

snarky film about the blue flower, one-part mockery and another part medi-tation. Novalis's blue flower has made its way into popular culture too. It has a mythology all its own. Keep an eye out and I'll bet you'll be surprised how often you see it crop up on a movie set, discreetly set in a background vase, or vaguely referenced in the romance book you're reading. *But what does it mean*? Let's try and answer that question the best we can, but along the way I want you to pay close attention not only to *what* it symbolizes, but *how* it symbolizes; that is, *how* we go about answering the question in the first place.

To try and "figure out" what the blue flower means is in a certain sense evidence of a misunderstanding about the nature of meaning, and of sym-bols. Symbols can't be "figured out," not completely, anyway. But that sort of answer is also annoying because it suggests we might not be able to get anywhere by considering their meaning, or worse, that they could mean anything. Neither is true. So let's walk through how we might try and "figure out" the blue flower in order to see how symbolic thinking works, and then we'll return to the problem of trying to "figure out" symbols in the first place.

To begin with, when you're trying to decipher a symbol, look at what it is: its parts, material, color, shape, etc. Ask yourself: what does a *flower* usually suggest in my culture, in my tradition? Novalis is not starting from scratch. Flower symbolism isn't new. We all know that red roses mean love, purple crocuses mean youth, black dahlias mean betrayal, and so on. We all read in high school the famous passage in *Hamlet* where Ophelia tosses a bouquet of flowers onto the ground, each one signifying in a unique way her doomed love with the Prince of Denmark. When encountering a symbol, the first thing to do is to notice there is a tradition backing it up, and that as a result, you already know something about its meaning. You have a head start, so to speak. What this means with regard to the blue flower is that *part of its meaning as a symbol is derived from stuff outside the book*. Novalis is us-ing a symbol with rich history, he is drawing from an inventory of symbols that already exist, with which we're all familiar (even if only roughly).

Symbolic thinking works *out of a tradition*. For most of us, that's the Western tradition, but of course you may be working out of other tradi-tions, or mixed traditions. The point is that we all have at our disposal a pre-existing inventory of symbols. Novalis is no exception. Notably, unlike in *Hamlet*, we never learn the blue flower's species, but the fact that it's a flower is important. We have some idea of what that means, almost intui-tively, because flowers are part of our cultural encyclopedia. Flowers are liv-ing things and they're pretty, so we usually associate them with beauty and evanescence, right? But how do we know that? We know it *because* of our tradition, our pre-existing cultural world of books, movies, plays, poems, holiday cards, old sayings, images, and a whole host of other associations that existed before we were born and will exist long after we're gone. Symbolic thinking is made possible by the pre-existing milieu of meanings and associations that make up our lived tradition, the culture into which we're born. Tradition isn't always stodgy. In some cases, it gives rise to the possibility of insight and innovation. The pre-existing inventory of symbols that make up our world allows us to know in some sense what a flower "means," even if we don't really know what, precisely.

Then Novalis innovates. He takes a traditional symbol and re-invents it. It's a *blue* flower. Not exactly rare, but not as common as say a red, white, pink, or yellow one. Ask yourself: what does *blue* mean? What references does it call to mind? Perhaps the night, or the twilight? Usually we think of flowers as bright and colorful, lively and life-giving. But a blue flower is more mysterious. Like the dusk, it is somehow in-between night and day. It might also remind you of sadness, as in "I'm feeling blue," or a longing for something, though you know not what. After all, to "be blue" isn't just to be sad about something, it's about being sad *in general*, existentially, deeply within yourself. Van Gogh's "Blue Period" wasn't just a time in his life when he was down because his dog died, it was a time in his life when he wrestled with the deepest of questions. What is my source of meaning? Why go on? Things like that. We know a blue flower carries the residue of yearning, longing, a sense that something's missing, of being in-between, of depth—like the blue ocean—a depth that seems inexhaustible and that can go on forever. We know this, again, because we can pull from our pre-existing knowledge of these symbols that arise out of the milieu of symbols into which we're born, which make up our culture.

Next, Novalis places the blue flower in a dream, in a vision. What is a dream? You sort of know, don't you? Think of what we think about when we think about dreams. Dreams are your deepest drives working themselves out in your subconscious. They are your hidden concerns, unknown even to you, in some cases. (Keep going.) They are your desires expressed in weird and mutable ways. Dreams make up the immaterial world, the concealed, subterranean caverns of our own minds. Placing the flower there means the flower is within us—lurking in the recesses of our psyches—but also somehow eluding us. And what does this elusiveness mean? Well, think about your own life. What do you experience when you want something you're unable to grasp, when the thing you want evades you. You probably feel a bit of frustration, and some longing. Maybe sadness, or even disappointment? But you might feel hope, too, hope that one day you will grasp it. It's funny how symbols "work" on you like that. It's like they come from "outside" of you, like they "act upon" you, inducing certain feelings and invoking specific reactions, almost without your ability to stop them or to choose them. The trick is to develop a sensitivity to those feelings and reactions. What does the elusive, ephemeral, twilight-colored flower *do* to you? What feelings does it generate? Therein lies much of a symbol's meaning, even if you can't say it out loud.

Now we can begin to put all of these threads together: flower + blue + dream. A web of symbolic meanings emerges. We have the contours of what the blue flower might just represent: it's something beautiful, mysterious, and compelling. It's something that calls to us in our dreams, when we're half-awake, like when we're caught up in the mundane, day-to-day insomnia of a routine life. It's the desires hidden within us and the desires pulling outside us. It is that "something more" that each of us longs for. It is the nagging tug, the sleepy vision, that comes to us like a soft and floral fragrance, a subtle perfume wafting across life's humdrum and hypnotic pace. It calls to us in a whisper. Although these are only outlines, the edges of a shadow, they do give us a sense of what the blue flower means.

This "sense" is important, and is a common feature of symbolic thinking. Although there is almost never a simple, one-to-one correspondence between a symbol and its meaning (e.g., blue flower = wisdom), there is a mélange of meanings that swirl together and that draw our attention in a certain direction. Symbols narrow our list of concerns to things within their interpretive domain, to considerations related to their potential referents. A symbol is like a gated fence encircling a large field: it provides a boundary of possible meanings, limiting our contemplative focus to thoughts within its borders, while at the same time giving our minds a space to wander. But the boundary is always porous, each gate allows new meanings to enter in, and other meanings can morph, and move out.

Symbols that do this well *resonate* with you. They "strike a chord," so to speak, rousing something within you (I usually feel it in my chest), and giving you the feeling that a truth has been conveyed, and that, like a gift, you have received it with gratitude. A symbol's resonance induces you to say, "Yes, that's it. That is what it is like," whatever "it" may be. Resonance is the deep, full, reverberation of meanings that develops out of a symbol's referents reinforcing and reflecting off each other. It is the synchronous vibration you feel in your soul when you're moved by symbolic truth. It is the experience of the symbol's many voices speaking together, and at the same time. These voices, these meanings, form a conversation with one another and invite you to tarry, to consider all the things they have to say. Resonance prolongs a symbol's impact. It makes it so that you carry the symbol with you and it helps you see it in other places. It calls for contemplation, quiet, and attention to your connection to the world around you.

In *The Roots of Romanticism,* Isaiah Berlin says that the Romantic symbol not only expresses something, it participates in the very thing it expresses. Take the flower, for example. Any old flower will do. Imagine a rose, let's say. A rose is pretty. When you give someone a rose it signifies affection, attraction, and beauty. Why? Because it is itself beautiful. It is attractive. It has delicate petals, a lovely aroma, and an alluring curvature. But we know that beauty is also *more* than a rose. The rose doesn't capture everything that is beauty. The rose is an instantiation of beauty—it is something beautiful—but beauty goes beyond the rose too. There are other instantiations of beauty that can say "beauty" in other ways: a child's smile, for example, or the softly fallen snow on a quiet pine forest. The point is that the rose both *expresses* beauty and *is* beauty. It is in part the very thing it signifies. Berlin notes that caught up in the Romantic use of symbols was the idea that "there is an infinite striving forward on the part of reality, of the universe around us, that there is something which is infinite, something which is inexhaustible."[5] But for the Romantics this presented a problem: our inventory of symbols draws mainly from finite things, from objects, ideas, colors, images, etc. Each has its limitations. According to the Romantics, you "cannot convey the whole of what you are seeking to convey because this whole is literally infinite" and all we have are finite glimpses, *les petits exemples* of the infinite thing we're expressing.[6] So things like the blue flower are in a way doomed to fail because there is no way they can fully express the infinite, or even the desire for the infinite. Nevertheless, for the Romantics, symbolic thinking was a key way to relate to the infinite precisely because the infinite expresses itself in and through the finite. In other words, for the Romantics, insofar as symbols do indeed participate in the thing they're trying to express we can get a glimpse of the thing, and there is joy in that. There is something wonderful about the flash of beauty that is a summer rain shower or a cricket's song. There is bliss in the taste of cool water or a crystalline winter morning. And there is a deep truth about our desire for something more, which is given over in Henry's longing for the blue flower. The desire to even know what the blue flower means—to "figure it out"—is itself an instantiation of our desire for meaning. That's how symbols work. That's why they're so enchanting.

---

5. Berlin, *Roots of Romanticism,* 101.

6. Berlin, *Roots of Romanticism,* 101.

The Albatross and Irreducibility

Gustave Doré, *The Albatross*, c. 1876, engraving.

Another famous example of symbolism and the power of symbolic thinking in Romantic literature is Samuel Taylor Coleridge's ghostly albatross. The bird appears in "The Rime of the Ancyent Marinere," the first poem in the 1798 version of *Lyrical Ballads* (Coleridge wrote *Lyrical Ballads* in collaboration with William Wordsworth). The poem tells the tale of a sailor who commits a heinous crime and is doomed to pay penance for it, over and over again. It's full of wonderful Romantic tropes: there are spirits and curses and icy seas and madness and gloom. It's really great stuff, honestly. Let's get our bearings on the context of the poem and then examine Coleridge's idea of the symbol up close. Doing so will allow us to see how, like Novalis, Coleridge saw symbols as the gateway to appreciating life's magic *through its mystery*.

Lyrical Ballads caused a stir when it was first published. Most of the poems are good, many of them are very good, and a few of them are masterpieces. But what scandalized society was the fact that Coleridge and Wordsworth made the conscious choice to write the bulk of them in normal, everyday language. Up until the publication of *Lyrical Ballads*, poetry was considered "high art" in the sense that it made use of extremely stylized language, complex cadences and rhythms, and often obscure and hard-to-penetrate references or allusions. Coleridge and Wordsworth shattered this mold by having the audacity to use regular old English words to get their lofty poetic points across. The language of their poems is not highfalutin or *haute couture* at all. It's quite accessible, actually. Indeed, the very name of the book—*Lyrical Ballads*—suggests that the authors intended to take more refined poetic forms like lyrics and mix them with more commonplace forms like ballads. Lyrical poetry is known for its refined musicality, its use of rhyme, meter, alliteration, consonance, and other complex literary devices. Think Shakespeare. Ballads, on the other hand, are often bawdy, folksy, and common. They tend to be songs of the land, or tunes about normal people doing normal—even silly—things. Calling the book *Lyrical Ballads* tipped the reader off to the idea that this collection of poems was going to do something new, something edgy: it was going to make high art out of low speech, and that's exactly what it did.

For the most part, Wordsworth's contributions to *Lyrical Ballads* "Romanticize up." They take a mundane thing like a boy hooting at an owl and give it a poetic charge that taps into its universal meaning. We saw a similar move by Wordsworth in the last chapter on sincerity, where he praised tombstone epitaphs for their simple elegance and universal appeal. In Novalis's words, Wordsworth gives "the commonplace a higher meaning" or "the semblance of infinity to what is finite." Coleridge's contributions on the other hand "Romanticize down." His poems are more fantastic, mysterious, and exotic. He writes about far-off lands, dramatic events, and ghostly specters. Poems like "The Dungeon" and "Rime of the Ancyent Marinere" capture Coleridge's concern with making the mysterious connect to the mundane. Like Shelley in "Ozymandias," Coleridge takes fantastical things and shows us how their extraordinary truth is actually rooted in the drama of our ordinary experience. "The Rime of the Ancyent Marinere" may be

Coleridge's greatest achievement when it comes to modeling this sort of Romanticization, this form of enchantment. Let's see how he does it.

"The Rime of the Ancyent Marinere" turns on one, inexplicable incident: the death of a bird. But it is precisely this inexplicability that leads to Coleridge's insights about symbolic thinking as a means to mystery, and to enchantment. The poem begins with a mariner, a sailor, old and grizzled, stopping a young man on his way to a wedding. The mariner has a "glittering eye" and reaches out to the young man, who reluctantly listens to his story. Despite the sheen of the old man's visage, his body is old and withered, more skeletal than human. He begins his tale. He once set out to sea on a beautiful ship, manned with two hundred sailors. Their voyage began without incident, "merrily" even, until a storm-blast came, driving the ship into a great sea of "snowy clift[s]" and "mist and snow."[7] Surrounded by massive chunks of ice that "cracked and growled, and roared and howled," the sailors became terrified, lost, and alone.[8] Out of the snow-fog—as if from nowhere—came an albatross: a great, white sea-bird with expansive, grey wings. The sailors rejoiced, taking the bird as a good omen, a sign of things to come, a sort of prophetic indication of salvation or hope: "Through the fog it came; / As if it had been a Christian soul, / We hailed it in God's name."[9] The sailors fed it with their own precious food stores and it joyfully flew around the ship. Immediately following the bird's arrival, the "ice did split with a thunder-fit" and the helmsman steered the ship through the ice, and into warmer waters.[10] The sailors celebrated the albatross, feeding it and entertaining it with "the mariners' hollo!" as it flew above the ship, bringing a "good south wind."[11] For nine days and nights it circled and perched on the mast of the ship, a haunting, familiar presence, "whiles all the night through fog smoke white, / Glimmered the white moonshine."[12]

The poem then takes a chilling turn. The mariner's face becomes contorted, tortured even, as he recounts his tale. The wedding guest, terrified, exclaims, "'God save thee, ancient mariner, / From the fiends that plague thee thus! Why look'st thou so?'" The mariner confesses: "'With my cross-bow / I shot the albatross.'"[13]

---

7. Coleridge, "The Rime of the Ancyent Marinere," 339–40.

8. Coleridge, "The Rime of the Ancyent Marinere," 340.

9. Coleridge, "The Rime of the Ancyent Marinere," 340.

10. Coleridge, "The Rime of the Ancyent Marinere," 341.

11. Coleridge, "The Rime of the Ancyent Marinere," 341.

12. Coleridge, "The Rime of the Ancyent Marinere," 341.

13. Coleridge, "The Rime of the Ancyent Marinere," 341.

Wait, what? Why? Why on earth did he do *that*? What in the world compelled him to kill the albatross? It was a good omen, wasn't it? Didn't it bring the warm breeze and break the ice and all that? Why would the mariner just shoot it? *What does the killing mean?* These are all wonderful questions, questions that open us up to the space of symbolic thinking. They are the kinds of questions that enchant us. You should be asking these questions. The poem demands we ask them. In fact, more than in the answering, the key to enchantment is in *the asking itself*.

The poem goes on. At first, the sailors were angry at the mariner for doing a "hellish thing" by killing the bird "that made the breeze to blow."[14] But the breeze didn't die down, even after the bird's death. It continued. The ship sailed on, underneath "the glorious sun."[15] All was well, and so the sailors changed their tune. Rather than seeing the albatross as a good omen, they began to think of it as a curse, the thing that "brought the fog and mist. / 'Twas right,' said they, 'such bird to slay[.]'"[16] But eventually the wind calmed. The ship's "sails dropped down," and the boat sat idle in the "silence of the sea."[17] The once-glorious sun became a "bloody sun," rotting the ships planks, despite their being "water, water, everywhere[.]"[18] The sailor's tune changed again. Dying of thirst, where "every tongue, through utter drouth, / was withered at the root[,]" the sailors began to blame the mariner for killing the albatross.[19] Its death was the cause of their misfortune. They took the dead bird and tied a rope around it, and "[i]nstead of the cross the albatross / About [the mariner's] neck was hung."[20]

What is going on here? It's a bit mysterious, isn't it? One thing's for certain: the meaning of the albatross is changing. It's morphing, moving, and mutating throughout the poem. The sailors struggle to make meaning of the albatross, just the same as we do. The albatross doesn't symbolize *anything we want it to*, but it doesn't seem to symbolize *any one thing* either. There's something going on about an omen, a curse, ill-tidings, etc., but also promise, hope, and possibility. It's a strange milieu of symbolic meaning all mixed together. Coleridge doesn't allow us to settle on a single signification, he doesn't allow us to claim the final verdict, or decide once-and-for-all what the albatross is all about. You might even say that the mariner's

14. Coleridge, "The Rime of the Ancyent Marinere," 341.
15. Coleridge, "The Rime of the Ancyent Marinere," 342.
16. Coleridge, "The Rime of the Ancyent Marinere," 342.
17. Coleridge, "The Rime of the Ancyent Marinere," 342.
18. Coleridge, "The Rime of the Ancyent Marinere," 342.
19. Coleridge, "The Rime of the Ancyent Marinere," 343.
20. Coleridge, "The Rime of the Ancyent Marinere," 343.

original sin was trying to do just that: trying to capture, master, control, or determine the meaning of the bird; that is, to reduce its meaning to one meaning and in doing so, killing it. The mariner disenchanted the albatross as a symbol by shooting it down. This is an important point in terms of the Romantic strategy of symbolic thinking. Often times we find ourselves to be the mariner, crossbow aimed at a symbol, trying to pin it down. We want to "figure it out," just like the sailors. But as the symbolic meanings of the albatross begin to build up around it we suspect that the albatross is sort of like a symbol of symbolism; that is, the albatross *resists reduction* and in doing so reveals to us the very structure of a symbol. Symbols point, they gesture toward, they participate in the thing they are trying to signify. Any attempt to explain what a symbol means with any sense of completeness and finality defeats the purpose of invoking the symbol in the first place, and so must always fail. Conversely, when viewed as an invitation to *explore* meaning rather than discover it, symbols become a source of great insight, wisdom, and enchantment. As we've seen, they present an opening, a space to consider the depth of a thing. They are like a landscape of meaning into which we are lured, with the choice to search the valleys and recesses for richness, and significance.

As the poem goes on, a number of magical and amazing things happen: a small skiff passes by with two figures aboard, Death and Life-in-Death. They are casting dice. Life-in-Death wins. She whistles, and all the sailors drop dead, save the mariner. They curse him with their evil eyes as their corpses fall to the deck of the ship. Alone, the mariner sails the seas, longing but unable to die himself. It's as if the curse of the albatross sustains him even though he would rather it all to end. Continued life is his punishment and his penance. One night he sees some enigmatic "water-snakes" swimming about in the ocean and he has an epiphany. Their unmatched beauty which emerges out of the blackness of night transforms him. Their smooth skin is a "rich attire" of "blue, glossy green, and velvet black," and they make tracks in the water.[21] Their grandeur takes hold of the mariner's heart. He achieves a second naivety, experiences a moment of enchantment in ecstasy, and exclaims: "A spring of love gushed from my heart / And I blessed them unaware!"[22] The mariner then does a funny thing, something he'd been unable to do up until this moment of enchantment, which reminds him of the stunning fact of being: he begins to pray. And as he does "from [his] neck so free / The albatross fell off and sank / Like lead into the sea."[23]

---

21. Coleridge, "The Rime of the Ancyent Marinere," 346.
22. Coleridge, "The Rime of the Ancyent Marinere," 346.
23. Coleridge, "The Rime of the Ancyent Marinere," 347.

In the end, the mariner returns home, guided by the ghost crew, now in angelic form. He is met by a boatman, a boy, and a hermit and each has a different reaction to his countenance. The boatman is afraid, the boy goes mad, and the hermit is shocked. We learn that the mariner's curse and penance must continue. He is destined to tell his story over and over again to passers-by, which is the story of symbolic reduction, death, and disenchantment. His story serves as a warning against the unknown and unnamed human impulse to master and control, to capture and kill the symbol. But there is a final irony in the poem: the very curse of re-telling is itself a performance of symbolic thinking. Symbols give a surplus of meaning. They can never be exhausted because the thing they signify is inexhaustible. And so, the mariner must tell and re-tell, he must say over and over again the truth of the albatross. He has returned, but he can never come home. He can never settle. He is more Abraham wandering the desert than Odysseus finding harbor in Ithaca. Enchantment is an ongoing, recurring conversion, enchantment is an eternal re-enchantment and renewal. It must happen again and again in an endless circle of re-making, an endless hermeneutic.

We could go on and on with this poem. It really is a masterpiece. But we've gotten far enough into it to make the point that symbolic thinking is a means to enchantment. That is my way of putting part of what I think Coleridge wants us to see in the poem. The albatross is the Romantic symbol *par excellence*. Coleridge is both showing us how to think symbolically, and how to avoid defeating the symbol. Notice how he allows a variety of meanings to accumulate around the bird but he never lets us settle on one. Notice also how he somehow sets the parameters for the bird's meaning without confining it too much. The albatross can mean a cluster of things—there are groupings and traces of meanings that attach to it—but none of them stick with any finality. They are always deferring to other meanings, offering different inflections, though generally within the same family of possible meanings: death/life, despair/hope, curse/blessing, isolation/community, wandering/return, reduction/surplus, etc. Like the albatross above the ship, we too must circle around these meanings, diving into some of them at certain times, like when they seem most germane to our experience, or when they speak to us with a resonance we simply cannot ignore.

The Tiger and Eternity

For readers already familiar with Romantic poetry, you might expect this section to be about William Blake's sublime composition, "The Tyger." It's a masterpiece. I love that poem. But I'd like to offer a personal example of symbolic enchantment in order to show how it operates on a mundane level, how it generates resonance and charges even quotidian occurrences with profound significance and value, how through our encounters with symbols we can experience moments of eternity piercing the veil of time. That's a strong claim, I know. I hope you'll indulge me. You'll be happy to know this section does involve a tiger, but not one with quite as much "fearful symmetry" and fire-burning eyes as Blake's. After all, the tiger in my story belongs to a three-year-old.

My son is a toddler. Like most toddlers, he has a stuffed animal. He loves it. It's a tiger. He sleeps with it, plays with it, brings it with him in the car, sings songs to it, shares his snacks with it, and does all of the other things any child would do with his stuffed animal. By most accounts, his interactions with the tiger are unremarkable. Child development and child psychologists tell us that his love for the tiger is normal, right, and healthy.

One day, I loaded my son and his tiger (or so I thought) into the car. It was raining. We were in a hurry. I was getting soaked. I buckled my son into the car seat, closed the door, marched around to the driver's seat, and drove off.

It wasn't long before I heard that familiar voice from the backseat.

"Where's tiger?"

Now, I've probably picked that tiger up off the floor of the car a thousand times, so without even looking I responded as I normally would.

"He's on the floor, buddy. I'll grab him in a minute when we get to a red light."

But my son wouldn't have it.

"No," he said, "he's not. He's not here." I could sense the uneasiness in his voice.

"Yeah, buddy, he's on the floor," I replied. "I'll get him as soon as we stop, okay?"

"No, he's not." His voice cracked. He was panicking a little, I could tell.

"Seriously, bud. I can't turn around right now. I'm driving and it's raining. It's not safe. You'll just have to wait."

"He's not here, dad!" He cried out, his worry and grief obvious. He began to cry. He cried hard. It surprised me, actually, just how hard he was crying. The rain kept coming down in sheets. We finally got to a red light. I turned around to look for tiger. He wasn't there.

"He's not here, dad!" my son exclaimed, through his tears. "He's on the road! At home!"

I thought for a minute. Had he fallen out of the car when I was loading up? Had I missed that? Was tiger in the street, getting run over and rained on? I started to panic a bit too. I looked at my son. The look in his eyes was despair, and loss.

"Okay, bud. Let's go back and look." I pulled over, shot off a quick text to let my folks know I'd be late, and turned the car back toward the house. As we drove up I saw tiger sitting in the street, covered in rain and mud. But there he was. I'll admit: I was relieved.

"There he is!" I said, surprising myself with my enthusiasm.

"Let's get him, dad!" my son added, "He's all dirty."

I pulled the car over, jumped out, grabbed the tiger, wrung him out a little, and got back in the car.

"Here you go, buddy," I said. "We found him. He'll need some love until he gets warm, and we can wash him off, but I think he'll be ok."

My son didn't say anything. He just held tiger tightly. He sniffed a little, his cheeks wet with tears. He closed his eyes. He turned his body slowly from left to right, rocking tiger in a hugging embrace. Then I heard a soft whisper: "Oh, tiger. You're okay."

It's easy to dismiss this story as just a day in the life of being a toddler. It's unremarkable, typical, and even a bit sentimental. You might think it's got nothing to do with symbolic thinking or enchantment. But I disagree. I think it's moments like these that in a profound way demonstrate our human capacity to think, feel, and live within a symbolic order. I think it's even more than that, actually. I think this story demonstrates the unique human capacity to raise a moment of mundane time into an experience of eternity, which is in part made possible by our ability to encounter the world through symbols.

Now, when I say "eternity" here I don't mean infinity, or some vague sense of everything marching forward along a timeline, as if things were going on forever and ever in a never-ending parade. By "eternity" I mean what the philosopher Erazim Kohák means by it; that is, that as human beings we experience moments of existence that in some powerful way pierce through our experience of everyday time, moments when we no longer experience time as a series of instances, marching along episodically, one after the other, black ticks on a clock's face. According to Kohák, there are some moments that we experience that are "out of time," or that come at us in a way that transgresses the typical, "before, now, after" of clock time. These moments are value-charged moments of revelation. They are moments in which the "perennial validity" of an eternal truth strikes us with an irreducible *haecceitas*, a "thisness" that speaks for itself and justifies itself in its very appearing.[24]

---

24. Kohák, *The Embers and the Stars*, 83.

It's tricky to describe these moments, but we know them from experience: the shock of a July-blue sky, the magic of a loved-one's laugh, the grief that comes with saying goodbye to a dying dog, the feel of your mother's hand on your back as she comforts you, the eyes of a hungry person asking for help. These moments are not trivial. They reveal the holiness of Being. They are the moments when we are most fully human. They disclose our powerful capacity to go out and meet the world—to encounter Being itself—and to raise it up to a moment of ultimate value, to transform through our joy and sorrow the passage to time into "the eternal validity of truth, goodness, and beauty."[25]

My son's tiger is many things, among them, a symbol. It is a thing that refers to something other than itself (devotion, comfort, assurance, love, etc.) but it also participates in the things it references (its softness comforts, its weight assures, its face smiles lovingly, etc.). Like the albatross, its meaning is irreducible. And like the blue flower, it draws upon a pre-existing inventory of meanings to convey its own. But it does more than that. It is also a repository for my son's affection. It is a receptacle of love, a recipient of devotion. It is "a thing cared for," and in being that, it becomes *more than a thing*, it comes to symbolize and to embody an eternal truth. It stands out from among other things, from all things, and in its existence my son experiences belonging, safety, and the mutual bond of I-for-you, which is the bond that subverts the tragedy of human alienation. The tiger-as-symbol opens up all of these possibilities, and in doing so becomes the vehicle through which eternity passes into the order of time.

Let me say a bit more about that.

The loss my son felt when his tiger went missing was not merely the disappointment a child feels when he loses a toy. A toy is an object, something mass produced, without identity or meaning. A toy is something replaceable, something unloved. In truth, there are millions of copies of my son's tiger-as-toy. You could probably buy one yourself, right now, on Amazon. But you cannot buy *his* tiger because for my son *this* tiger is not an object, it is a thing that he loves, a thing loved, singularly, and without reservation. It has become *own*, not object, not possession. Worn smooth by nights of hugging and petting, the tiger has become a symbol of what it is to love, what it is to imbue something with ultimate meaning. Tiger has sat next to my son during countless meals. He has been friend, companion, playmate, and comforter. In the order of clock time, the tiger will vanish. Just like all of the toy tigers—and you and me, and my son too, in fact—all will disappear in their turn, overtaken by the horizon of finitude. All will be

25. Kohák, *The Embers and the Stars*, 83.

forgotten. But the moment of eternity that is manifest in my son's love for the tiger will remain forever because in his love and care for it he has raised it up out of the march of time and into eternity. Eternity not in the sense that years from now people will know about the tiger. Of course, they will not. But eternity in the sense that in his care for the doll, in his conviction that it is of ultimate value lived out in his love for it, love itself stands out in all its glory. In his devotion to the doll, eternity ingresses everyday life, the eternal pierces the veil of time. This cannot be denied.[26]

The tiger is a symbol, and symbols open a space for eternity's ingress into time. They are not what causes it to happen, but they do make it possible. The fact is, we are swimming in symbols, rich symbols, not just cliché ones. We can see now that to be human is to think symbolically, to act symbolically, and to generate meaning with and through symbols. Because symbols draw from a rich cultural inventory they are always pregnant with meaning, swollen with a myriad of references. Like the blue flower, they say something to us, almost intuitively. We are often already familiar with their connotations and signals because they come to us from our own traditions. But like the albatross, they resist reduction because they are pointing to and participating in something more than themselves, something more than the medium that they constitute. They invite interpretation, endless interpretation, in fact, as we trace and contemplate their references over and over again throughout our lives. This confluence of saying and not saying, reference and participation, and endless interpretation is the value-laden landscape of human life.

It is in part because we have the capacity to experience the world symbolically that we also have the capacity to recognize the arrival of eternal truths. These sorts of truths often come to us in and through symbols: donning black to mourn, giving a gift, kneeling in prayer, all express through symbols (color, item, gesture) an unsayable truth, a truth that is no less true because it is unsayable. My son's love for the tiger is true, and the tiger symbolizes the possibility of deep and abiding concern for another. As a symbol it opens onto the possibility of love's ingress into time. But the tiger must be loved in order for that truth to arrive. Symbolic truths are not deficient truths because they are unsayable truths. In many ways, they are *more* true than empirical or articulable truths. When we experience moments of eternity we do so within the milieu of symbolic life, of symbolic living.

26. My thinking in this paragraph is deeply informed by Kohák's account of eternity and time in *The Ember and the Stars*, particularly on pages 106–9. I borrow heavily from his thinking. While the tiger example is my own, my analysis of it mirrors Kohák's analysis of a similar "Pandy Bear" phenomenon, which he explores on those pages. I credit him for the insights and language I've used to describe this phenomenon.

As we'll see in the section below, you can attune yourself the world of symbols that surrounds you and heighten your awareness of the way in which we as human beings imbue the world with value, the way we raise time to eternity. You can cultivate a sensitivity to your own miraculous capacity to experience the world as a place, not just space, to love and to grieve and to be struck by the beauty of an autumn moon or moved by the kindness of another's generosity. You can develop in yourself the ability to experience a world of symbols, a world of enchantment.

Enchantment Strategy #4: Symbolic Thinking and Poetic Contemplation

As you can see, symbols are powerful tools for re-enchanting the world. They're much more than just literary tropes or things that stand for something else. They are part of a broader cultural milieu and age-old traditions. They go to the very heart of what it means to be human. To raise your awareness of your own, natural tendency to think symbolically and experience the world through symbols is to heighten your attention to the way in which we as humans imbue the world with meaning, and to experience the world as a meaningful place. It's true: we can't but think symbolically.

In this chapter, however, we've tried to unpack the depth of what symbolic thinking really means, and to examine how our penchant for symbols opens up the possibility of poetic contemplation; that is, a way of encountering the world as a place ripe with meanings and referents, ones that direct our attention to deeper things, things that make life resonate. Poetic contemplation is a double-sided activity. On one side, it means that when you encounter a symbol, you consciously reflect on *what* the symbol means to you, what it's telling you to think about, and then tarrying there a bit and reflecting on its meanings and truths. On the other side, its noticing *how* a symbol works on you, how it both conveys meaning and destabilizes it, how it refers to something other than itself and participates in it, and how it serves as a vehicle for eternity's ingress into time. It's one thing to think symbolically (we all do that), it's another thing to *contemplate poetically* the symbol. Poetic contemplation pays attention to the "what" and the "how" of a symbol. It's where the magic really happens. Let's see how it's done.

Step 1: Let Go of "Getting It"

One big reason why people tend to shy away from poetry in general, and Romantic poetry in particular, is because they're afraid they won't "get it." Poetic language seems unnecessarily esoteric. Poems make weird references to obscure people or places like "the Visigoths" or "Arcady." Even when poems seem straightforward, many readers have this sense that there's something else going on, that the truth is underneath the surface of the words and rhymes. It's like the poem is a mine and you're the miner and the task is to dig into the poem and extract its hidden gem—its true meaning—in order to say you really understand it. For some it's like a mystery to solve: the poet hides the secret in the words and lines and the you must decode the message.

But that's not what poetry is about. Poetry is not a game of cat and mouse. As readers, our task is not to "get" a poem, as reluctant as we might be to let that desire go. Poetry—and the poetic use of symbols—are about resonance. Poetry and symbols deliver truths that cannot be said in any other way. Sure, you may need to have a working knowledge of some basic poetic ideas in order to comprehend what you're reading, and sometimes that takes a little work (a Google search here, a dictionary there), but the point of engaging a poem is not to "figure it out," but to encounter it, to be moved by it. The same is true for symbols. The first step in discovering the enchantment of symbolic thinking is to let go of "getting it." Let go of the feeling that you need to decode the symbol in order to understand it. Resist the drive to pin a symbol down to a singular meaning. Don't kill the albatross. Instead, embrace the plurality of meanings that the symbol conveys. Trust that, to a large degree, you already have a sense of what a symbol means because you live in the cultural milieu out of which it emerges. Rather than worrying about how to reduce a symbol's meanings to one, consider all of them (or as many as you like). Revel in them. Explore them. See them as a rich repository of potential significations that can enliven and deepen your understanding of a feeling, issue, idea, or experience. A good symbol allows you to look at all the edges of a thing, to roll it around in your hands (or your head) so to speak, to examine its contours, shapes, and textures. It keeps saying, "look here," "notice this too," and "see, there?" It invites you to consider the different angles of a truth without feeling the need to say once and for all say, "I get it." On Monday it might say one thing to you, and on Tuesday, something else. There's beauty in that. Let it be.

Novalis's blue flower is a good example of the mercurial nature of a symbol and how we can embrace its multivocality. But there are other, more common examples. Imagine you have an uncle. You and he are very close.

You've always admired his keen sense of humor, bright smile, and playful demeanor. At every family picnic he's there, laughing and helping, a moving reminder of the joy of family and the truth of a good man. Imagine that he loves muscle cars. He's constructed a small garage on a cheap piece of land and that's where he builds and works on them, just as a hobby. Now, imagine he's grown old, and developed Alzheimer's Disease. He's become frail, and often seems lost. At family gatherings he's quiet and keeps his hands folded in his lap, his eyes darting about. He says little, and smiles less. Now, sadly, imagine he's passed away. He's left a small inheritance to his wife (no children) and nephews and nieces. A few days after the funeral his wife, your aunt, comes to your house and brings you a set of keys to a 1965 Mustang Fastback. She tells you there is no car attached to the keys, it has rusted away and was taken to the junkyard when she was cleaning up the estate. She tells you that, before the Alzheimer's set-in, your uncle planned to restore the Mustang and give it to you as a gift because he had a special affection for you, but now all she has are these keys. She wanted you to have them.

I know that for some people the keys might not mean much. They're just a trinket, a memento. Maybe that's true. After all, they're keys to a car that doesn't exist. But as a symbol, they are so much more. What—symbolically—do these keys mean? A little poetic contemplation goes a long way. The keys mean many things: a loving uncle, a smile at a family picnic, a kind hand. They mean work and craft, skill and patience. They mean the joy of a fast car and the freedom it brings. They mean youth and death, a life that—like the Mustang—dissolved into the ever-flowing river of time. They mean a bond. They mean that you were thought of when you weren't around. They mean remembrance, mourning, and grief. They mean all this and more. The key to the keys-as-symbol is that they are not reducible to any one of these meanings. You can never "get" the keys. Instead, you can, contemplate them, hold them, explore them, and appreciate the way in which such a small, useless thing carries so much weight in the world, how they touch eternity. Let their meanings resonate. Let the keys' symbolic meanings ebb and flow, calling to mind all that can and cannot be said about the life and death of a good person. That's the first step in poetic contemplation.

Step 2: Draw from Your Inventory

We can see from "The Rime of the Ancyent Marinere" that to think symbolically in the Romantic mode is not just to use language as a set of symbols, or to simply recognize the use of conventional symbols, like "red means stop." Symbolic thinking is more than that. Thinking symbolically is a way

to enchant the world, or to experience its enchantment. As an enchantment strategy, symbolic thinking means that you develop a keen awareness
and sensitivity to the cultural context into which you're born, to become
familiar with the inventory of signs, symbols, references, and significations
that make up your cultural encyclopedia, and to draw from that wealth and
wisdom to charge your everyday life with a variety of meanings.

One thing to notice about this idea of "an inventory of symbols" is
that you don't get to choose which inventory you're working with. In a very
important sense, you're thrown into your world, into a place and time and
culture that was already there before you showed up. But that's a good thing.
In fact, it's precisely *because* the culture into which you're born preceded
you that you have an already-developed inventory of symbols from which
to draw, and to make references. Look around you. Your world is full of
symbols *you already know*: trees mean life, age, wisdom, growth. A fireplace means hospitality, warmth, cheer, and companionship. A book means
knowledge, conversation, and contemplation. Your child's face means imagination, hope, and possibility. Where did these significations come from?
How do you know—almost intuitively—that that's what they mean? Part
of the answer is that their initial associations have been percolating over
thousands of years. For millennia poets, authors, painters, singers, lovers,
mothers, priests, fathers, storytellers, etc., have drawn on and developed
these symbolic references in order to make sense of their lives and give them
the magic of meaning. And now they are available to you, a rich, profound
encyclopedia of symbols, all at your disposal. Use them to enchant your life.
When you see a single candle burning in a dark room, notice the connotations and references it whispers: quiet truth, light and revelation, solitude
and reflection, human aspirations, knowledge and mystery.

Never forget that the meaning of a symbol is not static. Even though
your cultural encyclopedia was written before you showed up, you can
still mess with the entries. In other words, symbols and their meaning are
malleable. The French philosopher Paul Ricoeur thought this was one of
the most amazing things about symbolic thinking. He was curious about
how new meanings emerge and so looked into the word "innovation" to see
what happens when we make something new. He found that innovation is
rooted in two other words: invention and inventory. To invent is to create.
And to inventory is to catalog. So, to "innovate" with a symbol is to draw
from the catalog of possible meanings that it brings with it *and* to use those
meanings in new ways, forming new combinations of meanings. A symbol
never means one thing, once and for all. It brings with it a set of cultural
references but you can always play with them, change them, shift them, innovate with them, in order to generate new, resonating meanings. Symbols

are therefore inexhaustible and represent an enormous opportunity to experience enchantment. To think symbolically is to soar like the albatross, to circle and swoop and dive into the rich waters of reference and signification that make up the world around us. Human beings are the kinds of beings for whom symbolic thinking is possible. That's an incredible thing to say. We should embrace that capacity, that unique side of ourselves. We should cultivate it, and enjoy it. Through the power of symbols, we can explore our greatest joys and our darkest fears. We can wrestle with grief, consider the meaning of our lives, and see the beauty of the sheer fact of existence. All of this is there, in something as simple as an autumn leaf. Unlike empiricism, which seeks to know and to master, symbolism opens us up to new visions. It invites us to explore and to innovate. It gestures towards the possible, and it participates in mystery.

Step 3: Romanticize Up, Romanticize Down

There are lots of ways to experience the magic of symbolism. While of course the Romantics are not the only poets to use symbols, they did leave us with a useful, two-fold structure to help us approach symbolic thinking as a means of enchantment. Through symbolism you can "Romanticize up" or "Romanticize down." You Romanticize up when you take a mundane, everyday object and pay attention to the parts of it that are mysterious, giving it an air of the infinite (desire in the blue flower, love in the Mustang keys, etc.). You Romanticize down when you take something fantastical, extraordinary, or unfamiliar and see in it the common but profound human truth to which it speaks (time in an ancient statue, penance in a wayward ghost ship, etc.). Once you've gotten over "getting it" and developed in yourself an appreciation for the cultural encyclopedia into which you're born, you can begin to experience the plurality of meanings a symbol provides and Romanticize up or down to your heart's delight. All it takes is some looking, some reflection, and some sensitivity to the way in which symbols and symbolic meaning present themselves to you.

To do so, you have to overcome the temptation to minimize the many meanings that emerge. And you have to be intentional about Romanticizing. When you go to the beach, for example, pay attention to the references of the sand, the ocean, and the bright summer sky present to you. Be willing to open up your cultural encyclopedia and see what's in there. In a scientific register, the push and pull of the waves on the shore is a byproduct of the moon's gravitational pull. It's gone on for ages and will continue to do so. It's physics.

But in a symbolic register we might Romanticize the beach up, taking this (literally) everyday phenomenon and seeing in it something more.
We might crack open our cultural encyclopedia to the "water" entry and
see that water already has a number of cultural associations attached to it.
For over two thousand years artists have used water to symbolize womb,
renewal, movement, birth, life, change, etc. Knowing this, you can see in the
push and pull of the waves the truth of time's relentless passing. The sand on
which you stand, although more stable than the ever-churning ocean, sifts
and shifts underneath your feet. Is there is no solid place to stand, no way
to avoid the world-as-change? And then there is the sky—bright and hot
and blue—which draws your eyes up, toward transcendence, toward a feeling that somehow union with the One might just be possible, that in some
way we might dissolve into the all-blue horizon of Being and experience a
moment of time-out-of-time. To see all of this in a simple ocean scene is
to Romanticize up, to experience an enchanted world rich with symbolism
and meaning.

One important point here: as you practice noticing and innovating
with symbols you'll start to see that you don't always have a clear, cognitive
vision in your head as to what they mean (e.g., "this means that, or "x means
y"). Rather, you'll develop an intuition of their meanings. Symbols will give
you an impression of what they want to say, an affect, really, more than a
thought. You won't necessarily say to yourself "sky means transcendence"
but you will feel the pull of transcendence when you look at the sky and
recognize your relationship to it as one rooted in symbols.

Don't be afraid to Romanticize down, too. Romanticizing down can
be an interesting way to experience enchantment. It's not as common as
Romanticizing up, I don't think, but it's just as powerful. The next time you
encounter something fantastic, marvelous, or extraordinary, ask yourself,
"What is the common human truth here, told in exotic terms?" Remember
how in "The Rime of the Ancyent Marinere" Coleridge used a wild and
surreal ghost story to get us to explore the rather common human experiences of guilt and penance, loneliness and alienation, and the desire to know
and master. By making the extraordinary connect to the ordinary Coleridge
Romanticized down; that is, he took what seemed fantastic and showed how
the fairy tale like setting and characters actually reveal something deep and
true of all of us, about our common human experience. We all know what
it is to feel guilt. We all know the drive to know and understand. These
everyday experiences are given a new life and depth when explored in and
through a fantastic tale. Consider such tales in your own life—those that
may seem to have little bearing on your experience of life or even seem

childish—and ask yourself, "What common human truth is this extraordinary experience disclosing?"

Take Halloween, for example. Halloween gets a bad wrap in the United States because it's perceived as an overly-commercialized and shallow holiday based on maximizing candy and costume sales. It's little more than a cheap opportunity to turn a profit. That's one way to look at it, for sure. But you might also look at what we do as a culture and ask why we do it in the first place. Why do we dress up like ghosts and goblins? Why do we do it at night? Why October 31st? What is all of this fantasy and role play and abnormal behavior about? Thinking symbolically, a layered view of Halloween can emerge, one that looks past or beyond the initial distaste of mass consumerism that marks it.

Halloween, or All Hallows' Eve, happens in-between fall and winter. It's a day at the threshold of the seasons. It symbolizes a passage, and a passing. It also comes when the world is dying: the leaves fall from the trees, streams dry up, and weakened animals are culled as prey. Death lurks about this time of year. Halloween is considered by many European cultures to be the day in which the veil between the living and the dead is thinnest, which makes sense, given the symbolic associations of threshold, death, and passage that make up the holiday's imagery. In fact, we dress up like ghouls to blend in with the other "real" ghouls that are said to come out from their graves and prowl around on All Hallows' Eve. And so, by dressing up, we participate in the symbolism of death and passing, and place ourselves within the mix of life and death. We can *in a playful way* explore our own mortality. Through symbols like ghastly faces, jack-o-lanterns, and cobwebs, we can live in the *as if* and for a moment consider just how close to death we really are, just how frighteningly mortal we are. But we can do it with a kind of comedic bravery because we have symbols, which allow us to look at things indirectly. After all, looking death directly in the face is, well, terrifying. Halloween's symbolic inventory gives us recourse to explore death without falling into despair. You see? We can Romanticize Halloween down, from the extraordinary to the ordinary, from the fantasy of ghosts to the everyday fact of death, and after a little poetic contemplation begin to see that through its symbols we are able to confront a profound and dreadful human truth: one day, you too will cross the veil; one day, you will know death.

Be ready to look with fresh eyes on cultural activities or experiences that you once took for granted as foolish or maybe even outlandish before you started engaging in this Romantic strategy. Romanticize them down. Look for the human experience they are dramatizing and see if you can't learn to appreciate the truth they're trying to convey. It can be kind of fun, actually. Go on, at the next "meaningless" holiday party, give it a try.

Step 4: Experience Eternity

As we saw with the tiger doll story, the capacity to experience eternity's ingress into time is a hallmark of the human person. We are the types of beings for whom Being is a question, as the philosopher Martin Heidegger puts it. For us, the question of meaning is always "there," always animating us, moving us, and inspiring us to make a world for ourselves. According to Erazim Kohák, what we discover when we turn off the electric lights of technology, put down our phones, and commit just a part of our four-and-a-half hours of daily screen time to paying attention to our surroundings is that the world actually has *a moral sense*. It appears to us a beautiful orchestra of order, a place where we belong.

Kohák doesn't mean "order" in the medieval meaning of order; that is, there is a God-up-high, a master puppeteer making everything happen for a reason. Nor does mean "moral" as in the Ten Commandments sense of moral, a list of dos-and-don'ts with which we must comply. He means that in the silence of a forest or on a winter walk we discover a rhythmic order, an almost innate experience of life as seasonal, paced, connected, and tied together. There is a rightness to it, an impression that all is as it should be. In moments like these, we are attuned to our capacity as humans to experience the Mystery of Being: *that there is something*. When we experience this mystery, we are moved by it and invited to celebrate it. It resonates in us. The mystery is fundamentally ineffable, and so we are called to "think it" symbolically, to contemplate it poetically, and to encounter it indirectly, through metaphors that both express it and participate in it, that gesture toward it and also bring it into our immediate experience.

As a practical matter, to encounter the moral order, to experience eternity in the way Kohák describes it, you must bracket your critical inclinations to view human values as cultural constructs (and so to minimize them), and instead affirm the validity of the truth the symbol presents. These critical inclinations are the voice of disenchantment. For example, you may hear someone say something like, "'Eternity' and 'order' are just humans making stuff up to feel better about their predicament. The cosmos is a big, scary place, and the prospect of a meaningless existence is hard to stomach, so in an effort to deal with it and comfort ourselves, we create things like 'eternity' and a 'order' to get by." That's disenchantment talking. That's the spin of the immanent frame. To encounter eternity, you must set aside this tendency and adjust your way of seeing things, you must shift from the "natural mode" to the "moral mode" of perception.

Let me explain. Normally, *naturally*, we experience time as a vast, flowing river, a chain of causation, one thing leading to the next. The cause precedes the effect. *This* happens, because *that* happened. When you perceive things according to this natural, causal mode, a funny thing emerges: life always appears one step away from you. You're always looking back (at a cause) or looking forward (to an effect). You're always perceiving things as derivative, the result *of something else*. There is great utility in this natural mode of perception (e.g., the ability to predict events, to analyze them), but there are also limits. The natural mode deflects our attention away from the present, from what is before us, now. Your friend's father dies. You see him mourning. You think, "How sad he is today, but time will heal his wounds. His dad lived a good life. Once the funeral is over, he'll have a chance to reflect, and he'll be okay." This line of thought is wrapped up in causation, naturally enough. The son mourns now, *because* the father died. The son will later heal, *because* enough time will pass. The truth of his grief is deflected into the moments that come before it and after it.

But perceiving grief this way—and joy, too, for that matter—neglects its present purity. It papers over its perennial truth, a truth that arrives here, now, in the cry of mourning or in joyous laughter. These are moments in which the eternity of love pierces the veil of time, when it is inscribed into the order of things. Viewed as a moment of value, not causation; that is, viewed in a moral mode rather than the natural mode, this inscription is also a transgression. It is a moment of time-out-of-time, a moment that exists apart from other moments because of its supreme nobility. The son's grief renders the moment holy, it lifts it out of the before-and-after and places it into the universal. It affirms the undying validity of sorrow, which is the human capacity to lament the loss of a loved one. Like the chill of a crisp autumn wind, you child's smile, or the skylark's song, the son's sorrow signifies the sacred. It *is* the sacred.

And where the sacred is present, so are symbols. Be on the lookout for them. Symbols are the language of the eternal. We take recourse to symbolic thought in moments of eternity-piercing-time because, as we have seen, it is hard to say the truth directly. Symbols give us the tools to celebrate and say the ineffable, as much as it can be said, anyway. They allow us to stand before the Mystery and honor it, and participate in it, too. The next time you're at a wedding, or a funeral, or a family gathering, pay attention to how we draw upon symbols to give voice to the experience. Pay attention to how we say the unsayable by reference to stories, metaphors, images, poetry, and song. There is power in symbols. They are guideposts to the eternal.

Once you've attuned yourself to the language of symbols, they'll begin to speak to you on their own terms. The world will appear to you symbolically, even without you doing much of anything. That's because the symbols were there before you showed up and you were born with the capacity to read them, to experience them. Symbols are an invitation to peer into eternity, to make the invisible truths of our human existence visible through material and mundane things. Bread can become the gift of life. Wine, the joy of merriment. The black veil speaks of our unspeakable sorrow. And the crocus signals our hope for a new day. At this stage in your practice, you simply need to let the truth made manifest through the symbol resonate with you. Let it move you. Accept the invitation to explore your human nature and experience existence through symbols.

On my fortieth birthday I went to a graveyard and wandered around, looking at the tombstones, of course, but also the grass and footpaths faded by hundreds of years of visitors, both alive and dead. I paid attention to the lay of the land and the little hints of life that paradoxically lived in tandem with the death surrounding me: a skittering squirrel, a sun-bathing cat, a passing priest. Each had a message for me: store up your loves, give yourself over to the warmth of Being, take seriously your call, move forward. Each whispered something eternal to me.

Symbols are not just made up things. They are a gift handed to us by those that have come before us, who have pulled them from the milieu of culture and made something with them. We are both their custodians and their beneficiaries. We are also their creators. We are free to make new meanings with them, to feel their resonance in us, and to use them to probe the deepest facets of what it means to be human. Through them we can poeticize the world, and touch upon eternity.

Concluding Thoughts

The word "poetry" is rooted in the Greek word *poiein*, which means "to make." When we Romanticize something, we make the mundane seem fantastic or the fantastic seem mundane. We don't idealize. We observe the world through the symbols that precede us with a heightened attention to their appearance, and we make meaning out of the symbol-world in which we live. To do so goes to the very heart of what it means to be human. The word "Romanticize" is usually used pejoratively, as though it's a bad thing. But it's not. To Romanticize (in the Romantic sense, that is) is to think symbolically, to contemplate poetically, to give the finite the dignity of the infinite, a dignity it deserves because it *participates in* the infinite. It means to see in the most wonderful, exotic, and alluring experiences a touch of human truth shared by all of us, across space and time. It means to make the invisible visible, to raise up moments of clock time into eternity, and to see the enchantment of a world charged with symbolic meaning. The world of symbols is always speaking to us, but we must attune our souls to its language. The beauty of symbolic thought is that it's always there, always available to us by virtue of the fact that we are human beings, and we are born into a world always already imbued with symbols. Look around. See them. Reflect on them. Innovate with them. Let them resonate. Let them enchant.

6

The Great Beyond

Seeking the Sublime, Finding Transcendence

Feeling the Cross-Pressure

"I'm spiritual, not religious."

"I don't believe in God, but I do believe in a higher power."

"Everything is made up of energy. It all goes back to the universe when you die."

"You have to make your own meaning. No one's going to make it for you."

These are our modern mantras, the sacred claims we chant to ourselves day in and day out in our disenchanted lives. They're the residue of our desire for something more, something other than a merely material existence.

You've heard them all before. Shoot, you may have even said them yourself. There's nothing wrong with that. It's natural. In fact, the most interesting thing about these mantras is exactly that: *they come so naturally to us.* It's as if they're obvious, incontrovertible. They give voice to our given view on things. Although each mantra is a little different, they suggest that whatever is "out there" is basically an expression of what is "in here." In other words, each mantra implies that what makes up the entirety of the universe is part of "the natural order." Even the one about a "higher power" when pressed turns out to be a claim about some vague intuition that "everything happens for a reason." Sure, there are still people out there clinging to fairy tales, those who insist there really is a God/Wizard-in-the-Sky, but the implications of these mantras are that we know that isn't really true.

They suggest that God-talk is just some people's way of finding comfort in a cold world. Organized religion is oppressive and out of vogue. Explanations or experiences that fall outside the purview of the scientific gaze are hokey, antiquated, and even a little immature. God, religion, and the transcendent are available to us as add-ons to an otherwise secular world, but the baseline assumption we seem to make is that, at the beginning and at the end of the day, this is all there is.

And that's the key. That's the unspoken premise behind our modern mantras: *this is all there is.* It's what Charles Taylor calls "the immanent frame." The immanent frame is our default, modern position. It's the pre-reflective sense we have right now, in our contemporary age, that everything we can know and experience is contained within the "natural order." There is no "supernatural order," nothing "beyond" or "outside" of what we can sense, measure, or calculate. The material world *is* the real world, which is the world described and explained by the social sciences, the hard sciences, data, statistics, research, etc. Taylor calls this our modern "take" on things, as opposed to our modern "beliefs," because he thinks (and I agree) that the immanent frame has sunk so deeply into us that it operates in our lives in an unchallenged way: we don't even know it's there. It's not something we choose to believe in, it's something we're born into. It's so deep *we don't realize* we're living within it. We just assume that it's "the way things are." That's why expressions that come out of the immanent frame, that reflect it and affirm it, seem so natural to us.

But there's a hitch. On the one hand, we live within the frame of immanence, a submerged worldview that assumes the natural world is all there is. But on the other hand, we have a deep desire for something more, for some truth beyond what we can taste, touch, or smell. The problem is, we don't quite know what to do with this desire for "something more." It doesn't fit neatly into the immanent frame. It makes us feel restless, but also silly, in a way. (Why am I sitting in this church? I *know* God doesn't exist.) We feel restless and silly and mildly confused about this desire for "more" because the immanent frame doesn't account for it, at least not in a way that we find satisfying. Instead of taking the desire for transcendence as a phenomenon in and of itself, we analyze it from within the immanent frame and spin it into a symptom of something else, some underlying material phenomenon. The desire for transcendence is "really" just anthropology. It's the product of humans stargazing around a campfire and wondering what else is out there. You see? It's natural. The same is true for other enchanting human experiences. We reduce them to material explanations. Happiness is a brain state. Love is a complex chemical reaction. Living within the immanent frame creates two, competing desires: the desire for transcendence, and the desire to see everything as part of the natural order. We're cross-pressured: we want to go out, but we want to stay in.

This pressure tugs and pulls us in different directions. We ask, "Is this all there is?" "But, what more could there be?" replies the immanent frame. "This is life. Isn't it enough?" Yes and no. We sense that while it's "true" that this is "all there is" we also feel like there's something else, something beyond the horizon, some "we know not what."

This brings us back to the modern mantras. Usually, this cross-pressure operates in the background of our lives, like a mood or an assumption. But sometimes we sense its tension more profoundly, like in moments of grief or joy (e.g., death or childbirth). We wrestle with the desire for more and try and describe it from within the immanent frame, using the language of immanence.

"I'm spiritual, not religious." What an interesting thing to say. What does it mean? It means that you recognize the importance of seeking something more, something beyond the natural order, but that you are so turned off by organized religion (for a number of good reasons) that you don't see it as a viable place to explore the "more," whatever it is. Fair enough. But there's another assumption in this phrase too. By "spiritual" we mean something like a certain mode of being, a kind of person animated by a particular set of concerns, that present to you questions about life's ultimate purpose or meaning. The spiritual person wants to enhance her life. She wants to flourish. To do so, she may spend a lot of time thinking about and working on her "soul," "spirit," "energy," or "self." She meditates, studies indigenous people's practices, reads popular psychology, and has a healthy yoga routine. She may dabble in Christian mysticism or go on a mindfulness retreat. All of these are good things, to be sure. But what's interesting about them for our purposes is their inflection *back toward the natural order*. They all reflect the spin of immanence that goes unnoticed in our modern culture. "Soul," "spirit," "energy," and "self" are all rooted in the idea that there is a "thing" here, in the world, that moves and flows through life. It's not "out there" somewhere. It's invisible but it's *here*. It doesn't "come from beyond" and pierce into our experience. No, it is the source of experience. It's what binds all things together in the here-and-now. Meditation heightens our awareness of it. Indigenous people know it because of their closeness to the earth (a colonial caricature, I know, but one often expressed). Psychologists analyze the way it works itself out in our embodied psyches. And "Eastern religions"—those practices unadulterated by Western values—have a truer grasp of it. Yoga and mindfulness work because they're grounded in empirical evidence. There's *science* to back them up.

Paradoxically, then, "spiritual" is code word for "natural." It's part of the vocabulary of immanence. Take a look at another modern mantra: "Everything is made of energy." It seems incontrovertible, right? After all, physics says so, the laws of thermodynamics, and all that? *Of course* everything is made up of energy. The idea of "energy" falls well within the immanent frame, so it's a legitimate thing to "believe" in. "Energy" is a scientific-enough word to be empirically legitimized, but a vague enough word to preserve (some) of the mystery of the "more" we desire. It's perfect. You can chat with your friends about religion at a BBQ and say you believe in "energy" without being laughed at. You can use it to suggest something like a god without actually positing one. Belief in it keeps you safely within the immanent frame. The same is true of "higher power" talk. What is this "power"? And what about it is "higher"? When pressed, most of us end up appealing to some nebulous (but important) notion within us that there has to be more to it than this, even if the word "God" isn't quite right to describe it.

We just can't shake the idea that there's more, but we don't have the language for it within the immanent frame. Words like "spiritual" and "energy" and "higher power" resonate with us because they somehow operate within the approved lexicon of the natural order but still give voice to a human desire for transcendence. That's what it means to be cross-pressured. You feel it, don't you?

For those of us that do feel it (and I think that's most of us), there's another thing to note about the desire for transcendence viewed from within the immanent frame, something quite troubling: whatever the "more" or "beyond" is, it's fleeting. It doesn't last. And that in some important way calls into question how important it is that we pursue it. Sure, the Buddha or Zen monks in some remote mountain abbey might be able to discover transcendence thanks to a lifetime of dedicated contemplation. But for the rest of us mortals, the press of everyday life gets in the way. Everyday life makes achieving any sense of permanent or durable enlightenment impossible, and so the pursuit of it seems, well, futile. The best we can hope for is a flash of insight, a moment of Zen, but not the lasting bliss of wisdom that comes with *true* transcendence. Simply put: kids, jobs, pets, holidays, chores, errands, retirement accounts, etc., keep us from achieving whatever "transcendence" might mean. That's just the way it is. Going "beyond" might be nice for some people, but it just isn't available to everyone. We have to learn to settle for the disenchantment that comes with living "real" life.

But disenchanted life is unfulfilling. Beyond our being good to our families and maybe accumulating some retirement assets, we don't really know what it is *to flourish*. The thought of "flourishing" is a big confusing mess of ideas, social expectations, desires, and dreams that all seem to be competing with one another. There's no clear path to joy, to fulfillment. Most of us think that "human flourishing" is something like having your ducks in a row and having the time to do the things you want to do. That's it. Go on, think of a person you think is flourishing. What's she doing? She's probably got a good job with plenty of income and savings. She's fit, self-assured, and generally in a good mood. She may or may not be in a relationship (though she probably is), may or may not have kids (but probably does), and she has the time to pursue her interests: travel, yoga, arts and crafts, hiking, wine, etc. If flourishing means anything to us, it's something like that. But pay attention. Again, like the other modern mantras, we see here that "human flourishing" amounts to making the most of the here-and-now, creating your own meaning, finding your own happiness, living your best life, all within the natural order of things. If flourishing means anything to us, it means to arrange the pieces of life in such a way that it maximizes your happiness, eliminates obstacles to your desires, and allows you to live in the present moment. Flourishing is something we do within the immanent frame, as part of the sensible world.

So where does all of this leave us? In many ways, it leaves us pretty well off, actually. Life within the immanent frame isn't all that bad. Really, I mean it. There's a lot of beauty here, and beliefs in energy, spirit, soul, and a higher power are pretty innocuous. Nobody's killing anyone else over whether the energy is blue or green or flows up or down. No one's dying for "a higher power." But that's just it. The immanent spin on everything allows us to soften the more militant forms of life that have in the past led to a lot of bloodshed and misery, but they also water down our deep human drive for something more. On the one hand, it's been advantageous for humankind to explain everything in terms of matter because it's provided some common ground. We all have eyes to see. But on the other hand, it bowdlerizes the human press to acknowledge and seek out experiences that exceed immanence. Immanent spin pushes to the margins our desire for transcendence, a desire that can be life-giving and enchanting. Is there another way?

The Sublime: Romantic Aspirations and Awful Delight

The Romantics took seriously our desire for transcendence. They did not reduce it to science, or explain it away in terms of an underlying condition. They didn't refer to it as "energy" or a "higher power," or anything like that. They thought of it poetically. Some saw transcendence as the appearance of the "wholly other," a moment of something completely alien breaking into our mundane lives. Others suggested a more intimate connection between this world and the beyond, arguing that we can access the transcendent *through* the immanent, although ultimately transcendence exceeds it. I won't parse out all the finer distinctions here, but I will say that I think they are fascinating and important, especially for scholars and those of you who have an abiding interest in Romantic philosophy. If transcendence really gets your juices flowing then I recommend a deep dive into these ideas. But for now, I want to take a few turns around the block, so to speak. I want look at the constellation of ideas that we consider "Romantic transcendence" in order to enrich your understanding of what they were so excited about and show you how it can relate to your life. By developing a sensitivity to moments of transcendence, you can experience life's enchantment, even living within the immanent frame.

In the late eighteenth and early nineteenth century a new word came into vogue: *sublime*. Everything was "sublime." Those delicious macaroons? Sublime. Ms. Halloway's sparkling new dress? Sublime. That mesmerizing moon last night? You guessed it: sublime. The word "sublime" had lots of different meanings during this time period, but it always pointed to something exceptional, something special, or something exquisite. It wasn't until 1757 when the philosopher Edmund Burke published his treatise entitled *A Philosophical Enquiry into the Origin of Our Ideas of the Sublime and the Beautiful* that the idea really took shape as a Romantic and poetic concept.

In *On the Sublime and the Beautiful*, Burke wanted to sort out the difference between beauty and the sublime. Both deliver powerful experiences, but what is the nature of these experiences? How do they do what they do? According to Burke, the major difference between beauty and the sublime is that a beautiful thing is enjoyable to behold, it induces in us a feeling of pleasure and has a social element, whereas something sublime strikes us with awe and wonder—terror even—because of its sheer grandeur and vastness. A delicate flower may be beautiful, but a roaring waterfall is sublime. "Beauty," he writes, is "that quality or those qualities in bodies, by which they cause love, or some passion similar to it."[1] But of the sublime he writes, "Whatever is fitted in any sort to excite the ideas of pain, and danger, that is to say, whatever is in any sort terrible, or is conversant about terrible objects, or operates in a manner analogous to terror, is a source of the sublime; that is, it is productive of the strongest emotion which the mind is capable of feeling."[2]

---

1. Burke, *On the Sublime and Beautiful*, 74.
2. Burke, *On the Sublime and Beautiful*, 35.

The sublime is a more powerful feeling than beauty. It's "the strongest emotion" we can experience. It's the experience you have when you stand on the north rim of the Grand Canyon and feel the dizzying disorientation that comes with being brave (or foolhardy?) enough to gaze across its immeasurable expanse. It's the wild sense of helplessness you feel when you're out on a boat in the middle of the ocean and you realize it could overtake you in an instant. It's the rush of fear and annihilation that shudders through you when you're on a safari and witness a lion unleash its fury on a fleeing gazelle. It's the moment of brilliant moonlight that breaks out of the clouds during your autumn camping trip, tossing its ghostly pallor over all the woods and reminding you there is but a hair's breadth between your being, and nothingness. That's the sublime, and that's what many Romantics thought could open us up to transcendence.

But the sublime and transcendence are not the same thing. This is an important point. As we'll see below, for the Romantics the sublime is an experience that can open us onto transcendence but the two terms are not equivalent. We're getting ahead of ourselves though. What's important for now is to notice something else Burke said about the sublime: you actually *like* it. It's a bit paradoxical. Notice how in none of my examples is your life *really* at stake. You're standing on the rim, not falling off of it. You're in a boat, not drowning. You're in a jeep, not being chased by the lion. You're camping—presumably with all your food and gear—not lost in the woods alone. This is precisely Burke's point: we can experience the sublime *because* we know that we are not truly vulnerable to the threat that we witness, and the terror it invokes. This safety-under-threat structure of the sublime allows us to actually take *delight* in the sublime, to bask in nature's inimitable and infinite boundlessness. The power of the lion, the pull of the canyon, and the pulse of the ocean call our existence into question without crushing us. We are able to stand in the face of the incalculable force of nature and experience its infinite strength without the fear of it consuming us. So, the sublime is a curious mix of power, terror, and obscurity, but a mix that gives us delight, albeit an awe-ful delight.

Romantics like William Wordsworth, Percy Bysshe Shelley, and William Blake took Burke's idea of the sublime and ran with it, poetically speaking. In their hands, the sublime became an opening onto transcendence, a way to awaken us from the monotony of a middling life and to help us snap out of our existential malaise. Through the paradox of *terror + distance + delight* the sublime reveals to us not only the fearsome fact of nature's power, but also the way our human minds respond to it with a sort of charged or heightened attention. This sharp awareness then draws us beyond the sublime proper into a way of being-in-the-world that is marked by a poetic engagement with it, one that is alive with the questions of "Who am I?" and "What is my place here?" and "What is my relationship to the world around me?" Bringing these questions to the forefront of one's life transforms it from a daily routine to something that aspires toward more and more creative interaction with life itself. In other words, the sublime can transform us, opening onto a form of life that is enchanting because it is charged with a sense of existential immediacy, and a yearning for more.

Now, the modern reader may hear all of this and think, "Oh, yeah! The Romantics we're really into just living in the moment! I'm into that too." But that's not quite right. Experiencing the sublime is not about living in the moment. It's about a confrontation within the moment. It's about *drawing from the moment* and paying attention to the way we as human people react to the grandeur of existence. We respond to it with an openness and awe, a kind of respect and creative celebration of the majesty of Being, which is accompanied by the lure of "something more," something beyond even being itself. Admittedly, not all the Romantics had a clear view of what this "something more" could be. Most of the more poetic-types never bothered to develop a full, metaphysical account of what the transcendent "is" (although, some did. E.g., Schleiermacher and Schiller).

Part of the reason for this vagueness is that the pull of transcendence is as much *felt* as it is conceptualized, and so poetic language might be a better fit for expressing it. The transcendent can be invoked *but not fully articulated*. It's a lived experience, part and parcel of being human. Nevertheless, some Romantic philosophers did try to explain it, and used words like God, Nature, Being, the One, and the Absolute to try and get at it as an idea. But parsing out all of these distinctions is beyond the scope of our inquiry. What's key for our purposes is that the Romantics did not assume life (in all its fullness) ends with life (as a biological process). They didn't give everything an immanent spin. They insisted there is more to life than what we can measure, know, and account for through the sciences. And the sublime puts us right in the middle of that "more" through its radical lesson of human insignificance. The experience of the sublime calls our existence into question in the deepest of ways, and in doing so, it provokes questions of transcendence. Sublime encounters force us to ask, "What is out there?" "Why is there something rather than nothing?" "What lies beyond human experience?" "How ought I relate to whatever that 'thing' is?" The sublime both humbles us and encourages us. It says, "You're nothing, accept it" and "There is more, seek it." The sublime kindles in us a desire for the transcendent.

From the Sublime to the Transcendent: Moody Monks and Magical Moons in the Paintings of David Caspar Friedrich

Most of the examples of the sublime I've provided so far are rooted in ex-periences of the natural world: cascading waterfalls, splashing moonlight, dizzying cliffs, pulsating ocean waves, and so on. Nature, for the Romantics, was a rich source for poetic and philosophical discovery. The Romantics spent a lot of time outside, literally in the wild, seeking out the sublime. Shelley was known for his rambles through the English, Italian, and Swiss countrysides. Wordsworth hiked Mt. Snowden in remote Wales. Coleridge wandered the isolated woods of the English Lake District. The German Ro-mantics were no different. Goethe, Herder, and Novalis loved the outside world, and in Novalis's case the subterranean world too. But they didn't *just* experience the sublime on a weekend jaunt. And they weren't adrenaline junkies, hitting the slopes for a rush of excitement and an *après ski* to cele-brate it. No, once these Romantics encountered the sublime, they pondered it, they stewed on it, they contemplated it, they called it to mind later "when in a pensive mood." And they tried to *create* it.

As we've said all along, you don't have to go outside to experience en-chantment. The same is true for encountering the sublime. As odd as it may sound, you can experience it in the comfort of your living room, although it *will* make you uncomfortable (which is kind of the point, after all). But how can that be? How can you experience the rush, the thrill, and the terror of a swelling sea while cozied up in a blanket, sipping a cup of tea?

The answer is this: according to the Romantics, *art itself can induce the sublime*. With enough command, the artist can produce in the viewer (or listener or reader) through the work of art the actual feeling of the sublime, the terrible delight that comes with confronting the vastness of Nature's power that opens us to transcendence. That's one of the most wonderful things about these Romantic artists. They worked tirelessly to bring en-chantment *to* us, to put it in front of our faces, and to heighten our attention to it in our everyday lives. The wonder of a sublime painting is that it can strike you with all the intensity of a thunderclap, and (thanks to the inter-net) you can view it from your own couch (although I will admit I think going to see the original is better). A sublime painting or poem can move you like the churning truth of an ocean wave. In a spellbinding poetic com-position, the Romantic poet William Blake used "mere words" to invoke the awe-inspiring power of a prowling tiger. Shelley created in his poem "Mont Blanc" a sublime experience of a remote Alpine landscape, where "Power" is "bursting through these dark mountains like the flame / Of lightning through the tempest" and where "[t]he race / Of man flies far in dread; his work and dwelling / Vanish, like smoke before the tempest's stream[.]"[3] All of this done with just words, and the words are in a book you can read from anywhere. There's magic in that.

Romanticism is replete with great artists who were able to create experiences of the sublime for the viewer, reader, or listener. I'd like to look at one painter in particular, David Caspar Friedrich, who in my mind provides the best example of how Romantic artists were able to create sublimity through their art, and how in doing so heighten our attention to the pull that there is "something more," something transcendent.

David Caspar Friedrich was of a melancholic sort. We know from his letters and writings and the opinions of his friends that he was a loner, and he spent a lot of time contemplating death and its potential meaninglessness. Not exactly the guy you go to for an existential pep talk. This seems natural enough given that from a young age little David experienced a lot of loss: his mother died when he was seven, his sister died the following year, he watched his younger brother drown while trying to save him after falling into a frozen lake, and his sister Maria died only a few years after that of typhus. That's enough death to leave even the most resilient person a little rattled.

Friedrich's preoccupation with death seems completely normal. He was religious too, and most of his landscape paintings set up a tension between life and death, darkness and light, dying and rebirth, and the vastness of existence and the finitude of human life. Despite all of the tragedy he experienced, it's important not to overly psychologize his artwork and reduce it to "a man wrestling with his childhood trauma." While that's certainly part of the story, his masterpieces offer more than that. Friedrich was a genius landscape painter. His works are striking, captivating, and disorienting. They invoke a grand sense of awe, and they direct our attention to the puniness of human existence. Most of us know him from his famous painting, *The Wanderer Above the Sea of Fog*, which depicts a contemplative nineteenth-century hiker with his back to us looking out over a mountain range drenched in clouds and hazy gloom. It's a nice painting, but its ubiquity in contemporary culture has dulled our senses to it a little bit, softening its ability to deal us a sublime blow. Other, less well-known paintings by Friedrich demonstrate just how well art can deliver a sublime encounter and call us out of our middling lives.

Let's look at two of them: *Monk by the Sea* and *Abbey in the Oakwood*.

---

3. Shelley, "Mont Blanc," 1104, 1107.

The Sublime and the Awful Power of the Sea

These two paintings are astounding. Friedrich was in his thirties when he painted them. Unlike many of his other works, they were not commissioned by a rich patron or wealthy art connoisseur. They were labors of love, internally motivated expressions of his deep desire to explore the drama of human life, and the sublime. They were painted together, over the course of a couple of years, from 1808 to 1810, and are meant to be viewed together. They are self-portraits. They're not like your normal portraiture, of course. Friedrich is only present in one of them. Nevertheless, they are self-portraits and can be read "chronologically," beginning first with the contemplative life depicted in *Monk by the Sea* and then with the funeral scene in *Abbey in the Oakwood*. Both offer sublime encounters, and both open us onto transcendence.

Caspar David Friedrich, *Monk by the Sea*, c. 1809, oil on canvas. PD-Art

Monk by the Sea is simply breathtaking. It's sublime, actually. When you first encounter it, *Monk* shocks you with its composition, which seems to swallow you up. By far, the vast majority of the canvas is covered in a stark, blue-grey sky. The clouds seem to slowly shift you from left to right as they move timelessly across the painting. Your eyes then move down the painting, through the corpse-like blue to the abyssal blue-black sea at the bottom of the image. The menacing waves are not monstrous though. They're subtle, small waves. They barely break a white crest. Their threat seems almost cannibalistic as they slowly well and swallow whatever enters them, churning up their own offspring, the creatures that lurk beneath. As your gaze moves downward you notice a figure at the bottom of the painting. There is a beach too, but not a warm and inviting beach. This is no summer frolic by the sea. It's winter here, an unnamed northern beach, a cold and uninviting wasteland. Flecks of snow settle in the sand. A handful of sea gulls float on the icy wind above the tiny figure who's turned away from us, his curved back in a posture of contemplation, a soft question mark on the precipice, pondering the boundless and terrible blue. That's Friedrich. He was infatuated with monks, medieval life, and religious contemplation. In this painting, he shows us his true colors: dark, somber, alone, chilling, and reflective. The image is completely uncompromising in its insistence that we look into the immeasurable power of Nature and see our insignificance, that we shudder at the sheer fact of Being.

Take a moment to just look at the painting. Stop reading and just look at it. Let it work on you. There's no rush. No matter what I write about it I can never do justice to what it does of its own accord. When you're finished looking at it, consider a few more things about Friedrich's treatment of the sublime in this painting, and what he might be telling us about transcendence. First, notice how he uses visual *obscurity* to show us how things in the painting are revealed and concealed. This is a classic technique in Romantic depictions of the sublime, and it's enchanting because it draws our attention and demands we consider things deeper than mere appearances. The monk is hard to see. His torso almost completely blends into the sea. But his legs are a stark contrast to the frozen sand, pronouncing his presence in the scene, feeble though it is. His shaved head is a dot against the infinite ocean, but a dot nonetheless. The little flecks of snow on the beach and the barely-cresting waves all suggest a deep abiding power moving throughout Nature, one that seems all the more powerful *because we cannot see its completely.*

Notice also the fact that, as terrible as the sky and the sea are in this painting, as sure as we are that the icy ocean could dash the monk (or us) against the rocks like so many ships or whales, we are *safe.* The monk is on the shore. We are outside the frame. Remember that the sublime arrives when we face the terror of the inimitable power of Nature without actually being vulnerable to it. This gives the sublime its signature characteristic: terror and delight wrapped up together. We are in reality unthreatened by Nature's menacing threat but we *feel* as if we are threatened, and we face it in all its fullness. Like the monk, when we look at this painting we stand on the precipice of nothingness without falling into it. We feel its pull without being pulled into obliteration. Friedrich originally painted this scene with a small ship on the horizon, but he later painted over it. The human fantasy of mastery over the seas which the ship symbolized has no place amidst the awe-fulness of the sublime (unless, of course, the ship is shown at Nature's mercy, or being pulverized by it.)[4]

Life, Death, and the Moon In-Between

Caspar David Friedrich, *Abbey in the Oakwood*, 1809 or 1810, oil on canvas. PD-Art

Abbey in the Oakwood is as thrilling to view as *Monk by the Sea*. In shares a similar composition: the canvas is dominated by a tri-colored sky moving this time from a brown-black to grey and then back to black. Here there is no sea, only the ruins of an old medieval abbey and the skeletal silhouettes of oak trees stretching beyond the abbey's ancient heights. As in *Monk by the Sea*, there are small figures at the base of the painting. A silent strand of monks march through the snow and into the abbey ruins. They are carrying a coffin. Inside the coffin is the body of the monk from *Monk by the Sea*. Remember: that's Friedrich. This is a self-portrait. The monks and the coffin and the cross that is their destination are barely discernible against the blackening snow and horizon. Obscurity and shadows shade all forms.

In the foreground lies an open grave. It's almost imperceptible, but once you notice it, you realize that it is like a corpse's jaw agape, mortality yawning wide. You can't unsee it. The monk's death suggests your own, something always close at hand yet also distant, concealed. Disregarded and crumbling tombstones protrude from the frozen earth, and only the slightest sliver of a waxing moon crests over this awful scene. What a terrible

4. For a taste of this, see Friedrich's *The Sea of Ice* (1824).

deathscape to contemplate. Terrible indeed, and yet, it is not our own death that the painting depicts, it is Friedrich's. We sense the finitude expressed in the painting—a finitude that will one day be ours—but somehow the image holds our own death in abeyance. *Abbey* provides a space where we can face mortality, feel its awful press, confront its inevitability, but not give ourselves over to it. The effect of the painting is simply sublime.

There's one more thing to notice about *Abbey in the Oakwood*, something that is only obliquely present in *Monk by the Sea*. In *Abbey*, Friedrich gestures toward transcendence. At first glance, we see only immanence. The monks' single file line and cold march through the snow give us a sense of time—linear time, clock time. We move through life putting one step in front of the other. The season too (it's winter) suggests the past is dying. We're moving on. The gravestones are in disrepair. Time takes its toll. The gloom, melancholy, and sadness of the painting remind us that things are and will always come to an end.

But then the painting makes an interesting move; or better, it moves us. We look up. Our eyes travel vertically, between the great oak trees, and we trace the delicate arch of the cathedral ruin. We notice the contours of a faint moon, slightly suggesting that there may be something else, something other than the march of time and the desolation of winter. For an instant, we're invited to consider that there may be more to life than simply living through it. The glow of the sky seems to pulse a bit, surging from some unseen source. Our eyes move down again, returning to the monks, and we see them from a slightly different angle. Then it dawns on us: they're about to celebrate a mass—a funeral mass to be sure, which is indeed a somber event—but a mass that plays out, in ritualized form, the drama of life and death, sacrifice and offering, and most importantly, the sacred moment of *kairos*, the moment of time-out-of-time, of transcendence. The ruins and the oak trees frame a sacred space. They are a way out. In fact, they are quite literally a portal, a door, a threshold to . . . where? The painting doesn't say. It only suggests. The answer remains obscure. Like the monk in *Monk by the Sea*, we stand in the sublime and wonder: *is there anything more?* This is the call of transcendence. The abbey and the oakwood are where we hear the call of the beyond. Look inside yourself and do you not see something analogous to these trees and this church? Do you not sense some obscure opening, small and well-hidden, pressing you to ask the question, *is there something more?*

I could go on and on about these two paintings. They really are a marvel. But I hope the point has been made that the sublime is enchanting because it compels us to experience the world in a way that is charged with an existential intensity and awareness, an experience that is truly extra-ordinary.

The enchantment arrives when we see there is another way to feel alive rather than the mundane, immanent way we normally plod through life. The sublime also has the possibility of opening us onto transcendence, or at least raising the question of transcendence with an immediacy that is uncommon in the day-to-day grind. This too is enchanting because it calls us to a heightened sensitivity to the magic of Being, and offers the possibility of an experience of life that may even go even *beyond* Being.

As we saw with other enchantment strategies, the sublime is not reducible to a simple psychological state or mechanistic explanation. It is an experience "at the margins" of science, and for that reason it has the potential to imbue our lives with a significance we simply cannot achieve when we see everything in terms of immanence. It's not so much that science fails to account for the sublime, but that it cannot give a *full* amount of it. That's not a critique of science. Science is not worse off because it cannot fully explain the significance of the sublime. It's just that science isn't concerned with the sorts of questions the sublime raises, questions the monk by the sea is asking: "Why is there something rather than nothing?" "What am I to do in the face of my own insignificance?" "How do I relate to the great swell of Nature that surrounds me?" "What is this pull for something more that I simply cannot shake?" These are *philosophical* questions. They are *existential* questions. They are *Romantic* questions.

Let me make one last point about the Romantic idea of transcendence before moving on to the enchantment strategy. As I mentioned before, the Romantic idea of transcendence is a bit nebulous. Many philosophers struggle to clearly explain what they mean by "transcendence." Some philosophers use the term to refer to the supernatural; that is, God-the-Big-Wizard or ghosts or some other being or world beyond this one. Others use it to describe a spiritual state of enlightenment, as in "I've transcended to another way of existing," or something like that. Still others use it in the sense of human transformation or re-orientation. That's how Charles Taylor uses the term, for example. For Taylor, "transcendence" means going beyond the self, aspiring to a higher ideal, in such a way that it reconfigures your own sense of being-in-the-world. It's a way of achieving human fullness by reaching beyond the goal of human flourishing, by striving for something more than material life, and then returning to material life, only this time with a new moral and existential orientation. It's not too much to say that, for Taylor, the transformation that accompanies transcendence leaves us with a new identity, a new way to engage life, not deny it. For him, this new way is the way of love. But you don't have to agree with Taylor's version of transcendence in order to appreciate the pull of "something more," or the sense that your mundane life isn't the whole story. It isn't. As we've seen here and throughout other parts of the book, existence is charged with meaning, beauty, truth, and wisdom, things beyond what we can see, taste, touch, and smell. It's a wonder we're here. Truly, a wonder.[5]

Enchantment Strategy #5: Encounter Something Sublime

Let's recap. To encounter the sublime is to open onto transcendence. The sublime induces within us an affective experience of the power of Nature, a weird but productive mix of fear and joy, terror and ecstasy. When we face the vastness of Being full-on, we are shocked into admitting our own insignificance. The ferocious power present in the tiger as she prowls the jungle floor forces us to face up to the fact that despite our feeling that *our* life matters, in some important ways, *it doesn't.* There is a truth to the fact that you and I are nothing. But that's not nihilism. Life still matters to the Romantics. In encountering the sublime, we come to understand that the revelation of our own insignificance imbues life with an existential force, it invites us to look up and wonder: *is there something more?* The sublime affirms the value of this question. It says, "Ask it, and keep asking. There is magic in it." The question itself enchants.

For some the fact that the answer to this question will never fully arrive is a source of great frustration. Like Friedrich's moon, we will only ever see a sliver of it. Unsatisfying though this may be, the *desire* is the point. It makes us into "love dogs," as the poet Rumi calls us: creatures yearning for union with the One who sustains our life. This yearning, this howling is the secret cup. The desire for transcendence is part-and-parcel of what it means to be human, and it is a condition for the possibility of an enchanted world. Rather than trying to explain the desire for transcendence away in terms of a "mere" psychological state, the Romantics prod us to live with it, and to be nourished by it. The desire for transcendence compels us to be poetic. It is sacred. It is our participation in the truth of Being, carried out in an eternal act of co-creation with existence: Being and the human person

---

5. We've looked primarily at Romantic paintings for examples of the sublime. Romantic literature is full of great examples too. If you're interested in exploring more of this stuff, try Shelley's "Mont Blanc," William Blake's, "The Tyger," or (for a longer read), William Wordsworth's *Prelude.* Coleridge's "Kubla Kahn" is the sublime for a psychedelic reader, while the arctic scenes in the final chapters of Mary Shelley's *Frankenstein* are sublimity for the somber-minded. Even Keats gets in on the action if you're in to time as a source of the sublime, see "On Seeing the Elgin Marbles." Honestly, you can't go wrong with any of them.

striving to become, to manifest, and in the process making truth as much as discovering it.

Step 1: Get Uncomfortable

When it comes to the sublime, remember what Edmund Burke said: you have to get uncomfortable. You have to seek out places and experiences that jar you, that terrify you even, in order to encounter the raw power of Being, and your place in it. But remember also that the sublime is not about adrenaline. You have to put yourself on the *edge* of danger, but not actually *in* danger. Why? Because in order to experience the sublime you also have to experience delight, which means you are safe, you are free from the actual threat of harm and can experience the deeper, existential threat the sublime invokes: the dread of your own insignificance in the grand scheme of things. It's strange, I know, but that's key to the whole thing. The sublime is not about taking a risk and getting juiced with excitement. It's *not* the feeling you get when you go skiing in the Rocky Mountains and bomb down the mountain at what feels like a hundred miles an hour. It's the feeling you get when you hike up them and after turning a wooded corner the trail opens onto a vast mountain vale full of windswept snow blasting you in the face, declaring its indominable force and indifference to your own life. The sublime is not about "the rush" or "only living once." It's about the terrible delight that comes with realizing your own finitude, which in a paradoxical way also heightens your love of it.

So when I say find a powerful place and get uncomfortable, I'm not saying run with the bulls, or wrestle a tiger, or bungee jump. Those activities are fine if you're into them but they do not invoke the sublime. To experience the sublime, you need to encounter the sheer fact of Being, the overwhelming power of Nature. You need to find a remote seashore somewhere and gaze into the infinite swell of the ocean. If you're lucky enough to actually see a tiger, stay in the car, but then consider its unbridled power. Notice how every creature in the jungle bows to its strength and grace, how its muscles ripple with unrestrained dominance. Find a place where you are safe but on the edge of safety: not the literal edge, the *existential* edge. Find a place where you feel the terror of being overwhelmed by Nature's force without actually being vulnerable to it. Be careful. Remember that putting your life at risk actually undermines sublimity, it does not enhance it. You don't need to tip toe to the edge of a waterfall to experience its intoxicating pull. Stand at the base and look up. Let its boundlessness thunder in front of you. That, not actual danger, is the key to experiencing the sublime.

Let me give you an example. William Wordsworth wrote about a time when he took a night hike up Mt. Snowdon and was struck by the sublime mix of fog and moonlight and ocean and rivers and mountainside. With a local shepherd as their guide, William and his friend got up at midnight and hiked the mountain. Their plan was to catch the sunrise from the summit. Mt. Snowdon's not far from the Welsh coast. You can see the ocean and the mountains as you climb. It's quite stunning, actually. This was a "[s] summer's night, a close, warm, night" and the mountains were covered in a "dripping mist / Low-hung and thick that covered all the sky[.]"[6] The small band soon fell into the mesmerizing trudge of a hike. William, ever-pensive, was lost in "commerce with his private thoughts."[7] All three marched along, "forehead[s] bent / Earthward," when all of a sudden the fog opened up and "a light upon the turf / Fell like a flash" and

> The moon stood naked in the Heavens, at height
> Immense above my head, and on the shore
> I found myself of a huge sea of mist,
> Which, meek and mild, rested at my feet.
> A hundred hills their dusky backs upheaved
> All over this still Ocean, and beyond,
> Far, far beyond, the vapours shot themselves
> In headlands, tongues, and promontory shapes,
> Into the Sea, the real Sea, that seemed
> To dwindle and give up its majesty[.][8]

Wordsworth goes on, but you get the point: there, amidst the domineering mountains, the eternal night sky, the haunting hoary frost, and in "the clear presence of the full-orbed moon" William encountered the sublime. He experienced the raw and incalculable majesty of Nature without putting himself in any serious risk. But he was uncomfortable, both in terms of his literal discomfort (hiking up a mountain at midnight through the fog) and his existential discomfort (the feeling of terror that comes with being exposed to Nature's unbridled force). However, because his life was not in peril Wordsworth was able to feel both delight and terror, discomfort and awe, all at the same time. In fact, it was such a powerful moment that he when he got back to his cottage he penned this section of *The Prelude*, which is a powerful poetic re-creation of his experience of the sublime that summer's night. And in one, final stroke of generosity Wordsworth through the strength of his poetry is able not only to represent that moment to us,

6. Wordsworth, *The Major Works*, 579.

7. Wordsworth, *The Major Works*, 579.

8. Wordsworth, *The Major Works*, 579.

but to *put us in it*. Read with the proper level of attention and imaginative engagement, we too can experience the sublime of the moon and mist on a hike up Mt. Snowdon, and our soul can "feed[] upon infinity."[9]

Step 2: Wait, Marvel, and Contemplate

The sublime offers at least two moments for serious and enchanting contemplation, two moments to marvel and consider the magnitude of Being. The first arrives when you're *in* the sublime, when it's happening to you. Think of the monk in *Monk by the Sea*. He's there, standing on the precipice of the seashore, looking out onto the ever-undulating ocean. What's he thinking about? What images cross his mind? We don't know for sure, but the sky and the sea and the clouds give us a pretty good clue. Perhaps he is considering what Herman Melville calls in *Moby-Dick* "the ungraspable phantom of life," that effervescent thing we think amounts to a meaningful existence but that shimmers only for a moment before breaking apart into nothing.[10] Perhaps he is pondering his own mortality, his own cosmological paltriness in the face of the ocean's vast indifference to all forms of life, whether within it or without it. Perhaps he is marveling at the merciless power of the ocean, "[p]anting and snorting like a mad battle steed that has lost its rider."[11] All of this and more, perhaps. Perhaps unsayable things, things that can only be felt in our bones and that shudder through us whenever we face the eternal darkness.

The point is that the monk *is marveling*, that he is *contemplating*. He's taking a moment to stand before the abyss and to consider it, deeply. He's not just passing by on his way to the nearest beach rental to grab a towel and a cocktail. He's not lounging at a resort half aware of the waves as he surfs his phone. He's alone. He's reflective. He's attentive. He purposeful. He sought out the sublime and decided to stand in it. You must do that too. To understand how the sublime enchants, you cannot simply experience it and then move on. It's not something you take a picture of and post on Instagram. You must give it your full attention. You must face it, marvel at it, and then *contemplate* it. The magic happens in the contemplation. You'll notice your thoughts move from straight-forward respect for the ocean's power (or whatever sublime source you're staring at), to awe, to fear, to a sense of fragility, and then, oddly, to appreciation, joy, and reverence. Slow down and let your mind and your body move through these reactions. Notice

9. Wordsworth, *The Major Works*, 580.
10. Melville, *Moby-Dick*, 3.
11. Melville, *Moby-Dick*, 307.

what emerges. Notice how now, after staring into the abyss, you see your friends and lovers with new eyes. Their insignificance to the cosmos renders their significance to you unfathomable. The world around you becomes charged with meaning. The sun shines brighter on your skin, the bird's song is sweeter. Your life takes on an immediacy and a beauty that was not there before. This is the wisdom of the ocean, the truth of the sublime.

Just to be clear, I'm not saying there's anything wrong with having fun at the beach, and that when you go you should automatically turn into a brooding Byronic misanthrope. Don't ruin everyone's vacation. What I am saying is that there is another side to the beach, there is another side to these experiences we have of Nature that call our attention to its plenitude and power. Taking a moment to stand before the sublime and letting it wash over you can call you to higher thoughts, a heightened sense of being, and a moment of enchantment. There is a certain bravery in that, a certain courage that comes with the curious soul's willingness to find the time to consider her life in the grand scheme of things, to stand on the precipice, so to speak. Once you're okay with being uncomfortable, seek out the sublime. Go and stand in it. Put your body in it. Be immersed by it. And don't rush. The experience will be powerful, I promise. The sublime may treat you like a stern teacher, or a crazed god. Be ready for either. It's hard to predict which it will be. Wordsworth's moonlight was more of a strike than a soft caress. Shelley's Mont Blanc rattled him to the core. The sea in *Moby-Dick* is for Ishmael both the cure and the cause of his melancholy. The great jungle cat in William Blake's "The Tyger" terrifies with its ferocity, calling even God's goodness into question ("Did he who made the Lamb make thee?"). The sublime is rarely gentle, but it always speaks truth.

Step 3: Lean to Live with the Question

Remember the moon in *Abbey in the Oakwood*? It's the only sliver of hope in the entire picture (well that, and maybe the Eucharist, but it remains unperformed). What are we to make of this moon? One way to read it is as a symbol for transcendence. To transcend literally means to *go beyond*, or to *go above*. The moon literally floats above the mundane, immanent life of the monks: the life of time, death, decay, and desuetude. It signals toward something more. But then we notice in the painting some other gestures toward transcendence. The abbey ruins are indeed ruined, but they somehow still draw us up, our eyes following their vertical lines into the ambivalent sky above. The oak trees creep up the image and lose us at the edge of their thorny fingertips. We can almost feel them ever so slightly releasing us into the night sky. What is Friedrich getting at with this curious intermingling of church and woods? Are they the same thing? Do they both direct us to the Absolute, one through human efforts and the other through Nature's? Or are they opposed, the oak branches taking us higher than human artifacts can achieve? Or do they work in tandem, mutually reinforcing each other's ability to fuel our human desire for more? It's hard to say. Like transcendence itself, the message remains obscure.

But one thing is certain: the moon calls us beyond the surface life. It beckons for a life enchanted. The sense of beyond the moon invokes is coupled with a sense of sanctity and sacredness. Transcendence is special. It's extra-ordinary. One way the painting accomplishes this sense is by juxtaposing the moon with the open grave and the coffin. There is a corpse in this image, as we saw, it is Friedrich's. There is an inherent power in a dead body. Go to a wake with an open casket and tell me you don't feel the room is heavy with a haunted weight. A dead body sanctifies the space around it. So to in this painting. The monk's corpse sanctifies the abbey and the oakwood, and the glow of the moon softly illuminates this sanctity and calls us to ask of mortality: *is there something more?*

In order for this question to enchant you, must be open to it. Don't skip over it. Too often in our modern world we want to spin the question of transcendence in terms of immanence and then dismiss or disregard it. When we feel the pull of transcendence, we follow it up by muttering to ourselves something like, "That's silly. Of course, there's nothing more. You're just afraid of death/boredom/meaninglessness, etc. Don't be a child." The desire for transcendence isn't just your immaturity flaring up, or your juvenile fear of death. It's more complicated than that. Charles Taylor argues that the desire for transcendence is part of what it means to be human. It's built into the very fabric of our being: we aspire, desire, we yearn. That's what we do. We deny something of ourselves when we deny this fact of our being, when we try and tamp down or psychologize our longing as simply death-denial or childishness. Our call to transcendence is a call to envision a life rich with meaning, one in which we are fulfilled and flourish, one that allows us to aspire to greater heights without denying the beauty of an embodied existence. In fact, you might think of transcendence as another word for enchantment. To experience a life enchanted is to go beyond a life of plodding time. It is to experience the moon as a moment of time-out-of time, rather than as an obscure light illuminating the slow march of clock time, a row of monks trudging through the snow. As we've said before, human beings are the kinds of beings for whom meaning is a question, and that question imbues life with a significance that is not reducible to psychological states or biological impulses. To experience the enchantment that comes from encountering the sublime you must remain open to the question of transcendence and not chide yourself for asking it. Don't dismiss it. Don't explain it away. Lean to live with it.

Where does living with the question leave you? Well, if you're able to resist the double temptation of either (a) answering the question (yes there is more, no there isn't) or (b) dismissing it (the question is silly in the first place), then you learn to live in the light of the moon. You learn to embrace that part of you that aspires. You affirm the question, you don't deny it. And in affirming it you allow yourself to experience the joy it brings with it, which can also be felt as sorrow. The joy comes when you experience the truth that life is, indeed, beautiful, and that there may be more than that even. The sorrow comes with the unsettling fact that you may never satisfy your aspirations, you may never reach the moon. But in allowing the question to resonate within you, you begin to experience life-as-depth. Life becomes dimensional rather than flat because there is always an opening onto more.

There's one, last, curious thing that happens when you learn to live in the cross-pressure of the question, something that only now, at the very end of this book, I am bold enough to say. Being open to transcendence means you open yourself to God. Not "God" in the popular sense, not "God" in the "Big Wizard" sense, but "God" in the sense of an experience that shatters our everyday form of life, that saturates our capacity to even have experiences in the first place, that calls into question the very limits of human knowledge, achievement, and comprehension.[12]

Now, I know what you may be thinking: "Mmhmm. Here it is. Here's the part where he smuggles in religion (Christianity in particular) and tries to convert me. I'm out." But that's not it at all. That's not even remotely close to my point. I'm not making a metaphysical claim about the grand order of things or advancing the idea that this all comes down to the presence of a Great Being. Quite the opposite, actually. What I mean by "God" here is God *after* God, or God *beyond* God; that is, the renewed sense of God-as-the-pull-of-transcendence rather than the (idolatrous) concept of God-as-Alpha-Being, or God-as-Great-Magician, or whatever. The word "God"

---

12. It's worth mentioning that subtle and sophisticated views of God—which have shunned the popular, naive Big Wizard view—are nothing new. Reflective practitioners across time, and from diverse religious traditions, East and West, have often rejected such ideas. For example, medieval theologians were not, by and large, a bunch of uneducated, superstitious dogmatists (despite this modern caricature of them). They were sophisticated thinkers, and they developed penetrating insights about the nature of God, and humanity. One could argue their theologies were more nuanced than our contemporary religious discourses tend to be. In any event, the point here is that thinking beyond God-as-Big-Wizard is a perennial philosophical activity, and the Romantics can help us reconnect with it.

can mean many things. For a lot of people, the word "God" basically means Being; that is, the Ground of all that is, the Source from which all things flow, the Thing that makes all things. But when you think of God as *a* Being among other beings (albeit a super-being), things starts to get complicated. Is God really a *thing* (even if "He's" the greatest thing?) If so, what's "behind" God-as-thing? What sustains God's existence? Or is God somehow beyond all things, even "thingness" itself? Like I said, it gets complicated.

Thankfully, we don't have to answer all of these questions in order for me to make my point about God and the sublime. On the whole, most of us can agree that the image of God painted on the Sistine Chapel ceiling—God-as-Big-Wizard—is *a visual metaphor* for God seen through human eyes. It's not meant to be a literal image of God. No one thinks God is a sixteenth-century Italian man dressed in pink flowing robes with a big white beard. Sure, we might use that metaphor to make a point one way or another about how we experience the Divine, but *we don't literally mean it,* and if we do, I think we're missing the point of art.

So what do we mean? Well, I think at least in part that by "God" we mean something like the call of the mystery of existence which compels us to a sacred life, that makes us yearn for a relationship with each other and the Other, and that beckons us like a horizon toward a mode of being that goes beyond the animalistic, anthropocentric, and adversarial world in which we most often find ourselves. "God" means *more*, it means the Other, excess, love, and gift. God is the innate human longing for friendship, the hope for human fulfillment, the call to overcome ourselves, and to return to life changed by having done so. God is the weeping widow, the child's smile, and the lovers' embrace. God is the snowfall and the summer dew. God is the hallowed yes that whispers to us in our darkest hour. You see my point now: the transcendence we encounter in the sublime opens us onto God, but it also shatters our old view of God. The sublime can take us *beyond* "God," to a rich and invitational sense of God that resists reduction and conceptual confinement. This God appears only after we have let go of God-the-Big-Wizard and allowed ourselves to live with the question, to embrace the mystery and drama of human aspiration, and to respond to the call of the divine.

Step 4: Return to Life Anew

At first glance, the real punch of the sublime seems to come when we open ourselves to transcendence and truly embrace the question of "something more." That's true, but there is another moment that is just as important for living the enchanted life that comes *after* this punch: the moment we go back to our middling lives, *changed* by it.

Once you experience the sublime—and perhaps the transcendent—your life feels different. Your day-to-day routine takes on a heightened sense of meaning. The world appears with a powerful immediacy and profound beauty that you didn't see before. It's a subtle shift though, not an earth-shattering one. It's not like one day you encounter the sublime and the next day your life suddenly has purpose, every day is a sunny day. As the Buddhist saying goes, "Before enlightenment, chop wood and carry water. After enlightenment, chop wood and carry water." Although Buddhist enlightenment and Romantic sublimity are not the same thing, there is an interesting parallel in the way Buddhists and Romantics talk about the effects of enlightenment and enchantment. In both cases, your everyday experience of life alters, and yet somehow, it doesn't alter. You "come back to life" a different person, but the change is more in the way you receive the world than in the way it appears to you. For Buddhists, experience of the world changes insofar as the enlightened person now experiences it directly, unfiltered, and absent suffering. Wood is still wood, and water is still water, but the Buddhist experiences them fully, in the truth of the present moment. For Romantics, everyday experience changes insofar as the enchanted person now experiences a world drenched in poetic meaning, where each breath contains the mystery of Being, and each moment is full of symbolism, love, and truth. That's the kind of change the sublime can usher in.

Practically speaking, after you experience the sublime, keep its lessons close by. Let its affects sink into you, let them become a part of the way you move about the world. The experience of plenitude and radical presence has a curious way of re-orienting you by disorienting you. Be reminded of the possibility of the sublime even when you're not facing it directly. Call it to mind from time-to-time. Wordsworth was famous for writing poems that re-presented the sublime, so that in the very recitation of the poem we could get a second glimpse, so to speak. His field of daffodils "flash[ed] upon that inward eye" even years later, yielding up more pleasure and more insight as he pondered them from his living-room couch.

Encounters with the sublime and transcendence have a way of seeping into our psyches. They settle into us and color the way we think about things. They can even affect the way we make decisions, and where we choose to focus our time and effort. For example, after encountering the sublime you might find more joy in the simplicity of an afternoon walk, now conscious of the powerful impulse that undergirds all of Nature. You see it now in its subtler forms, in the sparrow's spring flutter or the autumn wind's warning. Cultivate these sublime lessons and you will come to realize that there's more at stake in our day-to-day life than just getting through it. There is now a little whisper in your heart, prodding you to ask: is there something more? The world seems different, and that makes all the difference.

Let me end with a note of caution: don't become addicted to the sublime. Don't mistake sublimity or the feelings it produces with absolute truth or a supreme form of being. The lessons the sublime teaches are more nuanced than that, more complex. The sublime teaches us less about absolute truth and more about different ways to "move about the cabin" of life. It's an opening onto a certain mode of being, not the doorway to the One Truth. Seek the sublime, but don't devote yourself to it. When you do encounter it, carry its wisdom with you. But don't let the excitement of the sublime lead you to think your "normal" life is somehow deficient or too banal because it's not as thrilling as the sublime. Quite the contrary. The sublime should imbue your daily life with a new sense of meaning, it should help you see the intoxicating beauty of quotidian life. The magic of the sublime is that it breaks you out of the illusion of normalcy and then allows you to see just how abnormal life itself actually is. Life is not a dull, material existence. It's a richly symbolic, poetic, and magical one. What you discover on "this side" of the sublime is not nihilistic nothingness ("I am just a speck of dust") but aesthetic brilliance ("My God, the world is full of beauty").

Concluding Thoughts

Edmund Burke taught us the structure of the sublime, and the Romantics revealed its religious implications. Through their sensitivity to the way the sublime opens onto transcendence, artists like William Blake and David Caspar Friedrich show us how in the moonlight, the monk's gaze, or the tiger's prowl there is a deeper question lurking underneath the powerful feeling of terrible delight we experience in encountering them. Call it God, the Absolute, Nature, or simply, The Question, the pull of "something more" seems doubly profound when standing in the face of existence's limitless power.

Let yourself be enchanted by that. Recognize that to be lured by the horizon is part and parcel of what it means to be human. You don't need to feel embarrassed by transcendence or try and explain it away according to the rules of the immanent frame. Talk about it with others, your friends or family, or even strangers. These sorts of conversations revive in us a curiosity about our place in the cosmos, and that curiosity provokes an interest in exploring the margins of a materialist view of things. Acknowledge the fact that there are experiences that reside somewhere between the mundane and the so-called supernatural, between the facts of science and myths of speculative theology. There are a number of meaningful experiences that call into question the limits of human knowledge without bowdlerizing the truth of our flesh-and-blood life. By resisting the pressure to explain everything away in terms of psychological states or eschatological ends we allow ourselves to live in the enchanting space of possibility, the magical middle ground of The Question itself.

CONCLUSION

Things like Fairy Tales

Tips and Tricks for Living the Romantic Life

Goodbye Disenchantment

M y hope for you in reading this book is that it helps you participate more fully in the mystery of life; that is, that your life becomes enchanted. An enchanted life is something uniquely available to us as human beings. Enchantment is possible *because we are human beings*. To be human is to be the kind of creature that can be enchanted, that can experience a world full of beauty, truth, and love. As you know by now, enchantment is not make-believe. It's not a delusion. It's not waving a wand and simply choosing to see magic where there really is none. To be enchanted by life is to live it in a different mode, to decline to reduce existence to a materialist explanation.

Keep in mind that enchantment does not deny science or the value of materialist accounts of life. They're not two, opposing options. Enchantment does mean, however, that you think there is more to life than matter. The human imagination, our experience of Nature, sincere expression, the sea of symbols in which we swim, and the pull of transcendence all contribute to a form of life that *includes* materiality, but goes *beyond* it. As human beings, we have the unique capacity to raise up moments of time to eternity, to make meaning through interpretation, to tell ourselves stories and narrativize our lives, and to locate ourselves within a broader milieu of signs, symbols, ideas, and histories. These capacities hold the potential for a life full of joy, a life imbued with a deep sense of awe and wonder about the world around us. They open the door to enchantment. They make it possible. This, in the end, is the lesson the Romantics have to teach us: it is because we are human that we can live an enchanted life, and so we should.

Living life this way means you leave disenchantment behind. You forgo cynicism. You free your imagination. You aspire to sincere speech. You celebrate Nature as both a dynamic truth and a disorienting force. You poeticize the world. And you remain open to transcendence. Living an enchanted life is not always easy. Our world is dominated by disenchanting forces. The fetish of shallow repetition that is capitalist culture, the reductive impulse of scientism, and the critical vitriol of pop postmodernity push back against the enchanted person's genuine desire to live as fully as possible. But we must remember David Foster Wallace's rebels. Today's revolutionary is one who breaks out of this cynical mold. She is the person who offers a third way, who declines to adopt a hermeneutic of suspicion at every turn. Rather than seeing her project as tearing down what's been built, she sees it as building up something new. Romantics find their identity in being *for* things, not *against* them. That takes bravery in a world dominated by snark and cynicism, materialism and "critical distance." But that's the Romantic call: be brave. And the Romantic promise is that in doing so, you will become enchanted with life. You will live it fully.

Things Like Fairy Tales

Once you embark on the path to the enchanted life you will begin to see enchantment all around you. It's there, in the nooks and crannies of everyday living. I want to leave you with a short list of "little chances" for enchantment, small moments built into your everyday life that provide occasion to experience enchantment. Now that you know how to use the deeper strategies the Romantics taught, these little chances will be easy for you to take a hold of and poeticize. Things like fairy tales, holidays, seasons, food, and even lighting can be great sources of enchantment. These little chances are ripe with meaning and offer a nice way to begin to weave into your life regular moments of magic and beauty. I offer each one as a suggestion, an opportunity. You don't have to "practice" all of them. Choose the ones that resonate with you and play around with the others. In the spirit of little chances, I provide only the briefest of explanations of each opportunity. I don't want to say too much. It's up to you to take what you've learned from the Romantics and apply it to your life. But it's worth it, I promise.

Let's start with an easy one: the four seasons. The seasons are a simple, natural way to experience enchantment. In fact, if you were experiencing any form of enchantment prior to reading this book it probably came in the form of an ambiguous joy or pleasure you felt moving through the seasonal year. To some degree we all sense the beauty of the circle of time. Notice how each season brings its own mood, its own truth, and its own message. Pay attention to what each has to say. Embrace all of them. Take a moment with your cup of coffee or tea and stand still in each of the seasons. Contemplate what you see, what you experience. What does the season say? Draw from your inventory of signs and symbols. Let your imagination pull things together. Feel the season sincerely. Spring is both renewal and rebirth, but it is also promise and greening and growth and color. Notice its sadder side too, for in every birth there is a shudder of death, a whisper which gives new life a sense of immediacy. Summer is vibrancy, fecundity, and fullnes. It beckons us to laugh and be warmed by the joy of friendship. Autumn ushers in a time of reflection and harvest. It shows us how life can flare into a stunning display of color just before it recedes into darkness. And winter brings its own somber story: life falls away, at times we are cold, chilled to the bone by what we are forced to face in this all-too-short moment we have with The Mystery. If you view your life in terms of circles that spiral around the seasons, repeating these truths rather than marching through them, you'll see each revolution as a deepening rather than a passage. The seasons mark the meaning of life, not just moments stepping you closer to its end. Experiencing time in this three-dimensional way allows you to embrace the winter when it comes while celebrating the truths of the other seasons too. Eventually, your concern for yourself may give way to a concern for the broader world, for your brothers and sisters in humanity. Circle time has a funny way of doing that. In the end, it leaves you fulfilled by the fact that what was to be done, has been done.

Holidays are another little chance at enchantment. Seasons are marked by holidays, and holidays can be magical. Approach them as ways to focus on the wondrous aspects of the seasons, and relish in the fact that, as we saw in chapter 5, humans are the kind of creatures who have the capacity to experience moments of eternity piercing the veil of time. Major holidays like Christmas and Thanksgiving (if you're in the U.S.) do this easily. It's hard to look around a table full of your friends and family and marvel at the beauty of a bountiful meal and not think to yourself that there is something deeply true in this moment, something eternal. We all know the sweetness in the soul that comes with a Christmas tree's sacred glow, when the lights are out and the house is quiet and the snow falls soundlessly outside. Life is difficult and full of suffering. But in that moment, there is joy, even if only an instant. Embrace the truth in that. Be enchanted by it.

As we've seen, other less "serious" holidays can have more enchantment to offer too, if you're willing to look beneath consumerism, cynicism,
and commercialism. Halloween calls us to a playful engagement with our
own mortality and allows us to explore the haunting fears that lurk inside
of us the other eleven months of the year. Summer holidays like Independence Day in the U.S. or May Day in England heighten our awareness of
the irrepressible human drive for liberation in all its forms, be it political,
sexual, psychological, or existential. Lesser known holidays like Imbolc or
Candlemas might be revived to remind us of their sacred truths. On Imbolc,
for example, February 2nd, we might take up an older cultural custom and
celebrate the first stirring of the seed that refuses to lay dormant, even in the
frozen ground of winter. Plant a small, indoor herb garden. Care for it until
the weather warms, when you can take it outside. The symbolism is clear:
spring will come again. Life will not be denied.

Holiday celebrations usually come with decorations. Wreaths, knickknacks, spiderwebs, lights, flags, etc., are all forms of what I call "atmo-
spheric enchantment." They set a mood and act as a reminder to us that
the time of the year is special. It has meaning. They are material references
that heighten our sensitivity to what's going on around us, and they nudge
us toward contemplative reflection. Like little sensory cues, they suggest we
consider where we are in the year's cycle, what the season means to us symbolically, and what poetic associations we can make between the season and
our lives. Decorations are often fun, but rarely trivial. Even silly decorations
can serve to increase our awareness of the truth of the season's turning. A
twinkling sparkler in the hand of a child as she dances in the twilight of a
family picnic can speak the deepest of truths, truths about our love for one
another and the freedom of a summer evening.

But of course, seasonal decorations are just one way to create an atmosphere of enchantment. There are other ways too. For example, the thoughtful use of lighting can bring an atmosphere of enchantment, regardless of
whether the time is aligned with a holiday or not. The buzz of electric lights
often conceals the intimate play of lamp or candle light and the secrets they
have to share with us. Go ahead, try turning off the lights in your house on
a cold January evening. Illuminate half a dozen candles and crack open a
good book (maybe some Shelley?). Let the flicker of the flames, the play of
the darkness and illumination, the subtle warmth from the wick, and the
luring seduction of the shadows speak to you. Let them enchant you. What
do they say? Not sure? Use your imagination. Look for symbolic meaning. Contemplate how it all feels. Let the Nature inside of the flame dance
around you and the objects in the room. Remember that Coleridge saw in
the ash of a dying fire the truth of Nature revealed, and Wordsworth saw the

sublime in a splash of mountain moonlight. Enchantment is there, in the candlelight, too.

Another little chance for enchantment lies in fairy tales. How long has it been since you considered the depth of a fairy tale? In our modern culture we've replaced fairy tales with super heroes, and folklore with Disney cartoons. Super heroes and cartoons serve their own purpose, but I think we lose something when we transform fairy tales into motion pictures, or privilege comic books over story books. Fairy tales tell us something powerful about ourselves, something that cannot be said directly and that can get lost in the big screen razzle-dazzle of computer-generated animation and snarky scripts written with an eye toward parents. In his book *The Uses of Enchantment: The Meaning and Importance of Fairy Tales*, the child psychologist Bruno Bettelheim makes the compelling case that fairy tales are a unique form of art and that through them children can work to "master the psychological problems of growing up."[1]

But fairy tales are not only for children. As adults we can read them with new eyes and a lifetime of experience. We can begin to see them as rich sources of meaning and magic. We recognize in the wolf of Little Red Riding Hood our own fears of external threats and dangers. We see in Hansel and Gretel the foolishness of blindly chasing one's desires. We find in Iron John the secret wound that so many of us carry throughout life. And we discover in Cinderella's sisters the seeds of our own potential cruelty and warnings against giving into our uglier selves.

The enchantment of fairy tales doesn't end there, either. Their settings, characters, creatures, archaic plot lines, and ambiguous moral lessons invite interpretation and imagination. They are a treasure trove of meanings. It is only in things like fairy tales that we can conjure in our minds fantastical places and use them to work through our own life challenges. Fairy tales are a kind of "Romanticizing down" in the sense that, like "The Rime of the Ancyent Marinere," they invite us to look at something fantastic, foreign, or miraculous and see in them truths common to all human experience. Viewed this way, fairy tales become wonderfully enchanting things.

We've spent a lot of time talking about poetry already so I won't belabor the point here, but I would be remiss if I did not offer one last reminder of the enchanting nature of poetry. Other forms of literature can enchant too, of course, but poetry held a special place in the hearts of Romantics because of its highly stylized use of language as a way to "see into the life of things," as Wordsworth put it. Poetry can be intimidating (although hopefully less so now that you've read a bit in this book), so start with something

---

1. Bettelheim, *The Uses of Enchantment*, 6.

approachable. Many poems you already know might just require a little quiet contemplation to open you onto an enchanting experience. Take for example Robert Frost's poem, "Stopping by Woods on a Snowy Evening." It's brilliant. You know it already, or have at least heard it: "Whose woods these are I think I know / His house is in the village though;" and so on. The final lines resonate in our hearts as a culture: "And miles to go before I sleep, / And miles to go before I sleep." It's a simple poem, but a deep one. Read it. And read others like it. Memorize one or two if you can so you have them with you wherever you go. Carrying their truths in your heart can allow them to deliver surprising insights when you least expect it. Imagine reciting Frost's words to yourself on some winter's day when you do indeed find yourself in the snowy woods and let the words call your attention to Nature's presence. Or imagine their truth if you were to recall them as you comfort a dying lover and face the tragedy-that-is-eternity: although their life will soon end, yours will go on. There is pain there, to be sure, a pain that perhaps only poetry can say anything true about. Enchantment is not always pleasant, but it is always profound.

There are other little chances, ones that I have not seen or thought of myself. Things will emerge for you that I cannot anticipate. Keep your eye out and you will discover them. Recently I've found the magic of a vegetable garden, something I never thought I would be drawn to or find enchanting. But now I see the garden as a living symbol of all life. I compose in my mind little poems about the redness of my tomatoes and the pleasure of the squirrels that eat them (usually before I do!). Food is also a great source of enchantment. Food is nourishment, gift, work, and generosity. There is a reason why in almost all cultures hospitality and "a seat at the table" are sacred invitations. Sharing food with another person says that there is something here for you, that you will not be left hungry and destitute, that when confronted with the Stranger I will choose invitation, not animosity. All of the great Abrahamic religions teach this truth, over and over again. The Catholic Church has developed a two-thousand-year-old ritual centered around this simple idea of breaking bread with one another. Specific foods symbolize different things: the sugar-pleasure of pie speaks only joy, the rich red sauce of a pasta dish says indulge, and be merry. The light aroma of a lemon-spritzed fish signals crisp oceans and warm days. It's all there, right under our noses. Breathe it in.

One thing many of these little chances have in common is the presence of other people. As we saw in chapter 4 (on sincerity), there is something unique about the way another person appears to us. Other people appear as *wholly* other; that is, no matter what you do to try and pin them down their existence seems to exceed your efforts. You can never *fully* know them. You can never capture all of their details, machinations, desires, meanings, etc. People are not objects. Rather than trying to lord *over* them, we ought to live *with* them. We ought to acknowledge their transcendence and honor their infinity. To me, that means we should engage in a never-ending project of trying to *understand* the Other, but not to *know* her. The difference here is that in understanding, you commit to an ongoing act of interpreting the Other: sensing, probing, appreciating, responding to, and poeticizing her as she appears before you in all her mercurial and mesmerizing otherness. Knowledge, on the other hand, seeks to identify, categorize, analyze, and reduce the Other to a "thing," so that she becomes like a cup or a car, another object in the world to manipulate and control. This is the central problem of *Frankenstein*: Victor creates an Other when he meant to create an object. Now he must learn to live with what exceeds him.

The presence of an Other introduces yet another opportunity to Romanticize the world (in Novalis's sense of the term). The Other is a call to celebrate the Mystery of Being. He or she *is* transcendence. The Other is the moon in *Abbey by the Oakwood*, proving there is "something more" to life than our own subjective experiences. There is something "out there," something beyond us, something that is other-than-you. Just that fact alone can be enchanting. Listen, I'm not saying you should like everybody, or that every person you meet from now on will suddenly become pleasant to be around, just because you're viewing things through an enchanted lens. Even if you appreciate otherness, people will still irritate you, and you will still have conflicts with them. But what will change is that you will begin to see the Other as a lifeworld, one full of depth, vivacity, complexity, and beauty. And one that you will never know. The other person is *fundamentally unknowable*. The result is that the Other, *any* Other, is an occasion for awe and marvel, an opportunity to bow before the The Mystery of Being. The Other is something sacred. The next time you're at a stoplight and feeling uncomfortable because the homeless person on the corner is looking at you, look back. Look into the face of the Other, and there you will see an infinite expanse. There is magic in it: dizzying, stunning, disorienting magic. This magic is transformative magic. It can change you. This is what Christians mean when they claim to see Christ in the face of the poor: Others, like God, appear as pure transcendence and call us into awe, and into responsibility. And when our encounter with the Other transforms into friendship or love, another form of enchantment emerges, one in which two people celebrate the sheer fact of the other's existence and take joy in the beauty of the Other. As Aristotle said, friends are "one soul in two bodies," and recognition of the fact that you share such a kinship with another person can magnify your life's meaning in ways you cannot anticipate. If that's not enchanting, what is?

The Dangers of Enchanted Living

Now that we've covered a handful of little chances for enchantment, I'd like to issue a warning about enchanted living. It may seem odd, but there are dangers in it. You can take things too far. Some Romantics did. At the margins, there may be a finer line than we'd like to admit between the Romantic life and giving yourself over to fancy and passion. Let's take a moment to learn a few lessons from those Romantics who may have gone off the deep end in their pursuit of the enchanted life.

First, there is the tragic case of Thomas Chatterton. Here he is, in his most famous portrait:

Henry Walls, *The Death of Chatterton*, 1856, oil on panel.

It's grim. I know. It's supposed to be. Poor Thomas Chatterton was a brilliant English poet who at the tender age of seventeen committed suicide after producing a flurry of fantastic poetry. His life, writings, and death left quite a mark on the Romantics, especially Shelley, Keats, Wordsworth, and Coleridge. In a way, his suicide was prescient of what would later become a macabre hallmark of many Romantic lives: an untimely death. Recall that Shelley and Keats also died young, Shelley by drowning at the age of twenty-nine, and Keats of tuberculosis when he was just twenty-five. A lot of ink has been spilled over Chatterton's death and the reasons why he may have chosen to take his own life. He was poor and struggled to make a living. He enjoyed both the praise and derision of his peers and patrons. He lived without a father. He was melancholic, and in his own words just three days before his death admitted to a friend that he had "been at war with the grave for some time now." He deeply desired public recognition as a master poet but was treated with contempt when his would-be benefactor Horace Walpole discovered that Chatterton's archaic-sounding verses were actually modern compositions. And he was seventeen, which comes with its own set of challenges. All of these circumstances no doubt conspired to lead young Chatterton to the bottle of arsenic you see in the foreground of the painting.

Chatterton's death issues a stark reminder to all those interested in Romantic thought and enchantment: the quest for meaning, truth, and beauty can leave you distraught when you struggle to find what it is you're looking for. At times, during your pursuit of the enchanted life, you may find that you cannot see the world as a source of meaning because some deep tragedy has struck. These tragedies are real, and they can call into question the very value of enchantment, the desire to experience the magical side of life. We often find it difficult to consider the beauty of the world when, for example, we are faced with the death of a parent or a spouse, or a child has been abused. The injustice of death or the mistreatment of the innocent are too grave, too overpowering to feel anything other than tragedy. Don't deny these feelings, and don't resist them. It's true: enchantment is not a panacea for all of life's heartaches. It is not a cure-all for any existential ailment you might have. Like most things, enchantment has its limits. And like Chatterton, you will still at times live in darkness, where no poem or painting can give you solace. That, sadly, is the way of things. But unlike Chatterton, you need not resort to self-harm. While enchantment cannot remove heartache, it can give you some tools to live with it, to experience it within the context of the great project of human meaning-making.

The fact that enchantment has limits and carries some risks does not mean it's a worthless endeavor. It only means that when pursuing the enchanted life, you must remember that it requires a certain measure of prudence, and you must set reasonable expectations for yourself. The danger in enchanted living is therefore two-fold. First, it can be dangerous if you expect too much of enchantment, if you think that by adopting the Romantic disposition you will no longer suffer, or that all of life's experiences will be pleasurable and beautiful. They will not. You will suffer. We all do. It's human, all too human. But by living an enchanted life you will have the tools and strategies to help you make meaning of your suffering, to speak of suffering with more nuance and complexity. Facing death through the words of a Robert Frost poem ("And miles to go before I sleep") does not make death more palatable, but it does express the moment of eternity present in death, and it creates a space for you to wrestle with and engage your loss. Through the processes of grief and trauma you can rely on these enchantment strategies to help you navigate them in a way that taps into the deeper truths at play in human suffering, and our own limits.

Secondly, enchanted living can be dangerous if you give yourself over completely to the passions it can engender. Like Chatterton, you can become consumed by your desire for romance, imagination, poetic insight, and emotional intensity. None of these are bad per se—indeed, I've been arguing all along that they are good—but too much of a good thing can make it dangerous, and enchantment is no exception. The key here is to pursue enchantment, to cultivate it and live within it, but do not become *obsessed* with it. Don't over-value it to the point that you neglect all other human considerations or obligations. It's one thing to experience the sublime on a summer beach vacation and quite another to leave your spouse and children in pursuit of sublime experiences like some extreme thrill-seeker. That's going too far. In some ways, enchantment is more like a subtle shift than a seismic shake in the way you live your life. It plays out in the way you watch an autumn leaf fall, or the way you speak to a friend. It isn't giving yourself over to the throes of passion and, like Young Werther, thinking that the more *intensely* you feel the more *alive* you are. Enchantment is not just about intense emotion. It's about imbuing life with meaning, learning to think symbolically, declining to view all things as "only" material, and embracing the human capacity to experience the eternal and the transcendent. Let Chatterton's life and death be a warning to us all that there are limits even to enchantment, but that does not mean we should forgo it. It means that we should be aware of them as we embark on our path to a richer, fuller experience of human life.

Another danger that comes with enchanted life is the temptation to embrace it so wholly that you become militant or dogmatic about it, and deny the value of other modes of being, including secular materialism. As I've said all along, secular materialism is not bad, but it is limited. Science is not the enemy. Capitalism has done some good. Deconstruction served an important purpose. None of these disenchanting forces are in and of themselves problematic. They only become so when they are adopted to the exclusion of all other forms of knowing. The same risk runs with enchantment. If you adopt an enchanted disposition and then assume it is the *only* or *best* way to live, then you've fallen prey to the same kind of reductive dogmatism of any other worldview. It's important to always recognize the contingency of your position and the limits of your view on things. Don't let enchantment become your new religion.

Lastly, there's the danger of Magic Wand Syndrome. This is the idea that all you have to do to experience enchantment is wave the magic wand of your mind and—*poof!*—there it is. That's not it. There is no magic wand. As we've seen, the Romantic life is a deliberate form of life, not just "thinking things" to make them so. It's not a parlor trick, and it's not pretending like everything is hunky-dory. It takes practice, intention, contemplation, reading, effort, risk, and compassion to pull it off. Enchantment is about letting things in, letting symbols, myths, Nature, sincerity, etc., stir in your soul. It isn't easy, and it isn't simple. Similarly, don't fall prey to the idea that you can "go back" to the Romantic period to achieve enchantment (or any other historical period for that matter). You can't go back. Living the Romantic life is not about returning to a "better time," to a golden age when we had it all figured out. The eighteenth and nineteenth centuries were just as fraught with turmoil, war, suffering, bigotry, oppression, and evil as ours is today. There never was a golden age. Living the Romantic life is about bringing the wisdom of the Romantics into your contemporary moment. It's about applying their lessons to today's concerns, and seeing what you can glean from them in order to live a fuller life now, in this world, at this time. You can't go back, but you can use these Romantic strategies to go forward.

Is There A Good Answer to Chloe's Question?

Let's return now to Chloe's question: How *not* to become a star?

In chapter 1, we looked at Chloe and her father's conversation about death as an example of what it's like to be disenchanted, to feel the cross-pressures of modern life. Chloe and her dad live within the immanent frame, where we assume "this" (what we can see, taste, touch, measure, observe, etc.) is all there really is. The world is de-mythologized or flattened, and culture is dominated by the forces of deconstruction, scientism, and capitalism. In this world, we feel the press of time marching on without us. We feel foundationless and anxious because everything is called into question and "exposed" as either a fraud or part of a broader ploy to gain power or oppress each other. We don't trust the media, our teachers, or ourselves. We're suspicious of everything, "all the way down." We're suspicious and anxious, which breeds in us cynicism because we feel the need to find a way to defend against a world that's assaulting us from all angles. Everywhere we look, from social media to Sunday dinner, we're challenged every time we try to find stable ground. Because of our disenchantment—our over-reliance on rationalization, mastery, and materialism—we have no recourse to other ways of thought, to what Percy Shelley calls "subtler languages" that address our human experience with depth and delicacy. We sense that as human beings our lives are not reducible to scientific or pseudo-scientific explanations, and yet we don't have the tools to think them otherwise.

Chloe and her father are left with a stark question, a question that seems to have no satisfactory answer. In our story, Chloe was contemplating death and her father told her that when you die you become a star. He told her this because he's a materialist at heart but doesn't want to tell his daughter the cold hard truth. He told her this because he's not convinced religion is a viable answer. He told her this because he hasn't had the time or the interest in investigating poetry, symbolism, folklore, legends, or mystery. He told her this because his disenchantment has left him without the tools to offer any other kind of answer. He told her this because *he doesn't know what else to say.* And yet, her question presses on: "What if I don't want to become a star?"

Isn't this the question we're all asking? Isn't Chloe's question *the* question, the question posed by all those who are disenchanted? It comes in many forms. What if I don't want to die? What if my life is meaningless? What if I love you, and the thought of experiencing your death causes me such fear that I can't sleep at night? What if I feel empty inside, like the world has nothing to offer? What if everywhere I look I see selfishness, egoism, competition, and scarcity? What can you say to me from within the immanent frame that will give me some sense of comfort, meaning, or perhaps even hope that my life and your life are not completely pointless? What if I don't buy your star story because it's a lie, and you and I both know it? What if I am on to the fact that you just made it up to gloss over a hard truth? *What if I don't want to become a star?*

I hope you can feel the press of the question. It's powerful. Is there a good answer to Chloe's question? In some ways the answer is, no. That's why we keep asking it. That's why it persists. And that's why for as long as humans have been around they've felt compelled to ask it (or some version of it). We wrestle with it through art, poetry, psychology, religion, science, work, and all sorts of other endeavors. But the question keeps pressing. So what should Chloe's father say? What should be his answer? What should a cross-pressured secular humanist living within the immanent frame tell his adolescent daughter when she's struggling with the meaning of death, and of life? You could write a whole book on just that question.

To be honest, I'm not sure there is a good answer to Chloe's question from where her father stands. I think he makes a valiant attempt though. He's smart, compassionate, and quick-on-his-feet. His star story is a stroke of genius, but it still rings hollow for some reason, partly because it's not rooted in anything other than his impromptu idea that a little girl needs a story she can believe in—even if only for a little while—and partly because it doesn't have the kind of deep, symbolic resonance that can invite interpretation and creative engagement throughout an entire life. It's a good try, but it ultimately falls short. It's a stopgap measure, not an answer to the question. You see, that's the problem with the disenchanted life, the life dominated by scientific materialism. Scientific materialism doesn't ask the Big Questions like "Why are things the way they are?" or "What should I do with my life?" or "What does all of this mean?" Scientific materialism is great at telling us how things work, but it doesn't tell us anything about why the world is this way, or why it is at all, for that matter. We need other forms of human inquiry for that, other methods for thinking those sorts of questions through. That's where philosophy, religion, literature, poetry, art, and music come in. That's where the humanities provide fertile ground for responding to these deeper human questions about the nature of life. And, as I've been saying all along, I think Romanticism is particularly well-situated to teach us a thing or two, especially today, because of its close relationship to the Enlightenment, which was the last big disenchanting wave to wash over human thought. So what would a Romantic father say to his daughter? How could Chloe's dad reply if he were enchanted?

Well, he could say something that from within the immanent frame might sound silly, ridiculous, even. He could say that when you die, you go to heaven. "But wait," you reply, "he's not a Christian! And besides, *heaven isn't real!*" I hope by now you see the error in this logic, but it's worth analyzing one last time, within the context of Chloe's question, to drive the point home regarding the pervasiveness of the immanent frame and what it means to accept the Romantic invitation to enchantment. Notice how quickly the "But-heaven-is-a-lie" response comes to you, how second-nature it feels. It might even come with a mild sense of nausea directed toward the word heaven and the Christian mythology that accompanies it. That automatic, unreflective response is exactly what it means to live within the immanent frame: it's our baseline, default assumption that heaven-talk is immature because we all know everything is *really just matter*, and an appeal to anything that sounds even remotely religious is just an add-on (and therefore, at the end of the day, a lie). Telling Chloe that when you die you go to heaven is at best cheating, and at worst, propagating a delusion.

But having worked your way through this book, as someone who now understands what it means to be enchanted, you might not feel repulsion at the idea of heaven anymore. Instead, you might ask yourself: *What is heaven anyway?* Use your imagination. Think symbolically. Let go of your cynicism. Remember the truth of Nature. Recall the insights of the sublime. Hear the call of transcendence. Does heaven need to be a literal crystal city somewhere up in the sky in order for it to be a significant idea that we can use to make sense of our human experience? Are we really stuck between the two extremes of either (a) heaven is not real so don't talk about it (i.e., secular materialism) and (b) heaven is a literal city in the sky so talk about it all you want (i.e., naive religion)?

My argument is that *both* of these views are mistaken. Both of them cheapen the idea of heaven as a meaningful referent in Western culture. The secular materialist and the naive religious person mistreat the idea of heaven when they reduce it to either (a) or (b) and force upon us a (false) choice. This reduction only trivializes the deep and powerful idea of heaven, an idea that has captured the human imagination for thousands of years, and has inspired an almost inconceivable amount of poetry, art, and philosophical contemplation. To name heaven for Chloe is to give her a "first dose" of the magic of poetic thought. It is to introduce to her (in an age-appropriate way) to the vast inventory of symbols, ideas, and references that we as a culture have developed over the course of centuries to confront and explore the question of life and death.

Heaven speaks with many voices. For a child it is indeed a place in the sky where mom and dad and grandma and grandpa go when they die, and it is a great source of comfort. For a teenager, heaven is the promise of tomorrow and at times a moral compass (whether or not the teen chooses to follow the compass is a question for another day). For a young adult heaven may be something to rebel against, a paternalistic norm that seems totally unacceptable (and through wrestling with it, insight and wisdom can emerge). For a mature adult it is an invitation to hope once again. For an older adult it is the vision of a good life, one lived in love and friendship and charity. And to the dying person it is the last wish, the *adieu* to life-that-is-beauty, a thing that will never pass into nothingness. Paradoxically, in the end, heaven becomes the life that one has *already lived*. Heaven is the peace that comes with knowing all that could be done, has been done.

Heaven is all of this, and more. Heaven is more real than real, in a very real sense. It is that which cannot be said with any finality or closure. It is the combined hope of all human aspiration, and the desire for the yet-to-come. It is steeped in tradition, truth, sorrow, and suffering. It is, in the fullest sense, a symbol. Chloe's father can say with a confident heart that when you die you go to heaven, and in doing so inaugurate Chloe into a lifelong inquiry about the nature of life and death and introduce her to the wealth of symbolic references about heaven-as-the-desire-for life (which it is), and these references can deepen and enrich her experience in the most profound and transformative ways.

Now, you might wonder whether Chloe's father was getting at all of this with his star story. Aren't heaven and the star basically the same idea? I don't think so. The difference between heaven and a star is enormous. Heaven is part of our cultural encyclopedia. It is an idea embedded in a broader context network of meanings, history, symbols, rituals, ideas, and language. It has a life of its own. It's part of the water we swim in. Asking "What is heaven?" over the course of a lifetime will yield ripe fruit because it is an idea that's had time to culturally germinate and grow through art, literature, music, poetry, and philosophy. Heaven is part of the wealth and wisdom of the Western tradition. Chloe's father's star story is cute; insightful, even, but it was just made up on the spot. It does not bring with it the rich tradition and multiplicity of meanings that heaven brings as an idea embedded in a broader cultural tradition. It's a disenchanted band-aid, not an enchanted answer. You can't blame Chloe's father for trying through, and even feeling a sense of pride about the star story. It does have a hint of fairy tale and magic too it, but it is also "shallow" in the sense that it does not draw upon the deep and enriching inventory of symbols and metaphors, the kind of multiplicity of meanings that can only develop in the slow maturation of time, meanings churned-up through the turning of history's diurnal course, converted into "thick" meanings after centuries of cultural comment and reflection. The star story rings true for a moment (maybe) but then fades as soon as Chloe discovers "it isn't true" after all. The idea of heaven is a powerful truth that goes beyond secular or scientific truth. There's nothing wrong with referring to heaven, but it takes an openness to enchantment and dealing with our own disenchantment to see that.

But if Chloe's father is simply too uncomfortable with symbols steeped in the Christian tradition to use them, he could appeal to other enchanted answers. He could tell her a story. He can respond with, "Once upon a time . . ." and launch into a fairy tale like *Snow White, Sleeping Beauty, Godfather Death*, or something from *Arabian Nights* (which is itself a collection of stories told to stave off death) in order to open a space for Chloe to explore her question through narrative rather than discourse. You might think that responding to the question of death with a fairy tale seems like a cop-out. It dodges the question. A fairy tale is not a straightforward enough answer for Chloe. It's not what she's looking for. But as Bruno Bettelheim tells us in *The Uses of Enchantment*, fairy tales are not just arbitrary stories. They can serve a developmental purpose. Through them children explore their fears, desires, yearnings, and unconscious drives within the narrative space of the story. Fairy tales are not modern inventions like Batman or *Frozen*, designed to entertain and turn a buck. They're time-tested stories that tap into human archetypes, and they can carry great psychological import for a child working through a challenging developmental stage. One of the wonderful things Bettelheim points out about fairy tales as an adequate response to a child's probing questions is that fairy tales succeed *because of their indirectness, their ambiguity*. Fairy tales say without saying. Rather than offering a rationalized explanation of a human mystery, they open a space for a child to explore the darker side of Being without explicitly tackling it head-on. In fact, according to Bettelheim, the story's success "depends to a considerable degree on the child's not quite knowing why he is delighted by it."[2] Chloe's father can wisely resist the temptation to "answer" Chloe's question and instead put her in a space of symbolic and imaginative exploration, a space where she can seek for herself the answer to her question. Fairy tales have been refined and retold over time. Their ambiguity is their strength. Bettelheim cautions parents against explaining too much, and letting stories and narratives provide a landscape for self-exploration and integration. And this works because, as the poet Robert Bly has said, fairy tales are "more than true."

There are other ways an enchanted father might reply to Chloe's question, ways I've never even considered. But I've spilled enough ink over the question for you to get the point: Chloe's question is remarkable, difficult, penetrating, and in a certain sense, *unanswerable*. That's why we need enchantment and enchanted strategies to respond to it. It calls for more than a material explanation. And that's really the key to appreciating the press of her inquiry. The brilliance of Chloe's question is its un-answerability. No single approach to life can give it an adequate response, including the secular materialist approach. It operates as a wake-up call and invitation to those of us living within the disenchanted space of modern life to look with new eyes at resources "outside" the materialist framework. Her question calls us toward poetic, aesthetic, Romantic, and even religious forms of knowing in order to equip ourselves with the tools we need to wrestle with the question, rather than resolve it. Each of us must spend a lifetime answering Chloe's question, or pretending like it isn't there. But if we acknowledge it, if we approach it from an enchanted disposition, we see that the "answer" is a lifetime of engagement in the poetics of Being. It's the endless hermeneutic of human meaning-making. Life itself is the answer to the question, and life

2. Bettelheim, *The Uses of Enchantment*, 18.

is a multiplicity of voices, meanings, and ways of knowing. The task we must take on is to remain open to these voices and resist the temptation to reduce the Mystery of Being to one method, one mode. To do so, to live openly to the magic of Being, is to truly live the Romantic life.

Bibliography

Ball, Patricia M. "Sincerity: The Rise and Fall of a Critical Term." *The Modern Language Review* 59 (1964) 1–11.

Berlin, Isaiah. *The Roots of Romanticism*. Princeton, NJ: Princeton University Press, 1999.

Bettelheim, Bruno. *The Uses of Enchantment: The Meaning and Importance of Fairy Tales*. New York: Vintage, 2010.

Blanning, Tim. *The Romantic Revolution: A History*. New York: Modern Library, 2011.

Bly, Robert. *More Than True: The Wisdom of Fairy Tales*. New York: Henry Holt and Company, 2018.

Boyesen, Hjalmar Hjorth. *Essays on German Literature*. New York: Charles Scribner's Sons, 1892.

Burke, Edmund. *On Taste; On the Sublime and Beautiful; Reflections on the French Revolution; A Letter to a Noble Lord*. Edited by Charles W. Eliot. Danbury, CT: Grolier Enterprises, 1980.

Burns, Robert. *The Complete Works of Robert Burns: Containing His Poems, Songs, and Correspondents*. Boston: Phillips, Sampson, and Company, 1855.

Byron, Lord George Gordon. *Byron's Don Juan, Volume III*. Edited by Truman Guy Steffan and Willis W. Pratt. Austin: University of Texas Press, 1971.

———. "So we'll go no more a-roving." In *Romanticism: An Anthology*, edited by Duncan Wu, 958. Chichester, UK: Wiley-Blackwell, 2012.

Caputo, John D. *On Religion*. London: Routledge, 2001.

Coleridge, Samuel Taylor. *Collected Letters of Samuel Taylor Coleridge: Vol II (1801–1806)*. Oxford: Oxford University Press, 2002.

———. "Frost at Midnight." In *Romanticism: An Anthology*, edited by Duncan Wu, 645–49. Chichester, UK: Wiley-Blackwell, 2012.

———. "The Rime of the Ancyent Marinere, in Seven Parts." In *Romanticism: An Anthology*, edited by Duncan Wu, 339–57. Chichester, UK: Wiley-Blackwell, 2012.

———. "This Lime-Tree Bower My Prison." In *Romanticism: An Anthology*, edited by Duncan Wu, 633. Chichester, UK: Wiley-Blackwell, 2012.

Dupré, Louis. *The Quest of the Absolute: Birth and Decline of European Romanticism*. Notre Dame, IN: University of Notre Dame Press. 2013.

Engell, James. *The Creative Imagination: Enlightenment to Romantic*. Cambridge: Harvard University Press, 1981.

Esterhammer, Angela. "The Scandal of Sincerity: Wordsworth, Byron, Landon." In *Romanticism, Sincerity, and Authenticity*, edited by Tim Milnes and Kerry Sinanan, 101–19. New York: Palgrave Macmillan, 2010.

Ferber, Michael. *Romanticism: A Very Short Introduction*. Oxford: Oxford University Press, 2010.

Forbes, Deborah. *Sincerity's Shadow: Self-Consciousness in British Romantic and Mid-Twentieth-Century American Poetry*. Cambridge: Harvard University Press, 2004.

Heidegger, Martin. *Basic Writings from Being and Time to The Task of Thinking*. Edited by David Farrell Krell. London: Harper Perennial, 2008.

———. *Being and Time*. Translated by John Macquarrie and Edward Robinson. New York: Harper & Row, 2008.

Heine, Heinrich. *Travel-Pictures: Including the Tour in the Harz, Norderney and Book of Ideas, Together with the Romantic School*. Translated by Francis Storr. London: George Bell and Sons, 1887.

Geddes, Linda. "How Staying Indoors Affects Your Immune System." https://www.bbc.com/future/article/20200521-can-staying-inside-weaken-the-immune-system.

Goethe, Johann Wolfgang von, and Stanley Appelbaum. *The Sorrows of Young Werther: Die Leiden Des Jungen Werther*. Mineola, NY: Dover, 2004.

Kant, Immanuel. *Critique of Pure Reason*. Translated by Paul Guyer and Allen W. Wood. Cambridge: Cambridge University Press, 1999.

Kearney, Richard. *Anatheism*. New York: Columbia University Press, 2010.

———. *The Wake of Imagination*. London: Routledge, 1988.

Keats, John. "Endymion: A Poetic Romance, Book I." In *Romanticism: An Anthology*, edited by Duncan Wu, 1398. Chichester, UK: Wiley-Blackwell, 2012.

———. "Lamia." In *The Poems of John Keats*, edited by Ernest De Sélincourt, 161. New York: Dodd, Mead & Company, 1905.

———. "Letter from John Keats to Benjamin Bailey, 22 November 1817." In *Romanticism: An Anthology*, edited by Duncan Wu, 1403–4. Chichester, UK: Wiley-Blackwell, 2012.

———. "Letter from John Keats to Richard Woodhouse, 27 October 1818." In *Romanticism: An Anthology*, edited by Duncan Wu, 1424–25. Chichester, UK: Wiley-Blackwell, 2012.

———. "Ode on a Grecian Urn." In *Romanticism: An Anthology*, edited by Duncan Wu, 1466–68. Chichester, UK: Wiley-Blackwell, 2012.

Kneller, Jane. *Kant and the Power of Imagination*. Cambridge, UK: Cambridge University Press, 2007.

Kohák, Erazim. *The Embers and the Stars: A Philosophical Inquiry into the Moral Sense of Nature*. Chicago: The University of Chicago Press, 1984.

Larmore, Charles. *The Romantic Legacy*. New York: Columbia University Press, 1996.

Levinas, Emmanuel. *Alterity and Transcendence*. Translated by Michael B. Smith. New York: Columbia University Press, 2000.

———. *Totality and Infinity: An Essay on Exteriority*. Translated by Alphonso Lingis. Pittsburgh: Duquesne University Press, 1969.

Melville, Herman, *Moby-Dick, or The Whale*. New York: Harper & Brothers, 1851.

Novalis. *Gesammelte Werke*. Edited by Carl Seelig. Zürich: Bühl-verlag, 1945.

———. *Henry Von Ofterdingen: A Novel*. Translated by Palmer Hilty. New York: Ungar, 1972.

————. *Hymns to the Night and Other Writings*. Translated by Charles E. Passage. Indianapolis: Bobbs-Merill Educational, 1960.

————. *Schriften. Dritter Band: Das philosophische Werk II*, edited by Richard Samuel, Hans-Joachim Mähl, and Gerard Schultz, 675. Stuttgart: Kohlhammer Verlag, 1968.

Ohly, Heather, Mathew P. White, Benedict W. Wheeler, Alison Bethel, Obioha C. Ukomunne, Vasilis Nikolaou, and Ruth Garside. "Attention Restoration Theory: A Systematic Review of the Attention Restoration Potential of Exposure to Natural Environments." *Journal of Toxicology and Environmental Health*, Part B. 19.7 (2016) 305–43.

Perkins, David. *Wordsworth and the Poetry of Sincerity*. Cambridge: Harvard University Press, 1964.

Praz, Mario. *The Romantic Agony*. 2nd ed. London: Oxford University Press, 1951.

Richards, I. A. *Coleridge on Imagination*. Bloomington, IN: Indiana University Press, 1965.

Robinson, Katherine. "Samuel Taylor Coleridge: 'Frost at Midnight.'" https://www.poetryfoundation.org/articles/70316/samuel-taylor-coleridge-frost-at-midnight.

Rousseau, Jean-Jacques. *The Confessions of Jean-Jacques Rousseau*. Edited by J. M. Cohen. London: Penguin, 1953.

Safranski, Rüdiger. *Romanticism: A German Affair*. Translated by Robert E. Goodwin. Evanston, IL: Northwestern University Press, 2014.

Schiller, Friedrich. "On Grace and Dignity." In *Friedrich Schiller: Poet of Freedom Vol. II*, translated by George Gregory, 337–95. Washington, DC: The Schiller Institute, 1992.

Schlegel, Friedrich. *Lucinde and the Fragments*. Translated by Peter Firchow. Minneapolis: University of Minnesota, 1971.

Schwartz, Regina, ed. *Transcendence: Philosophy, Literature, and Theology Approach the Beyond*. London: Routledge, 2004.

Shelley, Percy Bysshe. "Mont Blanc." In *Romanticism: An Anthology*, edited by Duncan Wu, 1104–7. Chichester, UK: Wiley-Blackwell, 2012.

————. "To a Skylark." In *Romanticism: An Anthology*, edited by Duncan Wu, 1215–17. Chichester, UK: Wiley-Blackwell, 2012.

Stendhal. *Love*. London: Penguin, 1975.

Taylor, Charles. *A Secular Age*. Cambridge: Harvard University Press, 2007.

Wallace, David Foster. *This Is Water*. New York: Little, Brown and Company, 2009.

————. "E Unibus Pluram: Television and U.S. Fiction." *Review of Contemporary Fiction* 13.2 (1993) 151–94.

Wordsworth, William. *The Major Works*. Edited by Stephen Gill. Oxford: Oxford University Press, 2008.

Yost, D. Andrew. *The Amorous Imagination: Individuating the Other-as-Beloved*. Albany, NY: State University of New York Press, 2021.